The Reluctant Adult
Revisited

An Exploration
of Choice

This book is dedicated to my two daughters

THE RELUCTANT ADULT REVISITED

An Exploration of Choice

The Victimhood Archetype and the Evolution of Consciousness

Jill Hall

Published in the United Kingdom by
InterActions, Stroud

Original edition
The Reluctant Adult – An Exploration of Choice
published 1993
This second enhanced edition is with new
Foreword, Preface, Afterword,
Appendices and index.

Original text © 1993 Jill Hall
This edition © 2025 InterActions

https://interactions360.org
contact@interactions360.org

ISBN 978-1-915594-06-8

All rights reserved.
No part of this publication may be reproduced
without the prior permission of the publisher.

**For further books
published by InterActions**
see our website
https://interactions360.org

Contents

FOREWORD by Richard House..................12
PREFACE TO THE FIRST EDITION by Sue Hatfield..............15
PREFACE TO THE SECOND EDITION by Robin Shohet..........18
INTRODUCTION..................20

Chapter One
PSYCHOLOGY IN INFANCY......................23
    The Structure of Language and Our Concept of Self............25
    The Relationship between a Causal Ontology and
        the Need to Blame..................27
    The Inevitable Failure of Mother..................34
    The Power of the Victim Archetype on Our Collective Psyche...37

Chapter Two
THE GREAT REGRESSION......................42
    Creative and Destructive Modes of Regression and
        the Child within..................43
    Regression and Licence to Blame..................45
    The Fallen Self..................47
    The Fear of Growing up and Our Resistance to Change........48
    Are We Essentially Flawed or Not Yet Complete?..............52
    The Shift of Focus from Mother to Self..................55

Chapter Three
RECLAIMING THE POWER OF THE INFANT..................60
    Recognition of Spirit..................60
    Infant Consciousness..................63
    What I Sense of My Own Beginnings..................66
    The Impotence of the All-powerful Mother..................68
    Claiming Our Initial Responses as Our Own..................69
    The Myth of Total Dependency..................71

Chapter Four

BACK TO THE SOURCE 73
    The Shock of Incarnation 73
    A Necessary Bio-focus at the Point of Conception 76
    Our Obsessive Avoidance of Death 77
    A Temporary Shutter Mechanism to Establish the
        Direction of Life 79
    The Extended Shutter and the Prolonged Eclipse of Our Awareness
        of Spirit 81
    Physical Dependence and Annihilation Terror 82
    The Prevalence of the Defended Personality: Regarding Feelings as
        Enemies 83
    The Possibility of Transformation: Conscious Participation in Our
        Own Completion 85
    The Use and Misuse of Our Mechanism of Emotional Regulation . 86
    Acknowledging Spirit and Releasing the Template of Repression 88
    The State of Wholeness and Libidinous Well-being 89

Chapter Five

SELF-CONCEPT AND MEANING 91
    Approaching the Self through a Hierarchical Structure of Meaning . 91
    The Implications of an Ego-based Concept of Self 92
    The Relationship between Our Concept of Self and
        Our Concept of God 98
    The Civilization of the Split Psyche: The Challenge
        to Become Whole 100
    How Dualism Serves the Victim Self-concept and Thus
        Engagement with the Victim Archetype 102
    The Implications of a Self-concept Based on Spirit 105
    We Are One Body 107
    The Limitations and Dangers of Hierarchical Models for
        Understanding the Self 109
    Change as an Inevitable Threat to the System 110

Chapter Six

THE CIRCLE OF SELF 115
    The 'Shields' of Self Reflection 116
    Moving through the Medicine Wheel: The Four Directions
        Expressing Different Aspects of the Psyche 118

The Dark and the Light Mirror 120
Balancing the Powers of the Four Directions 121
The Direction of the South 122
The Direction of the North 128
The Direction of the West 132
The Direction of the East 138
The Space of Pure Consciousness at the Core of Each Self 142

Chapter Seven
HOW RESPONSIBLE ARE WE? **144**
Determinism Sits Uneasily with Our Lived Experience 144
The Unnecessary Choice between Free Will and Determinism . 146
Paradox as the Vehicle for Elucidating Free Will 148
Personal Responsibility Rests on Knowing Ourselves as Both
    Defined Entities and Ceaselessly Interconnecting Energies .. 149
The Necessary Distinction between Creating Our Reality and
    Controlling Others 151
The Different Levels Involved in the Process of Choice 153
The Wheel of Responsibility:
    A Multi-dimensional Model of Choice 155
The East: the Source of Choice – Our Original Intention 156
The South: The Responsive Self 160
The North: the Place of Choice and Decision-making 164
The West: Obedience to the Voice within 168
The East: The Freedom to Actualize Our Self 171

Chapter Eight
THE WHEEL OF VICTIMHOOD **176**
The Distortions Brought about by Our Engagement with the
    Victim Archetype: The Wounded Child 176
The Frozen Responses of the South 181
The Re-enactment of Old Fixed Positions in the North 182
The Passive Resignation and Refusal of Consciousness of the West . 184
The Fanciful Dictator of the East 186
The Distinction between the Circle of Reaction and the Dark
    Mirrors of the Wheel of Responsibility 187
An Analysis of a Classical Victim Situation: Rape 190
Exposing the Levels of Choice and Non-choice in an Episode of
    Rape 192
Sexual Abuse, Grooming, and the Real Victims 201

    The Importance of Understanding Guilt in Its Social Context .. 203

Chapter Nine
THE DYNAMICS OF POWER **206**
    The Initial Collusion of Infant and Mother: Impotence and
        Protectionism 207
    Powerlessness and Violence 209
    The Difference between Taking Responsibility and Taking the
        Blame 211
    Psychology as Prior to Sociology and Politics 213
    Primal Self-betrayal and the War within 215
    Insecurity and Consumerism 217
    The Demand for a Perfect Society 222
    The Level at Which Radical Change Is Possible 223
    Serving the System: The Power Games of the Impotent 226
    Depowering the Game by Accessing Another Level of Being .. 228
    Rescuers and Martyrs 234
    The Pseudo-security of 'Being in the Right' 235
    The Redundancy of Comparisons and Competition 236
    An Example of Self-empowerment 239

Chapter Ten
FREEDOM AND DESTINY **241**
    Creating Our Own Lives 241
    How, Then, Can Life Be So Unfair? 244
    The Greater Clarity Afforded by a Multi-dimensional
        Model of the Self 248
    The Nature of Self-generation 251
    An Example of the Transformation of a Frozen Response 256
    The Physical Experience of Releasing a Frozen Response 259
    Accepting the Damaged Self 260

Chapter Eleven
TOWARDS FULL ADULTHOOD **266**
    The Tide of Life 274
    The Importance of a Non-linear Approach to Change 279
    The Part Ego Plays in Our Fulfilment 282
    A Brief Recap of Our Present Predicament 283
    Spirit-in-matter 284

Appendix One
THE POWER OF THE CHILD 290

Appendix Two
VICTIMS CAN'T FORGIVE 294

Appendix Three
THE VICTIMHOOD ARCHETYPE: HEALTH, ILLNESS, COMPLIANCE,
CAUSALITY AND HUMAN CONSCIOUSNESS 299

ABOUT THE AUTHOR 323
INDEX 324

Foreword to the New 2025 Edition

> We are passing through the victim archetypal mode at this
> stage of evolution.... Victims can overcome their victimhood.
>
> Jill Hall

It would be impossible to exaggerate the evolutionary importance of this book. I have read stacks of books in my life, as student, professional academic and seeker for Truth. For me, a book is a great one when it is at least as fresh and relevant decades after first publication. In that sense, *The Reluctant Adult (Revisited)* is a very great book; and it deserves to be a global best-seller.

I have been fortunate to encounter many great minds in my professional life; and any dispassionate reading of this book (were that possible!) should conclude that it has been written by one of the greatest minds of the author's generation. Jill Hall could surely have written many more books; but if there was to be just one magnum opus from her pen, then what you will read here really couldn't be bettered. Less is emphatically *more* – as I'm sure Jill would say herself.

You will read deep wisdom about our human condition and the evolutionary juncture human consciousness has reached, with an acuteness of insight and engaging complexity that would be hard to equal. I know of no-one else who could have written this book, or anything close to it. Relatedly, it becomes clear on reading *The Reluctant Adult* just why Jill Hall was a 'straight A' philosophy student – save for the fact that she had all her own ideas and insights, and refrained from piggy-backing on the authority and previous writings of others! *Thank heaven*, I find myself thinking.

In my published review of the first edition from 1995, I wrote that 'A full experiential engagement with the dynamics of victimhood is, I believe, crucial in fully understanding the import and implications of Hall's ideas.... In any adequate account of the human predicament, the ideas set out in this book must surely take up a central position…. Soberingly, it could well be that engagement with the victimhood archetype may be the only hope for our future healthy evolution as a species.' Thirty years on, grandiose though it may sound, I stand by every word.

Jill Hall has a deeply stirring writing style. She has a striking propensity to pose questions – an erudite device that fits very well with the difficult, momentous subject matter she's grappling with. Her recurrent use of short parenthetic passages is perhaps symptomatic of a mind that is holding so many levels of understanding at once, and so does her level best – within the confines of the written-word medium – to make sure that no important stone of understanding is left unturned and thought about.

There is much new material in this new edition: two seminal articles on victimhood penned in the mid-1990s, a long interview from 2021 looking at the Covid 'pandemic' via the victim/persecutor/rescuer dynamic – throwing quite new light on the extraordinary events of that period; and a new detailed index.

Some might wonder about the practical relevance of the ideas in this book. From my personal experience, they have supreme relevance. Sue Hatfield's excellent foreword to the first edition is well worth a close reading in this regard. As with Sue, my own journey has been hugely impacted by the ideas in this book – ideas I first encountered in a lecture Hall gave at the University of East Anglia in the early 1990s.

Once exposed to these ideas, one sees how the victimhood mentality, and the associated 'Drama Triangle', are continually playing out in all human relationships and institutions – usually unconsciously. It's by becoming conscious of how victimhood insinuates itself throughout the interstices of our lives – psyche and behaviour – that we'll then have the capacity to transcend it, and so to advance the evolution of human consciousness.

Another example of the practical application of these ideas comes from the pioneering work of Skeena Rathor and her Co-Liberation work. Skeena writes: 'In our work on Co-Liberation – of being free – Jill Hall's describing of what it is to be in a triangulation of reluctance in feeling and making meaning of the world, as balanced adultifying human beings, has served our root-analysis work for the why and how of Liberation. We are enormously grateful for Jill's light of sight in seeing the shapes that our war-, control- and domination-paradigm casts over us. In pulling these shapes out of the shadows, we can let the light move through us once more. Jill Hall's work is a paint-brush for Liberation.'

Will *The Reluctant Adult* become a global best-seller? That will surely turn on the extent to which we're ready as a species for its challenging message. I hope that we are – but I fear we might not be. Perhaps this book is many years ahead of its time, and will become a global phenomenon many years into the future.

Jill Hall takes on the biggest questions facing humankind in *The Reluctant Adult*. In Chapter 9 (page 228) – a chapter which should be mandatory reading for all political leaders – she writes the following: '*Everything that we can possibly do to deny the validity of victimhood in our own life is our essential contribution towards fulfilling the evolution of humanity*' (her italics). Thus, we need to drop looking to external leaders to liberate us or improve our lives – for as Hall writes, it is *our own* victim attitudes that 'increase and reinforce our victim state, and help to bring about the persecutory behaviour of politically powerful leaders...'. So 'it is a collective responsibility to shift the power of the Victim Archetype'; and it is only at the individual level, extricating ourselves from victimhood's grasp, that the archetype can be transcended.

We are emphatically not helpless and impotent to bring about real, genuine change; for as Hall resoundingly argues, only by *each and every one of us* individually relinquishing our addiction to victimhood can we achieve the next stage of human evolution. This is something we can all do, no matter what our race, creed, age or income level. And a careful reading of *The Reluctant Adult – Revisited* shows us how to do it.

Richard House, Ph.D.
Retired university lecturer in Psychology and Education Studies
Stroud, UK, May 2025

Preface to the First Edition

A little over four years ago I attended a lecture by Jill Hall at the University of East Anglia, the subject matter of which was very much a foretaste of this current book. I listened attentively, nodding my approval along with others in the audience and at the end went home, aware of some questions raised by the talk, of having found it interesting and challenging, but quite unaware of what it had stirred in me at a deeper level. It was only when I arrived home and closed the door behind me that my true response to the evening's talk began to come to the surface. Quite suddenly I became aware of feeling a surge of anger; I felt furious with Jill, angry and hurt at what I began to feel were the implications of what she was saying.

At the time I was in the first stages of therapy, of a journey of unfolding the patterns of my life, and barely beginning to understand my part in what felt then like a tragic drama. I saw myself very much a victim of life's circumstances; particularly a victim of my parents' seeming inadequacies. What I had heard that evening just didn't fit with what I then believed had been the reality of my childhood. Surely, I thought, if it wasn't my mother's fault that I felt the way I did, that my life had turned out the way it had, then it must mean it was my fault. If she was not to blame, if she hadn't got it wrong, then it must be me. I remember very clearly standing in my sitting room as the realization dawned on me: what Jill was saying was that I was to blame, I was the one who had got it wrong; and I was furious with her; she was blaming me, the innocent victim. Such was my logic at the time. Still firmly embedded in the mould of the victim, I couldn't then see beyond the position of blame – if, as Jill claimed, it wasn't Mother's fault, it must be mine.

At the time the only way I knew to make sense of my distress, of my feelings of inadequacy and impotence, was to embrace the idea of the wounded child and guilty mother. I had no sense of my part in creating the reality which I now found so painful; no sense of being a cause unto myself; no sense that I could shift things around and come to see reality some other way.

Much has changed for me since that evening: the long process of therapy has for me borne fruit. I have indeed 'shifted things around', and I know that the pull of that energy of victimhood is still there – and at times surfaces with all the force it ever had; and I know also that I can see life otherwise. In the beginning I needed to blame, and blame I did, with all the force of the wounded victim child I nurtured within me. That was part of the journey, part of the healing; I needed to live out that aspect of me in order to move beyond it.

And what lies beyond that is the understanding that it isn't about blame. My mother was no more the cause of my pain than I of hers: we jointly created, my mother and I, the reality that was our relationship; and each of us is responsible for how we perceive and how we respond to that experience. I could now choose to re-create, to re-experience, the reality of my childhood in this present moment and respond quite differently. I came to understand that it is not a fixed reality, but shifts as my relationship to myself shifts. It is a wonderful feeling to go beyond that position of blame and to know myself as my own causing: to move beyond seeing as a burden, to accept it as a responsibility, and to know that in such responsibility lies freedom. I realize now that Jill was simply spelling out that by claiming our intrinsic wholeness as an infant, we could come to enjoy the richness of true adulthood.

So it was in some sense a very different 'me' who came to read the manuscript of this book. I think if I had read it two or three years ago I would have hated it and responded much as I had to that evening's lecture. Now as I read, it was with more openness and understanding; the subject matter was familiar to me; many of the ideas sat easily alongside my own; I had covered this ground in my own journey, and my understanding had grown along similar lines. And yet as I read, it was still there; I could hear beneath the surface all the old responses, the 'yes buts' that met each new point, each challenge to my old distorted logic: I could feel in me still the victim hooked into blaming, the wounded child seeking redress. But no longer caught within the power of the Victim Archetype, I could also contact some other response that held me and carried me through as page followed page. A book that once would have felt like a blow became, as I read on, a gift.

I am thankful that my journey, in life and in therapy, has been as it has; thankful to have met with Jill and to have shared part of that journey with her; and thankful now to read this book with the insight and understanding that has grown in my talks with her over the years. This book is for me now less a challenge than an invitation; it is offered with love and written with grace. I experienced a sense of triumph and satisfaction as I came to the final pages – and turned to the beginning and started to read it all again. It is an important book, that comes at a time when we are perhaps ready to open and hear what it has to say; ready to move beyond our blaming, beyond our victimhood and know that we can respond to the reality of our lived experience in a more creative way.

It may be that as you read this book you will become aware, as I did, of the 'yes buts', of the pull of that victim energy, of the part of you that feels blamed and angry at the very idea of not blaming. I would ask of you that you note such responses and read on, for the later chapters unfold the complexity of the activity of choice with recognition and compassion for our experience of non-choice. Be willing to put the book aside and return to it later. It is not, as I said, an easy book; but it could change the quality of your life.

Sue Hatfield

Preface to the Second Edition

I am delighted this book is being republished over 30 years after the original publication. It is very timely.

Central to the book, as I understand it, is the Victim Archetype, brought about because of an over-identification with the wounded child who can never recover from the faults of the mother figure, and has at some level been blaming ever since; and not just her, but the world of which she is a part. This error stems from an over-identification of ourselves as just physical beings when indeed in the early part of our lives, we are very dependent on our carers, principally our mothers. But if we see ourselves as spirit which cannot be harmed incarnating into a physical body, then the premise for the Victim Archetype, the innocent helpless child, disappears, and with it, the addiction to blaming. This tendency to blame is supported by causal thinking which is always seeking to find the cause of our unhappiness in the external world.

I hope in this brief summary I have done the book justice. It really challenges not only our Western materialistic notions of the human being, but how they are at a subtle level supporting much of the world of psychology and psychotherapy, which looks for cause in early childhood. By giving spirit its rightful place, we are invited to go past this paradigm, seeing ourselves as able to choose, moment by moment, to feel separate, or recognize an interconnectedness with all that is.

In the last 30 years there has been a welcome addition to the psychology literature of using the here and now (existential), and many spiritual teachers who also emphasize the importance of being in the now. However, the author's central argument, I think, still holds – that we are at some level addicted to the thought patterns that keep us feeling separate, in the past and blaming.

The author explores some of the reasons that might explain the prevalence of victim consciousness, a consciousness which contributes to a health-and-safety culture which is neither healthy nor safe; a fear of litigation, and the litigation itself that abounds in many helping professions as well as in the world at large; and some of the premises of psychological theory which colludes with a world-view that does not serve us. In inviting us to remember that as well as physical bodies, we are spirit and therefore connected to all that is, we no longer inhabit a dualistic world full of them and us.

Given the state of the world, the book is a very important contribution to understanding how we have got into this state, and how we can move beyond it.

Robin Shohet
Psychotherapist and author

Introduction

This book started with a challenge. A great friend of mine, a Jungian psychotherapist, said one day during a discussion that I seemed to have avoided knowledge of my 'helpless self' which, she believed, was part of the fundamental furniture of the psyche. Provoked by this suggestion I embarked on an extensive inner search in order to come to terms with that aspect of myself which I was, perhaps, refusing to recognize.

I had been filled with fearfulness as a child. I was late to socialize and generally took a long time to get used to the world. I seemed ill-adapted to my environment in every way. For years I was plagued by an onslaught of frightening images every night, and each evening I dreaded the approach of darkness. Growing up was an enormous improvement. But in spite of all this fear I did not experience myself as helpless. I have never known a time when I did not have a strong sense of self. I always felt that I was the centre of my activity and that it was 'me' who was doing the living. I felt very alone but not helpless. But now, spurred on by the challenge of my friend, I did everything I could think of to find this 'lost' bit of myself. However, the more I searched, the more I experienced, instead, a sense of my inner power – power to be myself. It was all most unexpected. And then the ideas that I have attempted to share in this book began pouring in on me.

By the time I started writing, the heart of what I had most cherished in my life as well as the beliefs in which I had invested an enormous amount of energy were falling apart, day by day. Devastating though this was, I was reminded, once again, that I need not enter a state of helplessness. Although I felt anxious, despairing, lost, depressed, it still did not seem that my condition rested solely on the forces that I experienced as impinging on me. And I found that whenever I could allow some movement in my perspective, the notion – and thus the fear – of helplessness would seem less real.

This book was born from my sense of the power that lies at the core of my being; and the deeper I searched, the more I knew such power could only come from what lies in us all – and in all things.

Let me say from the outset that I make assumptions about many things – in fact about all the things that most interest me. I make assumptions about spirit, the self and human nature. It seems to me that this activity is a part of the process of responding creatively to life, and so I make no apology. I trust that it is clear that I am offering only my viewpoint. If I keep accentuating that fact then communication will lose all immediacy and become hopelessly cumbersome.

And so I have chosen to speak directly of matters that are deeply important to me. I wish to share my vision of our psychological state of development as a species. These ideas are underpinned by many years of working intimately with hundreds of people as a psychotherapist – that is my grounding. However, the core theory arose out of a series of dream states. I would wake up at night with a phrase or a word on my mind and recognize that it carried a certain energy. I would start writing. The 'theory' emerged. It seemed to have a vitality and authority of its own. I have tried to express it in a somewhat 'respectable' form, but it has not been easy. I can hear people remarking, 'But where are her references?'. Although I have been enormously upheld by all the thinking of past and present philosophers and psychologists, scientists and artists – absorbing ideas like breathing air and receiving continual stimulation – I decided not to make the writing of this book an academic project. In fact I had to ban reading during this period because I became all too easily overwhelmed with new thoughts whenever I received fresh input of any kind; and I knew that this book would never get written if I explored the subject any further.

I also did not want to stray too far from the immediacy of the core idea. It was some reading in the field of Social Psychology (which I just happened to do because of a debate going on about Family Therapy with some colleagues of mine) that made me decide on the ban. The reader may notice the different quality of the writing in Chapter 5, when I did make use of some of the material I read around hierarchical models. Otherwise, as far as I know, no book has influenced the basic direction of my thought. It has arisen out of my experience of life and from different levels of my consciousness. This experience includes my training in Biodynamic Psychology with Gerda Boyesen. She communicated an extensive, immediate and vital approach to the embodied psyche for which I am enormously grateful. Some years later I came into contact with the teachings of the American Indian peoples in the wilderness of New Mexico, and experienced once more the impact of an enriching new 'language of the psyche'. Both simple and subtle, it became the tool through which I incorporated a whole unlived aspect of myself. But I also found it extremely difficult to do justice to this 'language' in the written word. (Hence my confusion about when to use capital letters in Chapter 6.) I have many times spoken the teachings, and that feels the appropriate mode of communication.

And so the assumptions that I make are not merely empty intellectual ones. They inform my life – and I enjoy my life enormously. They work for me. I wonder why it is that something seems less of an assumption if someone else wrote about it somewhere else and a note is made of that fact? Why does something have more authority, the further removed it is from its direct point of entry into the arena of shared thought? It is an academic habit to be ashamed of making assumptions. We all make them all the time. The important thing is to clarify what they are and look at their implications.

Chapter One
Psychology in Infancy

In our Western culture, psychological theories of human nature and development tend to encourage or legitimize the blaming syndrome. I do not wish to embark here on a detailed critique of such theories, but I invite those who have the interest and the energy to engage with the ideas of those who have been influential in this field – with Freud, Winnicott and Bowlby, Klein and Piaget, Laing and Grof. Notice how they all draw on the notion of cause and effect, which is so built into the very structure of our thought that we seldom question it. We barely recognize it as an assumption. And I shall be exploring later how this approach to the psyche goes hand in hand with the emotional position of blame.

For all the innovation and subtlety supplied by new thinkers and practitioners in the field of psychology and psychotherapy, we are still operating within a Freudian framework of thought. Freud is the 'Isaac Newton' of psychology, our basic reference point; and however much we may criticize his thinking, we have not dared to move beyond him. We have not yet allowed the foundations of our understanding of the human psyche to expand and shift and turn around in the way that physics has embraced transformations in its understanding of matter and the material world. Thinking related to the 'universe within' has not kept pace with thinking related to the universe without. We have not had our 'Einstein'. Many may see Jung as such; but although he did vastly extend the arena of study and explored new inner terrain, claiming both our primitive inheritance and a new psychic empire for Western thought, the foundations of psychology held firm. We are now in a Neo-Freudian age. We accept neurosis as the norm. We operate from our 'wounded child'. However sophisticated our intellectual abilities and achievements we are still, collectively, very young in our psychological development.

Just as Einstein's concept of reality evolved out of the clarity and brilliance of Newton's offering to physics, so we who would understand the psychological aspect of our being are indebted to Freud, however deeply we may disagree with him. We build on each others' ideas, and many diverse thinkers put forward a piece of the puzzle, an element of truth, as well as help us see what does not fit or where next to look. However urgently we may need to discard old thought structures and point out their flaws, we cannot help but learn from that which we select to leave behind. The whole process of unfolding knowledge is a joint communal human happening.

And thus we evolve. I believe that we have now digested Freud; that we can thank him – especially for drawing our attention to the power of the unconscious mind to shape our reality: we can thank him, and move on. I believe that the time has come to go beyond causal thinking, just as it is also time to place therapeutic work on the 'wounded child' within a broader, deeper context for understanding human nature.

Freud was a patriarchal thinker, and such thinking is no longer underpinned by any evolutionary necessity. The thrust of masculine energy needed for differentiation on the psychological level (mirroring the earlier thrust which gave physical form and shape within the primaeval continuum) has taken its necessary course. We have developed egos. We know of our separateness. And having latched on to this knowledge with enormous energy, we are plunged into the twin terrors of isolation and dependence. The lived contradiction can only lead to self-destruction.

If we remain stuck at this evolutionary point of concentration on the newest aspect of human consciousness – the ego – then we shall retain a philosophy of divisiveness which cannot help but give rise to social and political systems based on insecurity, competition, suspicion, threat and conflict. Power is the currency of our interactions; we engage in countless variations of the impotent/omnipotent dynamic. This is the offspring of ego domination and an over-weighting of masculine energy. We have lost sight of the truth that we are only separate on a certain level of being; ego consciousness can only, by its very nature, provide us with one aspect of reality. It is necessary that we now integrate our ego within the context of the larger self and allow awareness of our interconnectedness at subtler levels of reality to support and inform our knowledge of our diversity. As soon as we connect with our whole selves we then also experience a connection with the whole of existence, and therefore with all others.

Meanwhile the ego, which is closely associated with the rational mind and concerned with negotiating its way amidst a world of objects, demands an external cause to explain our unsatisfactory behaviour. We are always looking for a cause to hold responsible for our difficulties, becoming, as we do so, an effect – a victim. I believe that the Victim Archetype is the most consistently active of all the archetypal energies in which our psyche engages, and is so embedded in our way of being that we are not really aware of it. We have not distanced ourselves enough from it to recognize its workings in us. Experiencing ourselves as victims simply feels like the way life is. Just as a fish does not know that it is swimming in water as opposed to moving through air, so we do not have awareness of our medium of interaction in relation to some other perfectly natural alternative that our evolution could offer us.

On the other hand, ideals which require a starting point outside of our lived reality do not provide an access point to our present experience, and so cannot illuminate how our psyche is actually dealing with the world. Unless such illumination occurs, we cannot see in what way it would be possible to alter our lives and come to create a different reality for ourselves. Our infant psychological state of development, with the concomitant propensity to blame, combines with our adult training in objective thinking, and the last thing that we think of studying is the very mode we ourselves live out from day to day.

The Structure of Language and Our Concept of Self

A crucial obstacle to our awareness is the fact that we are so deeply and unconsciously influenced by the structure of our language that we cannot see what we are imposing upon ourselves and our world. Our rational thought is given form through language and we assume such thought mirrors reality. Our rational linguistic model demands subject and object, actor and acted upon, 'before' and 'after', and we take this to be the structure of the world and how life operates. Language prescribes for us a linear ordering of data suited to cause/effect thinking and thus suited to 'victim' thinking. Our language serves the Victim Archetype. We have the subject who causes the action, and the object who receives the action.

What is more, ruled by linear either/or logic, we have *either* the agent who performs the action or the *object* acted upon. Our language also insists on a clear division between active and passive verbs, encouraging us to think that we either *do* something or have it *done* to us. Unaware of the power of such thinking, we are set for blaming and abdication of responsibility. We become either an agent or a non-agent, as opposed to seeing ourselves as interacting agents and entities of equal status. 'You make me feel angry' is a common type of statement in our everyday lives, rather than 'I felt angry when you said that'. We imagine that we are either 'doers' or 'receivers', rather than experiencing ourselves as simply partaking in different modes of activity, each of which helps to shape our reality in its own way. And we have no sense that we are creating, by this way of thinking, the ideal soil for the Victim Archetype to take root.

Once we have acknowledged the difference between the structure of language and the structure of reality, then we can see that rational thought alone can never adequately inform us of the nature of the universe. And yet it has become the only means that is given respect. It has come to the point when only the fruits of rational thought count as sound knowledge. In this way we divide ourselves from the very reality we are attempting to live. Rational thought is not the most fitting mode with which to know the universe in its richness and fullness, and thus is not a fitting mode with which to know ourselves. Rational thought is linear, as language is linear, while reality is living, ever moving and multi-dimensional. We must approach the wholeness of our inner and outer reality, if we would know something of it, with our whole selves, which includes the part of us which is non-linear. We need to approach our truth with the aspect of consciousness that is not confined to the linear. In other words, the ego is far too limited to take on such a task.

Just as we have not yet integrated our ego within the self, so we have not yet fully recognized (let alone integrated) the two great systems which influence us: the primary system of 'being and doing', which is living, dynamic and multi-dimensional; and the secondary system of language and rational thought, which seeks to exclude, categorize, pin down and fix in order to name events, objects and concepts. These two systems seem utterly incompatible, as if we were destined as human beings to be at odds with ourselves and our world; but this is so only if we try to fit them together *on the same level of being*. As long as we imagine the ego to be the Self, we shall imagine that our language mirrors reality. The first step is to recognize the incompatibility rather than evade it. Only then can we come to an appreciation of the different *levels* of experience that these systems address. Reductionism cannot help but cheat us of our humanity. Just as we have to accept the Self as the larger field within which the ego operates, so we have to accept that a dynamic multi-dimensional reality is the ground or field within which language and rational thought play a part only.

When, therefore, we attempt to devise purely rational models of the psyche, we unwittingly serve the deep-seated attitudes of victimhood and blame that underlie our civilization. The Victim Archetype can be very subtle in its manifestations, and emerges in a great variety of rational disguises. Psychotherapists, whatever their background, would no doubt be horrified to see themselves as actually colluding with the perpetuation of victimhood, even as they struggle to assert the value and necessity of 'taking responsibility for yourself'. It is important to pay attention to the experience of 'the wounded child' in each of us but only as a stage in the process of healing. It is equally important to ensure that attempts to understand human nature are not being made from that same, wounded place.

The Relationship between a Causal Ontology and the Need to Blame

The most effective of disguises for our legitimization of the blaming syndrome is the long-established respectability of seeking external causes for phenomena. Civilized societies feel somewhat superior when noting how primitive peoples see the external world in a very subjective way, personalizing the elemental forces and activities of the natural world about them. We are proud of our ability to recognize the outer world for what it is, not realizing the deep abuse we have wrought on ourselves, and on our understanding, by confusing *distinction* with *separation*. We have come to misuse our capacity to make the distinction between 'inner' and 'outer', and instead *separate* self and environment.

This non-sensical habit has given rise to a fragmented way of being. It may at first seem surprising that such dislocation, in fact, clouds our ability to distinguish between self and the world. In making a false and absolute divide between self and other, subject and object, we are actually more likely to fix internal material 'out there' and never recognize it as ours, rather than allow a fluid movement between the two – which, I imagine, was the experience of those in more primitive, grounded communities. This is the price of ego development – a necessary stage in the evolving psyche; but does not our present predicament as a species call for us to move on to the next stage?

The fact that modern physics now elegantly emphasizes the falsity of these divisions has not yet taken root in our everyday thinking, although it is more and more spoken of and written about. The philosophical implications of advanced science have still to percolate through to the deeper layers of our consciousness. Meanwhile, our ego consciousness eagerly absorbs the powerful material achievements and promises of scientism. Even the more reluctant imbibers remain semi-saturated. We regard the objective world, cleansed not only of gods but also of suspect human meaning, as the only source of reliable knowledge. We are not going to fool ourselves. We are bent on looking at 'real' causes (which means mechanistic causal chains) and 'hard' facts. We can only trust what is 'out there'. From this shared base, the giant systems of capitalism and communism have taken form. We concentrate our attention on the material achievements and riches that have emerged from what we consider to be the bold acceptance of bare truth. The inheritance of scientism is still in us, whatever eminent scientists are saying or however ardently New Age groups are reinvesting the world with new meanings. No magic must be allowed, and mystery is to be overcome. Only 'objective' knowledge counts.

And so naturally psychology, in its own diverse ways, also focuses on external causes in its attempts to explain who and why we are as we are. External, that is, to the existential I; the experienced Self. Even when conceding the importance of the inner world of the psyche, *formative* power is deemed to lie outside of this self.

The psyche is slow to let go of a framework that it has deeply assimilated. It is slow to let go of scientism even though science itself is, as it were, going beyond itself, and has evolved so far that it is spilling over its own presuppositions and calling in new ones. Science cannot make sense of its own findings without expanding the conceptual framework and the very axioms that gave rise to those findings. The motion of particles at the quantum level cannot be explained in old-fashioned causal terms; explanations have to be cast aside unless completely novel thinking is invoked. Leading biologists are also beginning to look at the notion of cause afresh, and are focusing on the concept of self-generating systems. They are beginning to look at organisms as causes and effects of themselves; not pushed about by external forces, but expressing their own natures. Physicists, too, are moving away from the idea of inert matter worked upon by separate forces; forces operate through messenger particles and are generated by the actual geometry of space/time. The universe is one, great, self-happening. Physics is increasingly becoming metaphysics.

Can we equally expand the basic assumptions that underlie our present psychological theories? Of course physics, being the 'hardest' and most respected and secure of the sciences, has the confidence to do this, whereas psychology, being among the 'softest' and youngest and most suspect of sciences, may be slow to take off its corset and relax into a new and ever-evolving shape. Matter 'out there' trails with it remnants of cherished objectivity, and so the probing of matter to its tiny sub-atomic limits is now allowed to bring forth mystery. Yet we fear that we shall disappear down the 'black hole' of subjectivity if we dare study our own depths with the same licence and imagination.

It is vital that psychology also takes part in the neo-scientific revolution of thought that is now upon us. If material existence is far too intricate and subtle a phenomenon to be understood through a cause/effect mode of thought, then surely we must let go the attempt to approach the human psyche from such a standpoint. When we come to try and understand the psyche, causal thinking is not only inadequate but is even positively dangerous. We are likely to set up deep confusion and distortion if we latch on to false 'causes'. In our determination to find a cause, have we not based our whole understanding of ourselves on some early *reactive* phase (oral and anal fixation and the Oedipus Complex, for instance)? It follows that we then justify and feed our inventive defence system, giving it primal value, primary status, and we allow this aspect of our psyche to dominate and mislead us. This also means that all of us (including psychiatrists and psychotherapists who set out to heal) are, without realizing it, reinforcing reactive behaviour in others, too, by treating such behaviour as *fundamental* to our nature. We are busy raising the status of the neurotic in us. We then struggle to comprehend the human condition through the 'grid' of our neurosis, abdicating the ability to suspend that frame of reference and allow a clearer picture of the undamaged human being to emerge. Defensiveness is taken up as the only sensible and realistic position. We assume both a necessary and a profound dependence on a 'special other', which in turn feeds the conviction that we are bound to be let down and betrayed. If we seek attachment, then we are bound to feel abandoned. So of course we had better be continually on guard to make sure that we are not hurt again. Given this state of affairs, it is not surprising that we believe that our needs can only be met by fighting for them or by devising ways of manipulating others. Our championing of the defended self is mirrored in our social and political arrangements, and it is hardly surprising that our international relationships are permeated with collective fear and distrust.

I believe that causal thinking is a completely inept tool for dealing with the multi-layered and highly complex operations of the human psyche. It is only efficacious when dealing with mechanical systems, closed systems or linear sequences. The human being is none of these. We need to evolve theories that fit how we actually are, and that therefore no longer block how we *could* be. Conscious beings are surely the most open of all material systems. I have witnessed the psyche as essentially creative, not mechanistic, although it can become somewhat mechanistic if we believe it operates that way. That is how creative it is. We evolve our own unique answers, our own unique responses, to the intricate situations in which we find ourselves, or which we actively seek or bring about. We are not mechanical dolls playing out a linear chain of events.

The mystery of the psyche cannot be unscrambled and spread out into distinct, conveniently understood causal sequences. We are not a string of little happenings, or even a cluster of many strings that can be untangled and teased out for rational examination. It may satisfy the intellect to select clear lines of psychological development, but do we not continually feel confused and discouraged by the inevitable 'steps backward' that we all experience? The psyche operates on many levels at once and learns in a more complex, timeless and circular manner. We cannot hope to translate the co-existing interconnections of a multi-dimensional being into a linear form, nor shall we ever grasp the operations of the psyche by drawing only on our rational faculty.

One can, of course, say that if 'this' event hadn't happened, then 'that' event wouldn't have happened; but this doesn't prove that the former event caused the latter event. They are connected in some way, and the later event is affected by the former event, but it could have been 'caused' by any number of former events. For example: If the farmer had not been standing outside his house at the very moment when my husband and I passed on our way to get the lawn-mower repaired, then we would have taken it to another place to get it mended rather than the one that he suggested. I would then not have shopped at a tempting little bakery nearby and eaten a cream cake. Did the farmer cause my eating of the cream cake? Ridiculous. Did the broken lawn-mower? Did my partiality for cream cakes? But what was the cause of that? I could pick on anything I fancied. And what would be the cause of my choice of cause?

The belief that we can isolate a definite cause (whether an individual person or happening, a system or even chains of events) denies the inescapable connectedness of all life; the one, grand, dynamic tapestry of existence. Conscious knowledge of this truth gives us our ultimate security. The act of selecting a particular cause, the very process of defining a cause, is a distancing activity: it brings about a separation from our own power. It also generates the predicament of experiencing both alienation from others as well as impotent entanglement with them. This cannot help but give rise to unbearable terror (usually buried at a level well below consciousness). Hence our diversions, addictions and denials – our tendency to block and resist life in an attempt to protect ourselves and gain fleeting relief from our chronic insecurity. Causal thinking is based on the subject/object split which leaves us with a sense of being adrift in the universe, mere objects for others as they are for us, and so having to *forge* connections and *make* relationships rather than experiencing that we are born into connectedness.

As causal thinking goes hand in hand with the *division* between subject and object (as opposed to taking subject/object distinction into account as just one, but sometimes necessary, mode of viewing life), it is based on unreality; it is based on a partial reality, a mere aspect of reality, which is claimed as a fundamental reality. And so causal thinking, if used to understand the profundity of our natures and the intricacies of our personal lives, is bound to misinform us and mislead us.

If simple external happenings are far too complicated for causal theory to make any sense, then how can we hope to use the concept fruitfully when exploring the more elusive workings of the psyche? We can be endlessly diverted by trying to select the particular cause of our feelings, ideas or actions. I am often struck by how the same event can be used to explain different, or even opposing, behaviours and thought formations. The fact that a child's mother left him at a specific age can be claimed as the 'cause' of his depressive personality and his tendency to collapse; or equally, it can be put forward as the 'cause' of another's ability to stand on his own two feet and not rely on anyone else. But shouldn't true causes carry predictive efficacy? Causal theory, when applied to psychological matters, relies on retrospective knowledge. We trace back only carefully selected connections; ones which we couldn't possibly have made without the benefit of hindsight.

Indeed, the only certain cause of any event is the interaction of the whole universe – that immense self-generating holo-movement; and yet in turning to this explanation we lose any practical application of the notion of cause. We become submerged in the massive and

Chapter One: Psychology in Infancy

infinitely complex interpenetration of activities. The value of cause as a concept is that it can be abstracted from its surroundings; it can be selected for its special potency and its essential relationship to exact and expected results. It is only useful as a concept if the connection between two events is predictable and repeatable. These conditions simply do not apply to the multi-layered happenings and activities of our human experience.

The only feasible starting point is myself – the Self. But I deliberately do not wish to suggest that we transpose the idea of cause on to the Self and let the Self carry its full weight. The concept of cause has such associations with mechanistic determinism that its use is all too likely to promote the notion of control. If we see the Self as causing everything for itself, then we shall see the Self as controlling everything, which makes interaction with other controlling selves an impossibility. The term 'cause' also evokes a linear mode of thinking which renders choice and free will unintelligible. (I shall be enlarging on this subject – as well as the connection between control and guilt – in later chapters.) It is far more satisfactory, both intellectually and emotionally, to assign causal thinking to the appropriate areas of scientific endeavour and leave it there. We then free ourselves to put forward the hypothesis that we human beings are each a creative matrix, a source of energy, living within a multi-level reality.

Cause is a concept that has played a valuable role in the development of the analytic mind and our ability to handle the practicalities of life. The concept has been powerful and fruitful. But now we need to free ourselves from its confines. For although the 'clockwork' model is contained in our universe, and has its due and fitting place, the universe itself does not operate that way, as quantum mechanics has revealed. It is too crude a concept for the subtler layers of being. The movement, the organization, of the basic (and ever more ethereal) 'stuff' of the universe cannot be held to an order of that kind. Neither can the ever-moving experience of human beings. This does not mean that there is no order or lawful behaviour in nature but indicates, rather, that it is intrinsic rather than enforced by external powers, unpredictable rather than fixed. Just as our sub-atomic 'substance' dances with an inexplicable order and unknown freedom, so do our psyches form and re-form, and come into their fullness with our known freedom – when we know of our freedom. If the less complicated organisms of our planet are now seen as self-generating systems, then how much more potent is our ability, as human beings, to generate ourselves – we who have both a concept and living consciousness of 'self'; a self which acts.

I contend that the time has come for those engaged in the discipline of psychology to let the concept of cause rest. It is especially important because causal thinking, when we come to explain *ourselves*, is so easily translated into impotence and blame. We seek a cause to hold responsible for our ills – the ills of *our natural functioning*. I am not now referring to what we label as pathology. We diminish our humanity once we view ourselves, or experience ourselves, as an *effect*. Causal thinking leads straight to victimhood. The emotionality of the psyche colours and confuses 'cause' with 'blame', and 'effect' with 'shame'. We are lost in a mire of impotence, omnipotence and guilt.

The Inevitable Failure of Mother

Now the trouble with blaming is that it not only entices us away from our own power; it also lands us (along with the linear causal theories that it shadows) with an 'infinite regress' problem. Where does our blaming come to rest? Both intellectually and emotionally we have the sense of never getting there; never reaching satisfaction; never touching source. It matters not if we use a 'Nature' or a 'Nurture' theory – genes, parents, foetal distress, birth, early conditioning, childhood trauma cannot take the weight of all that they are called to bear as *explanatory principles*. *They fail to explain why the human race is the way it is*. And even if theories based on them may temporarily alleviate our distress and confusion, where do they leave mother?

Neo-Freudianism still reigns, and the infant is the focus of attention. Caught in the cause/effect model, it is bound to be the case that the more sensitively the theorists or practitioners look at the infant, the more guilt they load on to mother. It is no good primal therapists simply stating, as they are sometimes careful to do, that mother is not to blame. If the emotions of a pregnant mother are the cause of her child's self-defeating behaviour patterns later in life, what chance does that leave mother to be who *she* is? We invade mother ever further with each new theory.

However powerful we make mother, surely she cannot be the cause of the whole human condition? Did not she herself arise within it? It is simply muddled thinking to make the flaw the cause of the flaw. Something must be wrong here. It is interesting that most theorists are men. But women, who sop up guilt like blotting paper, would no doubt do little better, even if they did create the opportunity to spend their time publishing books on the subject. Look at Melanie Klein with her concept of the 'bad breast'. And Alice Miller, while taking up a valuable counter position to the later Freud in her championing of the actual lived experience of the hurt child, is as demanding on mother as any man. No answer is provided for *her* redemption, and so our general human predicament remains as much an enigma as ever. The child must indeed be listened to respectfully and her or his experience accepted; and the child knows itself as a participator in events even when under duress and appalling manipulation.

A human being can never be a puppet. If we count our young as ultra-sensitive and psychologically delicate – rendering them hopeless victims of tougher and naturally abusive parents – then the human species is doomed. Unless we balance our concern with the damaging events of childhood with an appreciation of our intrinsic resilience, unless we take note of our enormous creative ability to devise ways of surviving, we shall remain circling within a fundamentally neurotic perspective, waiting for the advent of 'proper' parents.

Even the richly subtle and benign theories of Gerda Boyeson require a paradise of non-thwarting mothers who enjoy nurturing or playing all day. The onus is always on mother to get it right, although it is acknowledged that she was once a hurt and wounded infant herself. As also was father, who is next in line as a thorn in the flesh of every child. (He fails to be the correct model, or give the ever-needed recognition to his children.) Lay bare the bones beneath the proliferation of theories that have flourished since the subject called Psychology took off, and there you see that the one who is truly held responsible for how we are is mother. The cause of our malfunctioning rests with her. Modern psychological theory has largely arisen within a capitalist ideological framework, and capitalism is based on the belief in the 'naturalness' of self-interest. And yet mothers, who make up a vast section of the population, are expected, in some inexplicable way, to be selfless. They must exist in order to fulfil the needs of their child. They must be a breed apart and not look to their own needs – or at least not until they have satisfied those of their children. If they dare to take account of themselves in the very way that is thought natural in others, then they apparently ruin the human race.

We insist that if we were not treated 'right' by mother then we can't live our lives properly. We are nothing unless she affirms us. Given such beliefs and expectations, it is hardly surprising that there is still, in spite of the important influence of feminist thinking, an underlying thrust within our culture to keep her in her place. For as long as we claim that our experience is primarily the result of external happenings, then maternal deprivation is likely to be top of the list. Mother is the favourite candidate to carry the burden of our distress. It all goes wrong when she fails to experience what Winnicott called 'primary maternal preoccupation'. Thus we victimize her with her own guilt, which becomes ever more refined as we modernize our social arrangements. And in some deep, hidden place within, we remain determined to wait, for a lifetime if need be, for her magic wand (or for father's turn of the key), as if we were mechanical artifacts rather than venturing out as live, creative entities.

You will perhaps be puzzled that I have not said more of Jung – that great and grand explorer of the vast field of the human psyche. He went far beyond Freud, extending the area of psychology into realms ignored or spurned by respectable rational thinkers and reductionist scientists. But although Jung ventured so far beyond Freud, he did not reverse the direction Freud had set. He did not release us, therefore, from the grip of the Victim Archetype and our fascination with it, although his theories do account for its extraordinary organizing power within our psyche and its inevitable expression in our behaviour. For all his acknowledgement of the human soul, his insight about individuation and his prophetic assertion in *The Answer to Job* that the destiny of humankind is to create more and more consciousness, Jung never really dealt with Mother. We are stretched by his thinking, but still do not know how we came to be as we are.

And then there is Abraham Maslow and Carl Rogers, as well as many other thinkers and practitioners in the field of Humanistic Psychology, who have deviated from Freudianism in a highly significant way by positing and focusing on the fundamental goodness of human nature. But they leave out the knotty problem of why, given that this is the case, we so readily and inevitably end up being neurotic and defensive. Why are we drawn to make such poor decisions for ourselves? Why are we so resistant to partaking in our birthright of joy and well-being? And so, with this troublesome gap in our understanding, mother tends to slip in once again to take the blame.

In the end, all these theories tend to imply that we are natural victims; that each member of the human race is unfortunately delivered into victimhood from the start, even if later, in some inexplicable manner, we attain the faculty of choice. *As long as we rely on mother as the answer to our human condition, then we shall engage in the Victim Archetype*, however subtle its expression. For there is, of course, no such thing as a perfect mother; and an imperfect mother, given full causal efficacy for our state of being, becomes a persecutor. However much we dress her up in sweetness and light, make an icon out of her and passionately cling to her, we shall nevertheless experience her as the great withholder and tormentor and frustrater of our needs. The breast has far greater power than any penis; our need for it is both primal and universal. When mother is invested with full causal status, childhood cannot then help but become littered with trauma like hidden (or not so hidden) land-mines, and we all become candidates for cure.

The Power of the Victim Archetype on Our Collective Psyche

Social psychologists such as Sullivan and Sampson, using hierarchical models in their analysis of social interaction and the formation of self-concepts, place archetypes as the highest order that generates meaning in human relationships. They are considered the most embracing of contexts that give meaning to our life scripts, contracts and speech acts. Indeed, they are such powerful organizing principles of the human psyche that in many cultures, they are given the status of gods and goddesses. If it is true that meanings are imposed on our stream of experience rather than being derived from it, if we are concept-driven rather than data-driven, then it is of deep relevance to our quality of experience to clarify our meaning systems. And as it is generally conceded that our modes of relating to others on all levels – personal, social and political – are far from satisfactory, then it becomes urgent to examine the context at the top of the meaning hierarchy, since that has the greatest power to generate such experience. We need to know what archetypes we function from and recognize the manner in which they organize our experience. Any change in such higher-order concepts would have substantial impact on all the lower-order contexts which engender meaning for us.

That which rules our unconscious mind plays an enormous part in producing our experience of external reality, and archetypes operate at the unconscious level. If the Victim Archetype is firmly lodged within our psyche, then 'feeling a victim' of external pressures, as well as of our own habitual patterns of behaviour, becomes a given – something 'we can't do anything about'. Unless mediated by consciousness, our fundamental beliefs, images and attachments are automatically translated into 'how things are'. If we would change our experience of the world then we must know of that vast hidden creative matrix, both within the collective and the individual psyche, which is ordering these events.

I believe there is ample evidence to suggest that the Victim Archetype has indeed become part of the structuring process of the psyche – a transpersonal dominant – and thus part of the structuring process of our personal, social and political arrangements. It may not often appear in our conscious self-image, but any deeper exploration of our inner conflicts and daily concerns does not fail to reveal its presence. The 'victim self' is found in 'normal', 'well functioning', 'healthy' people as well as in those termed inadequate and overtly unable to deal with their lives. The socially recognized victim – the victim of crime – carries and expresses this archetypal energy for us all in its most obvious form. And, of course, enfolded in each victim self lies a persecutor, but often well disguised as a persecutor of that same victim self. Blaming is the shared mode of both aspects of this archetype. Buried deep within us all is the dependent, frightened, hungry infant longing to be loved – to be taken over and made to feel good – and meanwhile occupied with blaming and trying to control the uncontrollable external world.

It is natural that we try to cloak this unsatisfactory state, this terrifying state, with a more comfortable and inspiring conscious belief – a story of adulthood and progress. However, the deeper unconscious organizing principle continues unabated, creating an inner psychic state to which we never fail to return. And thus we are out of sync; and a mass of contradictory beliefs play their part in our general confusion as to who we are. The great cry for liberty, equality and fraternity never takes root. We do not often relate as equals – we are usually either one 'up' or one 'down', victim or persecutor (or rescuer), child or parent. Modes of inequality form the persistent dance of human relationships, although, of course, we change positions in different contexts, and may even generate much variety within the same basic framework to which we have limited ourselves. Such interactions provide the perennial subject matter of psychotherapy – a relationship which is, itself, always vulnerable to an imbalance of power. It is hardly surprising that our attempts to heal the psyche mirror one of the most powerful prevailing modes of operation *within* the psyche.

Victim thinking, causal ontology and reductionist science have all gone hand in hand: they reduce complex systems to their elements and assume they are all determined in their motions. Victimhood flourishes within a materialist framework, a framework which affords the combination of deep psychological insecurity plus opportunities to relieve our fear by engaging in apparent control of a world which has been conveniently divided into bits. Never mind if we ourselves are determined; at least we function as the determining agents of lesser beings and the 'dead' world. And do we not, at the same time, gain the 'freedom' of not being responsible for ourselves as a species? Of course anomalies arise. Extraordinary phenomena keep cropping up and having to be explained away, just as experiences of real choice and creativity continue to punctuate the 'we cannot help it' mindset. So far these anomalies have not loosened the grip of the Victim Archetype, just as they have not done much to uproot out-dated scientific assumptions. We tend to put a circle around these occurrences and say 'how interesting', or 'it can't be true', and then carry on in the same old way. Or we give them a definite label like 'co-incidence' or 'telepathy' or 'hypnosis', which somehow seems to contain their implications from spreading beyond that cognitive box.

Our evident resistance to transformation could be our great teacher. Whenever resistance occurs it provides a clue; it shows us what next needs to be explored. The minute we experience resistance, and recognize it as such, we could be on to a rich vein of potential self-knowledge. It offers us a thread to the unconscious belief system which is holding the power to shape our present reality. We are protecting a basic belief, a cherished form of being, that we sense *has* to give way. Resistance is most active when the old belief system is both fundamental in its organizing capacity and out of date. Perhaps, at this stage in our collective development, we are expressing a final defensive flurry before allowing ourselves to 'see' the Victim Archetype at work in our lives. In that seeing we know, too, of our possible freedom.

I hold that the Victim Archetype is the most consistently active of the vast range of archetypes that our psyche calls upon. It holds the entwined power of two of the most fundamental of all archetypes – Infant and Mother. When they lock together in the collusive embrace of impotence and protectionism, generating blame and guilt, then we, as individuals and as a species, are caught in victimhood. I believe that until we disengage from the energy of this archetype we can never grow up. And unless we grow up we may, instead, become extinct. It is crucial that we do not block the next stage of evolution; that we allow ourselves to reach maturity. It is hardly possible to transform our personal, social and political lives from a position of imagined powerlessness: from a profound belief that we have no real freedom of choice or responsibility for our experience. Put differently, if we continue to see the Mother Archetype as more potent than, or as prior to, the Infant Archetype, then we create the Victim Archetype as the underlying influence which gives birth to our attitudes, our thought structures and our feelings, and we cannot move forward into adulthood. We cannot claim our wholeness and live as healthy human beings.

The answer is not to extend beyond mother (and father), in the hope of escaping from this state of affairs, only to latch on to poorly arranged genes or inadequately constructed social environments as the cause of our troublesome tendencies and strangely destructive behaviour. Whatever fascinating and telling discoveries we might make in these areas, focusing on them *as the source of our human predicament* will only seduce us into placing our power outside ourselves once again, rendering us equally vulnerable to the activity of blaming, and stripping us of responsibility for being as we are. We would still be taking on an essentially victim position, and victims can never construct a wholesome or a desirable society. They cannot help but call forth persecutors. Someone must hold the disowned power.

There is widespread agreement that human nature is at best a puzzle, and at worst a mess. We are the only species doomed to malfunction as we start out on life – before we have hardly begun. And yet we are so beautifully designed. The intricate workings of our bodies are a pure wonder, and the range of our mental faculties a marvel. Something doesn't add up. Perhaps we just have to look at everything the other way round. Perhaps we have to start with the infant in each of us.

Chapter Two
The Great Regression

If we donate the power to organize the human condition to mother, then we are bound to be drawn back to the womb like a magnet; the only safe place is the womb. The only way to be powerful ourselves is to be within the orbit of the powerful one – to be merged with her as one. Our libido becomes fixated on fusion. Music, song, dance, literature, painting – all show forth our deep and perennial yearning for romantic love; that strange, ecstatic state when we are immersed in the loved one – both energized and powerless, affirmed and yet lost.

The goal of prolonged fusion spells disaster, not bliss. Human beings are constituted in such a way that we cannot stay fused, and it is therefore a state that calls for its own destruction. For a being destined to unfold as a unique individual, merging brings forth a longing for murder. At an unconscious level, both partners lost in a pact of utter dependency wish at times to kill the other. It is not only the infant that rages but also the mother; she, too, has to carry the dark secret of her momentary surges of desire to annihilate the one she so absorbingly adores. If we seek fusion as a fixed state, we are doomed.

Attachment becomes our preoccupation, coupled with the driving need to separate. We often spend a lifetime compulsively swinging between these two poles of misfortune. We do not know how simply to be present *with* another. We experience all too little of true giving and receiving, true nourishment and attention, in our central relationships. Some may seek out special courses in 'Human Development' because, it seems, our human potential has a poor chance of being actualized at home, however many times we rearrange its occupants; however many times we alter the membership of the family.

Psychotherapists who work with re-birthing describe the

interesting phenomenon of their clients almost immediately attempting to go back into the womb after their heroic journey out into the world. Short lived is the joy or pure relief of survival. It seems that we are convinced that the best place to be is in the womb. But this desire, this behaviour, is blamed on mother's lack of proper maternal preoccupation; a disposition which, presumably, she is meant to have retained or gained in spite of having been subjected to its lack by her own mother. The belief is that if mother does not gear her existence around that of her child, then everything goes wrong. We see those 'in love' repeat this belief and this situation. Some magic 'other', who fits our needs to perfection, is the great and only answer to life. Mother (or lover) must be attached to us and solely to us. Once she has been given primal power, attachment is confused with survival.

Among other things, this makes our birth a 'death'. We then experience one of the most natural and essential of happenings as a calamity, and rate it as a severe and long-lasting trauma. What an introduction to life. Our survival drive, which directed us outwards into the world, curls back on itself. On the inner psychological level we all too often spend our lives scurrying backwards towards the 'womb', in spite of our marvellously developed physical state and mental skills. On some level, it seems, we are all determined to stay infants. Regression is not a special phenomenon that occurs only in a psychotherapy session: it punctuates our lives.

Creative and Destructive Modes of Regression and the Child within

I want to emphasize the difference not only between conscious and unconscious regression, but also between regression and the ability to connect with the child in ourselves.

When we regress we are drawn back to old feelings, old behaviour, old patterns of being. This phenomenon allows us to engage with the source of our habitual energy circuits and re-enter uncompleted emotional cycles. Such a process is freeing if we regress with conscious awareness that we are regressing, and manage to complete feelings which were interrupted, diverted or blocked – gaining a direct sense of how we could allow our energy to move more freely in future. It is entrapping, however, if we regress unconsciously in order to play out familiar positions from our past which cannot help but generate repetitive feelings, thoughts and behaviour that are often quite inappropriate within our present reality. Whenever we do this, we become programmed beings rather than creative beings. Moreover, most of those old, hidden programmes are based on fear, and were taken up by us when something 'went wrong'; when we judged the situation as too painful to bear, or deemed it too dangerous to be ourselves or express ourselves. They make up the defended or over-adapted child, both historically and as a feature of our psyche. Our lives will scarcely be rewarding or fulfilling if we keep returning to those episodes in our past which were most unsatisfactory and let ourselves be ruled by the outdated choices and decisions made to fit those occasions. Our ability to regress can thus be used either creatively or destructively.

It is an entirely different process when we choose to contact and express our intrinsic child energy – a quality of energy which exists within us whatever age we might be. The inner child, as a mode of being, is part of the rich repertoire of co-existing 'selves' that are ever available to us. Far from catching us in old patterns of the past, this child energy expresses itself in freshness and spontaneity, in playfulness and curiosity, now, in our present lives. We would be greatly diminished and handicapped if we left the 'child self' behind for good. It is this aspect of the psyche that can participate in life as a child of the universe, experiencing profound security and joy in that immediate sense of connection with the life force within and without.

But why is it that we are more likely to be drawn backwards into regression and repetition of our past fears and pains than we are to move forwards and call on our healthy, enlivening inner child? Emotional energy has the urge to complete itself, and the fearful feelings are the ones which we interrupted and blocked. Thus, it is the painful situations which we so sought to avoid that we are, paradoxically, compelled to repeat. We set up the same emotional dynamic again and again, hoping always for a different outcome – a magical, fairy-tale resolution. We are trying to 'get it right' this time. It may look like madness or masochism, but these obstinately espoused repetitions arise from our underlying drive to heal ourselves: to suffer our healing; to complete, and so clear out of our system, those crippling, fear-ridden feelings. Fighting them merely locks them, and locks us in them. Feelings need to flow, just as our life-blood needs to flow. If we give our feelings due attention, then we can experience them as subtle, inner physical movements that come in waves. And it is important to allow these movements, these waves of energy, to complete themselves, for then we are released to experience fresh feelings which fit and express the living moment – whatever that may be for us.

Why, then, is self-healing relatively rare? Why do we not more often complete our old, half-lived emotional cycles and liberate ourselves? Why is it that regression, albeit such a common phenomenon, so seldom fulfils its self-regulative and creative function?

Regression and Licence to Blame

Could it be that at this stage of our psychological development as a species, we are attracted towards our infant selves for an even more enticing reason? Only from this position can we really fully blame mother. Everyone is agreed that a baby is helpless and at the mercy of mother's moods and needs, her actions and omissions. As infants we have a right to be furious, to whimper and complain and demand and charm. All behaviour is legitimized, and no behaviour is our fault. The compelling vacuum of non-responsibility. We have an enormous investment in returning to this place. As adults with full, retrospective knowledge of later hurts and trials, traumas and failures, we can enter the infant position wondrously kitted out with an array of anti-mother weapons. We can blame with the full emotional force of the infant and the mental acumen of the adult. If we slip into regression we can more easily hide our refusal to know who we are; we can convince ourselves that it is mother who should define us, she who should supply our self-definition. By this time, of course, there will be other candidates ready to receive the familiar material. What would be judged ridiculous in a grown man or woman feels exactly *right* if we regress. Thus, 'infant' parents, too, can indignantly blame their children for their own failures and disappointments – or anyone else who will fit the bill. And so, of course, we do regress – again and again and again.

And if we resist this temptation then we proudly turn to self-blame instead. It seems a morally superior, and thus a more advanced, position. We call it 'being grown up'. We get hold of the idea that to be a responsible adult, we simply have to leave off blaming our parents and get going on ourselves instead. And so we wallow in unworthiness. But however sophisticated our methods, in such blaming we are not being the responsible people we purport to be. Blame is not synonymous with responsibility although many use the terms interchangeably in our culture. 'I am responsible' so often means 'I take the blame'. A noble action?

If we see life through a filter of guilt, then we can spend a lifetime switching between self-blame and self-vindication. When we blame ourselves let us look to see if it is not, in fact, with the causal fix of the intellect and the blaming energy of the disgruntled, rageful infant; or, perhaps, the resigned and tired and hopeless infant. 'Its all my fault. I'm hopeless. What can I do?' Collapse, and wait to be rescued. To use a phrase of Jung's, 'The hammer beats itself'. So often we believe that we are not blaming anyone at all when we are engrossed in clobbering ourselves – telling ourselves off for being useless and stupid and obsessed with the idea that 'if only I hadn't done so-and-so, then…..'. We get so used to putting ourselves down that we do not recognize the activity. It is so automatic that it slips past our attention. Self-persecution often takes place unnoticed. It is 'displaced blame'. It has nothing to do with taking responsibility for ourselves. We have simply learnt to be our own victim by promoting our own private internal persecutor.

We can even use psychotherapy, as we can also use religion, not to actualize our fuller natures but to berate ourselves in an ever-more distanced or sophisticated mode. When we are being responsible we use our judgement, not to blame ourselves but to discern what is really going on in an interaction and distinguish the various levels involved, rather than use it to apportion guilt and innocence. (The latter activity of 'passing judgement' is a social activity appropriately exercised in relation to the violation of social laws and, for that purpose, is set apart and marked by ritual of some kind. For this purpose we have Law Courts and definite legal procedures.) The energy of blame clouds good judgement and diverts attention from what is actually taking place in any given interchange.

I wish to emphasize that although living from a basic *position* of blame gets us nowhere, it is essential to recognize and acknowledge actual *feelings* of blame as they emerge from within us. If we are filled with a feeling of blame, as we are all bound to be at times, then repressing it or denying it only increases its hold over us, and locks it within us. At some point that emotional energy will leak out in a variety of indirect ways. We need to accept these feelings, allow them, and not judge them, in themselves, as bad. They simply are. Indeed it is important to give attention to any negative feelings that we experience towards our mother or father, or towards anyone or any situation, and let such feelings flow and clear out of our system (which does not necessarily mean expressing them to those involved). It is no help to pretend to rise above blame just because we know intellectually that it is an escape from taking responsibility. We can never go beyond blame by fleeing the knowledge of it in ourselves. We cannot come into our wholeness through avoidance of any aspect of ourselves. The beginning of our freedom from blame is the compassionate acceptance of the blame which we are actually living.

'Jesus said, "If you bring forth what is within you, what you bring forth will save you. If you do not bring forth what is within you, what you do not bring forth will destroy you". *The Gnostic Gospel of Thomas.*

The Fallen Self

In order to escape from the intolerable burden of persistent personal self-blame, we may perhaps go back to the first Self, or Collective Self, or Archetypal Self – poor old Adam. He, of course, passes on the burden of guilt to Eve. All very familiar. The natural world, represented by the serpent, also takes part of the load. We get plenty of cultural approval for this solution. Here is a wonderful external (yet securely internalized) cause for our messy and unsatisfactory condition. And it can never be disproven, because neither 'he' nor 'she' nor 'it' is actually 'out there' and vulnerable to verification. There is no one *there* to question. They remain forever safely in the shadows of pre-history and enshrined in myth. They are untouchable: the supreme, eternal ancestors who fertilize and generate, for ever more, our fallen state.

And so we can tell ourselves that it is not our fault because we are born into sin, even if we do have to be sorry for any particular sin that we may commit. As we are bound to perform some sin or other it doesn't make a lot of difference; we are guilty before we begin. We can safely exhort ourselves, in good company with others, to relax (if we can) and get away with a reasonable quota of transgressions for a normal person, keeping any extra hidden if possible. And so we jog on in the same old way and know nothing of true responsibility or fulfilment.

The Fall can be seen as the most basic form of collective psychological resignation. An archetypal Rescuer is called for. The different religions of the world supply a variety to choose from. We can ride along on their superhuman goodness which we, of course, given that we are just 'ordinary' people, know from the beginning we could never achieve. That is the great pay-off for being a worthless worm and a miserable sinner. At least we have found an answer to the problem of living which is suitably external to us. We only have to make our choice of Rescuer, or Redeemer, and that isn't too difficult, as we can always follow the prevailing belief system of our culture. It is sad how we miss the most vital communication of our greatest teachers as they live, each in their own way, the human mystery.

Relying on The Fall and a Rescuer to explain and take care of our human condition can be seen in terms of collective regression and collective infant blame. We have simply upgraded the hunt for an external cause to account for how we malfunction, as well as our hunt for an external solution, by placing our focus on a respectably higher 'spiritual' level. The infant-in-us will always crave salvation from an external source, just as it depends on the ever-giving breast from outside itself. Infant psychology will necessarily expect meaning to be given, by right, from a source 'out there'.

The Fear of Growing up and Our Resistance to Change

Yet what is this need to keep blaming all about? Why are we so reluctant to take responsibility for ourselves? It seems that we are strangely

Chapter Two: The Great Regression

resistant to really growing up. Is it because growing up, from the infant point of view, has come to mean 'taking' the blame? Fear of adulthood is an extraordinary state of affairs, and so unlike what we can discern of other living organisms. Why is the development of our psyche lagging so far behind our biological development? The human nest, the family home, does not serve only the very young. It is not just an initial base from which to venture out into full psychological autonomy. Few of us are ever truly free of the old family modes of interaction, and we set up new 'mothers' and 'fathers' and 'siblings' in every subsequent situation which affords us the opportunity – every time we relate to an authority figure.

Even when we go on to create our own families, or other groupings, the new system in which we participate will all too likely serve the same dynamic all over again, ensuring that the familiar patterns of interaction churn on unimpaired, however stifling or unproductive they are shown to be. And then we can moan, and blame, and call it stability. Do not most family systems do everything possible to 'keep things the same'? Our resistance to psychological growth – while at the same time so conscientiously nurturing and desiring *physical and intellectual* growth – our reluctance to move towards psychological maturity and autonomy, are mirrored in our deep and widespread fear of change. Even when we long to act differently, and when new ways of handling our relationships are obviously called for, change is experienced as a threat to be warded off – a crisis, rather than being accepted as the natural movement of life.

Forward movement, at least minimally, is an absolute requirement for any biological system. Why, then, do we so often flee into fusion, and tirelessly pursue the impossible state of fixed modes of relationship with others? Is it because of our initial fixation on mother, and our insistence that she must remain static and ever present for us? We favour the homeostatic tendency in our nature over the transformative capacity, instead of allowing these two modes of being to complement and balance each other. We engage in the endless search for stability and equilibrium above all else when these characteristics are the mark of inorganic systems. (This term is fast becoming outdated, and I use it now only to make a relative distinction.) In so doing we betray our organic and dynamic nature. An equilibrium which is fixed or held is incompatible with life and with learning. We seek the very entropy we also dread.

Does this preoccupation with repeating the familiar stem from ignorance of our fundamental security – the security which flows from knowledge of the dynamic, everlasting being of timeless spirit? If we conceive of ourselves as purely material entities and have no apprehension of our essential indestructibility, then all change is a threat; we read it as a possible death; and death, of any kind, must be avoided at all costs. The linear ego cannot recognize at what level the death is occurring because its literal mode of making judgements precludes it from distinguishing between the different ways of dying. And so, without awareness of spirit, change is suspect, and we respond to it by resisting it – the homeostatic tendency within the psyche will always win out.

Only spirit can provide equilibrium *at another level of Being* which is both sure and yet not static. This is the experience of peace. (Spirit manifests in matter as the living principle of balance which, in a dynamic universe, cannot help but call forth continual change.) Meanwhile, detached from the source and ground of our being in spirit, we hunger for the illusory safety of physical and psychological fusion, and vainly endeavour to create fixed modes of relating on the very level on which life demands continual movement.

We seem to have made a habit of habit. In spite of our pursuit and enjoyment of trivial changes to stimulate and divert us, we do anything to hold on to old ways and beliefs. Our absorption with passing fashions cloaks our obstinate determination and commitment to remain 'just as we are' on the psychological level, at whatever cost. At this level we resist change with all the ingenuity that we can muster – ingenuity which matches our talent for creating superficial change on the outer material level. As change in external styles of living escalates, so our fixated inner natures stand out more clearly (and perhaps puzzle us more deeply). Could this be the hope of our times?

It may be that we are nearing the limit of self-diversion. The gap between our frenetic obsession with superficial outer change and our profound resistance to inner psychological change, the need to fight for the freedom to rearrange political structures while keeping safely within the same basic frame of reference, the disturbing dichotomy between our drive towards external development and our internal determination not to budge from old habits – all are becoming more and more evident and uncomfortable. We are obviously out of balance.

Given our present stage of psychological development, change means growing up – leaving our infant position behind, that all-too-familiar position from which blaming others feels utterly natural and legitimate. We 'infants' know something is wrong all right, but how can that state of affairs be our fault? It must be those others, the 'grown ups'. Or it must be 'their' institutions. If we are operating from an infant state of mind, then change will be associated with having to become responsible; and that is the last thing we want. How can we become responsible for ourselves, for who we essentially are, when we don't yet know who we are. *It is terrifying to claim our whole nature when we sense, at the same time, that something is amiss, when we intuit that something is awry at some very profound level.* Anyway, how can an infant be expected to contemplate the nature of human beingness?

And so we go round and round in circles of avoidance, pivoting around the one sure notion that *something* is wrong with the way things are. Is it not evident in all our social and political organizations – organizations which we feel dictate to us even when we are in positions of power? We share a collective intuition of some kind of 'wrongness'. But instead of seeing this as a sign of our incompletion as a species (and a creative starting point for our transformation), we regress. It all seems too much to cope with.

Could it be that we are teetering on the brink of the next stage of evolution, and it is so much easier to sink backwards than to press forward into uncharted territory? And once regressed, we blame; and once we blame, then we are unlikely to want to grow up and become the blamed. And so we circle on, determined infants, and unable to step out into real growth and fulfilment. We resist any truly significant psychological change by means of the diverse and wonderful inventiveness of the psyche itself; a psyche divided against itself. We spend our energy on proliferating and refining our own special styles of defence; defence against self and others. We can only break the vicious circle of regression and blame by turning to find the source of our resistance to change.

Are We Essentially Flawed or Not Yet Complete?

Most religions, because of their very nature, try to go back to source, to origins; but because their search is undertaken through the troublesome grid of 'good and evil', they are likely, in the end, to produce some version of the Fall. Even monotheism has its shadow side. Once God is some kind of entity and we only admit of one such being, this entity bas to be good. Any other prospect is too appalling to contemplate. And, of course, by definition, a single God must be all-powerful, as 'He' is supposed to account for everything that is. God is the ultra-meta-explanatory principle. So how can a good and omnipotent God do such a botch job and create this strange species called human beings who are, it seems, intrinsically unbalanced and at odds in their rate of development: inner development not matching outer development. Is the God of our infant human race also into blaming; blaming cloaked in mercy? It seems that we have evoked a God who says that it is our fault. We haven't done it right. We took the wrong choice at some vital point.

I find the systems of belief that lie behind myths of our fallen nature no more satisfactory than modern psychological theories. *They are all thin on why, as a species, we seem to have such a marked propensity to make poor choices rather than productive ones.* Even the profound and subtle thinking of Buddhism has nothing very helpful to offer on this troublesome question about the origins of our waywardness; it is stated that the Dharma wheel, by accident, started turning the wrong way. And the answer that is tirelessly put forward by Western theologians about the necessary conditions of 'free will' just isn't good enough. *Why doesn't the lovingly given power and privilege of choice at least stand an even chance of going either way?* Why this sense of being doomed, from the beginning, to fail? Once the wrong choice is made, it is not difficult to see why trouble multiplies for a dynamic, complex being; but why is the wrong choice so much easier to make than the right choice?

No account of human nature, ancient or modern, religious or scientific, has ever satisfactorily explained why such beautifully designed beings get it wrong so much of the time; why such intelligent beings are so unfailingly stupid in such vital areas of our lives. They say, 'If only we did "this" or "that", we'd be all right' – but they never account for why we don't do 'this' or 'that'. And although some people attain access to another level of consciousness and a more profound view of reality by meditating for years in remote and peaceful places, or by transcending stress in extraordinary circumstances, such a way of life cannot be the answer for the human species as a whole.

It seems that this powerful myth of the Fall, embedded in our Collective Unconscious and Conscious, must not be bypassed or ignored; that it demands to be properly and fully understood. If not, it will go on influencing most people's experience as they live their day-to-day lives, because experience is shaped by belief. The contents of the media – the prevailing slant of the media – is a clear expression of the fact that we have come to settle for the stronger pull of the negative. We feed back to ourselves, and prove to ourselves that human nature is sick. We literally sicken ourselves. We can only study ourselves with our own minds and we believe that we are a 'faulty model'.

Is it not rather that human nature is incomplete? We are not so much 'bad', as 'unfinished'. Except, that is, for certain individuals who, refusing to regress and blame, somehow or other manage to come into their fullness during their lifetime, finding their wholeness, their wholesomeness. But those of us who are still caught up in an infant psychological state of being are bound to view such persons as essentially different from the rest of us. We dub them saints, gurus and mystics. Once this distance is established, we are back in our same old quandary.

Perhaps what we need to do is to seek contact with the adventuresome and curious 'child' in each of us and, in this way, redirect the enormous energy which is presently invested in regressing backwards to our troublesome blaming infant. Can that alive and fascinated 'child', which is intrinsically part of our psyche, discover how to *live* ourselves into completion and wholeness? Can the responsive 'child' – responsive to life itself and seeing with fresh eyes – let go of our old belief in our fallen nature? Our greatest danger, our greatest betrayal of life, is to view it as *essentially* flawed. If we see it that way, it will be so.

We need a new theory, a fresh way of seeing ourselves; a way of *living* ourselves. We need a new account, a new human story, that frees us from the intellectual ungroundedness of 'infinite regress' and the psychological paralysis, wastage and negative recycling that is brought about by blaming. As I mentioned earlier, even theories that deeply accept and affirm how we have turned out to be (such as those in the Humanistic Psychology tradition) still claim, at base, that the trouble lies with the mother and father who constricted and thwarted us. If only we could have been left as lovely natural children. And birth has come to be regarded as a trauma; as almost too much to expect us to go through. There's always something wrong with how it is. Our blaming is often very well disguised, but it's there. We need a theory that is blame-free; a theory that does not depend on external causes to account for who and how we are and yet faces the challenge of our malfunctioning and our poor choices – our evident resistance to life.

It seems to me that we shall make little headway with the creation of a transformative new human story unless we acknowledge how pervasive is our need, our determination, to remain an infant. We obstinately remain the wounded child – injured, needy, innocent and ruined. It is indicative of that mind/body split, which is deeply embedded in the thought of our culture, that we are not more puzzled by the fact that the body heals itself with such innovative brilliance and speed, while our psyches keep re-opening the old wounds and relentlessly travelling down ill-functioning neurotic pathways. Such contrasting performance of psyche and soma should challenge us into new ways of thinking about ourselves. If the lower-order level of soma (as we assume it to be in our culture) is so highly successful, then is not the higher-order psyche up to some game in its repeated failures? And could it really be the case that what we consider to be the crown of creation – the human mind – is necessarily as fixated and inflexible as it appears to be? A mark of evolutionary development throughout all living things is the attainment of greater and greater complexity, mobility and freedom to act. How is it, then, that the most highly evolved species in our world, having shown itself to be enormously innovative in other areas of operation, organizes itself with such a lack of flexibility when dealing with those feelings, thoughts and behaviours involved in human relationships? It is all the more extraordinary when relating with one another is the most fundamental of all human activities. We would none of us be here without the breast, or someone to produce a bottle. We are born as social beings.

So the behaviour of our psyche is most suspect. Surely such a highly developed aspect of life should have a natural ability to operate differently. On the other hand, is it really so strange that the most complex known organism on earth is still, in some respects, in its infant state? We are behind all other less complicated species in our *completion*, for we have so much more to complete. Human consciousness is young. It has just begun. We biologically adult human beings continually regress because indeed we are, psychologically, at an infant stage of our development. I find it hard to imagine how the plant system could improve itself (all 'improvements' are engineered by humans for human purposes). It has evolved an elegant and fitting order. Does not a flower symbolize perfection, beauty and even truth for us? Do we not use flowers to communicate love to another and to mark our greatest celebrations and most profound and sacred rituals? But which of us could not spend hours reiterating ways of improving the human race? We spill out 'oughts' and 'shoulds' with hardly a thought.

The Shift of Focus from Mother to Self

Rather than holding on to old stories of sin, could we not spin forth new ideas of how we might come into a fuller completion of ourselves? What is the next shift of consciousness that could release a clearer mind and freely flowing feelings? We know such states are within the range of our human potential because individual human beings have lived to show us so. The archetypal Christ figure states, 'I am the Way, the Truth and the Life'. The infant psyche naturally interprets such a statement as referring to the Christ outside of us; he, in his person, is the answer to the riddle of our ill-lived lives, the example to follow and the model to copy. Or else, in some mysterious and sacred way, it is he who will 'do it for us' – *instead* of us – rather than showing us, once and for all, that it can be done. But with a shift of emphasis, could we not understand this powerful statement to imply that *every* 'I' is the way, the truth and the life? The full Self expresses its own unique way of being in the world, *is* its truth, and allows the richness and energy of the movement of life. Perhaps the fully individuated man, the Christ, is telling us to look to ourselves for the answer – not look to our insulated egos but to our whole and integrated selves. It is our Self that is the new starting point. That is the shift of the kaleidoscope of human thought that we require; the shift from the excessive, and often unconscious, focus on getting from Mother (or 'other') to Self-focus.

But first we need to dare to engage with our infant psyche in a fully conscious way so that we can truly come to know this infant self. We can never grow up by running away from our infant nature or by spurning it. I believe that *our powerful need to regress has an evolutionary basis. We regress because somewhere deep inside we know that we must start at the beginning.* We know that 'In our beginning is our end'. But we must alter the level at which we approach our infant self, or we shall simply be caught in the wounded blaming child, demanding rescue and protection; fearfully refusing change and resisting the very state we most need to claim – self-responsibility.

So we make our choice. We are all drawn back to infanthood, as is fitting at this stage of our development as a species, and we have various options. We can continue to remain with our wounds and play out the ruined human being; we can endeavour to discover our early wounds in order to heal ourselves; and we can go further and enter into our beginnings at another level, allowing our consciousness to expand into a fuller knowledge of the being who incarnated into this world. If we undertake this third course we come into an apprehension of spirit, and the balance of the psyche is utterly transformed.

The time is ripe for us to let go of the former option and take up the latter two – the choices of fulfilment. The development of the ego as an aspect of human consciousness is now achieved. It has given us a perspective of differentiation and we now know ourselves as differentiated beings. The ground is thus prepared for the process of individuation to take place. But the ego has also given us the illusion that we are 'grown up' because the ego is orientated to perceive a world of external objects; and viewed as external objects, we *are* grown up. We are also more advanced in the operations of the rational mind than we are mature on the emotional level, and the ego associates itself with rationality. As I mentioned earlier, our development is uneven and we are, at this stage of our human story, rationally sophisticated emotional infants with adult bodies. The fact that our ego is itself more or less fully evolved further adds to our impression that we are grown up; but ego is not the most fundamental aspect of our psyche and does not carry the essential vitality to 'grow us up' psychologically. We cannot achieve psychological maturity merely because our ego has reached a high level of its development. And if we inflate the ego and mistake it for the full Self, we shall never grow up. Only deep organismic unfolding, which at some point energizes our clear decision to be an adult, can bring us into full maturity, and that process is constricted and inhibited if we do not acknowledge spirit.

In recent years, social psychology theorists and family therapists have claimed that the Self is forged via social interaction and can best be described in terms of social-interaction patterns rather than in terms of what is referred to as a monadic, ego-centric entity. This, in effect, negates the existence of the individual (at the very level at which differentiation as an entity is applicable), and can be seen as a 'flight from blame' because it implies that there is really no one there to blame. It thus still falls within the blaming mode of thinking. What is more, it is especially important to claim a sense of individual self within the operations of a family system, or else we simply repeat the 'sins of the fathers'. Who will break the chain? The discarding of the concept of self as an entity at this social level, existing in its own right *although never in isolation*, is a high price to pay even for the relief of not apportioning blame. If we are all and only 'relationship', what is it that is relating or being related to?

At some level we may indeed not be an entity – just as at a subtle level a table is not a 'thing' but is a process in the continual act of formation through interlocking movements of energy (although it is preferable that we perceive it in its grosser mode if we wish to eat off it). So, too, if we wish to act responsibly, or know of or speak of the psyche, then we need to treat ourselves as entities; at the level at which we perform actions and study psychology, we *are* entities and are discernible as such.

The objection to calling ourselves 'entities' may stem from the fact that we tend to assume that the term implies a closed system, and that is something we can never be – among other things, we breathe. But just because human beings are open systems does not mean that we have no boundaries of any kind and cannot function as a recognizable whole within a larger field of being. However, the minute we label the particular entity that we are – characterize it – we are liable to objectify and *fix* ourselves. This is our dilemma; this is the act of violence to beingness. We are ever-changing entities participating in the act of formation, not fixed objects. The virtue of assigning relatively 'meaningless' proper names to each of us to mark our status as individual entities is not only a matter of practicality; such a procedure points to the existence of each person as a being in the world *and tells us no more* – it tells us nothing *about* our nature, but announces *that* we are. It is a non-story and thus leaves us free. No wonder naming a human being is both awesome and ordinary; no wonder it is often carried out as a sacramental act.

To make sense of my experience I find it necessary to claim that I myself, as a human being, am an entity, ever fluid and evolving, and thus I infer that others are, too. I experience them as such. But because we are unique entities, it does not mean that we are monadic, ego-centric entities. I suggest that we are polyadic spirit-centred entities in unceasing relationship and interconnection with other entities. Given this, our approach to knowing the entity that we each are needs to be both varied and imaginative, open yet rigorous – depending on what aspect of our experience we are addressing. We can never know a multi-layered reality (within or without) by means of one method or approach. To limit ourselves to a scientific model would be as inappropriate as it would be to embrace only a meditative medium of discovery. And many different languages are needed for expressing what we find – literal description, metaphor, images, mathematics and art forms of all kinds. The richness of being human and the responsibility of being self-conscious are awe-inspiring; an enormous challenge. Self-image and concepts of self are certainly built up through social interaction, but how can we possibly state how a self is forged? The self-aware 'I' is the most profound of mysteries.

To quote Peter Russell, 'Trying to describe the self is rather like setting out with a torch to search for the source of the torch's light'. I propose that we have to take 'self' as a given, as an axiom of human experience. It is a necessary starting point, both logically and experientially. Can we even begin to explore our inner world (a common human phenomenon) if we cannot meaningfully claim to be a self? And if we wish to escape incessant regression (as well as an infinite regress), then the only context for self is the Infinite Itself – the infinite that resides both within and without each self.

Chapter Three
Reclaiming the Power of the Infant

Recognition of Spirit

It seems to me that unless the spiritual dimension of life is taken into account, psychological theory flounders; it is not just a matter of being lopsided. Unless this dimension is taken as fundamental to human beingness, we are trapped into blaming of one kind or another – doomed to victimhood and perpetual immaturity.

If we do not admit to spirit at all then we may find that we have to admit, instead, that we are actually reductionist materialists. This conclusion may be unwelcome to those who would rather define their position in less stark terms, especially now that an increasing number of eminent scientists are beginning to discard the limitations of the once-respectable materialist framework. Many would perhaps prefer a more open and congenial description of their belief system – or would prefer not to have to stand by any particular belief system at all. But if we do not, or feel that we cannot, take on the notion of spirit as a living reality, then the mind is left unsupported in a limbo realm, and all too soon becomes equated with the workings of the brain. It is interesting that the German word 'Geist' means both mind and spirit, and we can see when grappling with Hegel how both stand or fall together.

So if we find that we are no longer comfortable with a wholly materialist philosophy and are drawn to consider the existence of a spiritual reality, then we also may be challenged to see that if spirit exists at all, then spirit must exist from the start: when we contemplate the nature of spirit we apprehend that spirit simply *is*. It may manifest physically in time, space and process, but it is not subject to these aspects of life. The whole essence of spirit is that it is not captured or limited or held by these concepts. Therefore we do not *develop* a spirit. It doesn't pop out of a mid-life crisis, even though we may indeed come into an awareness of spirit during the search for new meaning that is common at that time of our lives. We can, of course, develop our understanding of spirit or our ability to access this level of being. In fact, this is usually a long unfolding process giving rise to much development – development of personality, thought, imagination and behaviour. Any direct experience of spirit has a profound effect on our lives. And so, I maintain, the part of our psyche that is developing (the ego/persona part) may hide or reveal spirit, and perhaps in a progressive manner; but spirit, itself, *is*. Either we humans are spiritual beings or we are not spiritual beings.

The developmental or process aspect of a human being, therefore, begins with the first meeting and multiplication of cells at conception. So where does the spiritual aspect begin? It is a false question. 'Isness' can't begin; it can only be. Our first biological instant is therefore one with spirit – spirit complete and whole. The utterly new physical process, located in time and space, is inseparable from 'old' or, rather, timeless spirit.

Is this perhaps why we have such a deep intuition to go back to source? Does it account for our perennial fascination with sources which, in this modern rationalist epoch, has, for the most part, been diverted into a concentration on causes and their effects? The physicist Paul Davies, referring to our physical universe, says, 'This very early phase – the first second of existence – is now the subject of intense study by theoretical physicists, some of whom believe that many of the features of the universe can be explained by processes that occurred then'. If we would understand the universe, then it seems that it is necessary to go back to source – to its very starting point. If we would understand our human beingness, then perhaps it is also necessary to go back to source – to a fresh instance of the formation of a human being. Perhaps we shall learn what we need to know by going back to any incarnation – by going back to our own incarnation. And as each of us has incarnated, we have direct access to such a source. We have direct access, in some sense or other, to an original point in the evolutionary process. We have each participated in the beginning of the unfolding of a human being.

Some physicists suggest that in our attempts to understand the birth of our universe – that mighty explosion of energy called the Big Bang – we need to imagine space and time infinitely shrunk to a point of nothingness. Thinkers of this persuasion consider the universe, in its initial state, as a 'bounded singularity'. (A 'singularity' indicates a point where things apparently cease to exist or become infinite.) Perhaps it would be helpful to go back in time and imagine our own origin in these terms – each shrunk to a point of nothingness which is, simultaneously, both a doorway to the infinite for spirit and the moment when our ego and our developing biological self cease to exist. (If we go forwards in time, death could similarly be construed in this way.) It could be illuminating to see ourselves as a 'bounded singularity', a fresh point of energy about-to-be-manifested in material form. We are each a unique starting point, a new instance of biological expression, drawing on the infinite – on All-That-Is.

As a source point of life, we contain our essence – or rather we *are* our essence, we carry our potential. How could we not then have the power to be ourselves? Furthermore, as participators in the unfolding secret of life itself, we are inextricably part of an immense process. Thus, we are never dependent on any one item or person in the universe or on any particular system for our essential quality of being. I put forward the hypothesis that we are each an original spark of life.

So, this 'bounded singularity' that each of us is at incarnation, this infinite point of material nothingness and potential energy, coming out of All-That-Is (just as the universe did before it), expresses itself in the specific mode for its coming into being – the meeting of sperm and egg. We start life at the connection point of time and timelessness. Our first biological instant is therefore at one with spirit; and spirit, by its very nature, can only be whole. The utterly new physical process is integrally connected with timeless and whole spirit. The infant, from the very beginning, is thus spiritually 'mature' – in the sense that, as spirit, it is complete and whole.

At this moment, as whole spirit in new developing body, are we not poised to 'choose' our way of being, our basic orientation to the world, more freely than at any other point in our lives? We are each a nexus of unique responses. It is we who respond to our mother, and to the external world, in our own uncluttered and unclouded way. Our responses, in our early days, are at their most authentic; they are most utterly ours. Pre-conditioning. Pre-persona. At this point our most fundamental predispositions, our deepest intentions, are given substance. Our newly embodied spiritual essence translates itself into the psychological mode, becoming the seed of our individuation. From the very beginning our most powerful conditioner is ourself. We generate our own unique nature, drawing in material from the outer world as part of our creative endeavour. Our environment has an enormous and vital impact on us, but it does not make us who we essentially are.

If we take time to explore deeply into ourselves with our full and open attention, we begin to sense more and more how the infant in us took up certain attitudes and positions, displayed certain preferences, and then responded to mother and the outer world in ways that expressed and reinforced those positions. Dare we call them 'decisions'? In any case, they were enacted by us as unique beings. And the more we ponder these 'decisions' (or our particular mode and quality of being), the more we ponder the ways in which we directed our energies and looked on the world, the more we feel them as *ours*. We sense how we responded to our incarnation – to our first expression as matter. We sense how we participated in our first interaction with mother and with the world. We experience ourselves as the agents of our lives.

Infant Consciousness

Perhaps this is the moment to say something about infant consciousness. Recent research indicates that the brain is neurologically sophisticated enough in a seven-month-old foetus to support consciousness (all the senses are operating), and possibly even self-consciousness. I have always been fascinated by a remark my daughter made to me when she was a few years old. Still held in a reductionist materialist mode of thinking myself, I had to keep it suspended within me for years without being able to make sense of it, and yet I was quite unable to dismiss it. She said, with such clarity and assurance it was almost shocking, 'Mummy, do you remember when I came up out of the water and saw you for the first time?'. And indeed, we did have eye contact before she was even fully out of the birth canal; I shall never forget it. I did not know yet whether she was a girl or a boy, but in that moment when our eyes met I experienced her ageless presence.

However, not only is there recent scientific evidence to support the possibility of consciousness in the well-developed foetus, but now that we recognize it as such, there is more and more experiential evidence to indicate that consciousness of a kind is present from conception onwards. This, of course, blows many people's minds – especially those minds that have equated themselves with the brain! To them it is bound to sound like nonsense. How can an embryo without a brain be conscious? And those who believe that the self is forged through social interaction must equally rule out of hand any possibility of some form of self-consciousness, however tentative and primitive a version of this phenomenon is attributed to early foetal existence. I grew up surrounded by the assumption that even babies were not conscious and didn't really feel anything, let alone know anything. I clearly remember my mother telling me so. We have had an enormous investment in disclaiming the innate power of the infant; in keeping the Infant Archetype as an expression of utter helplessness and pristine innocence. The 'tabula rasa' concept of the infant mind that was adopted by rationalists of the Age of Enlightenment renders the infant a pure prey to mother and father and all other social forces – the perfect conceptual backdrop to encourage the flowering of the Victim Archetype.

Perhaps it is easier to approach disturbing and revolutionary ideas about foetal consciousness from the other end – by looking at death. We now have well-documented cases of near-death experiences which lend support to new theories that are gaining scientific attention. In fact, scientific evidence is growing for some sort of extra-neurological memory system that does not depend on the state of development of the brain. The existence of such a faculty certainly renders the near-death experiences more understandable to us. The brains of the people having these experiences of death are non-functional from a medical point of view. So how is such consciousness possible? That is what places these experiences in a different category from dreams of dying or death.

There are many carefully recorded cases of people who are declared dead by doctors, only to recover and report every detail of what occurred in the operating theatre. More remarkable still, they describe events that went on at the same time in other rooms in the building. They accurately recount exactly what people said, the expressions on their faces, what they wore, and many other things that they could not possibly have seen, even if their eyes had been open – which they were not. This is consciousness of another order to ego-bound consciousness. It is not subject to the same space/time limitations, although it still deals with images of discrete objects and a material world. It is more comprehensive in nature; it has some kind of overview or meta-position. It could be seen as freer or more powerful. And yet the brain is not, apparently, sending out signals and making neural connections. The brain is static and judged to be dead.

So why, if consciousness does not rest exclusively on brain function, cannot a cell or cluster of cells possess consciousness of some kind? – perhaps some very simple and transparently clear order of consciousness. It could possibly be called 'essential consciousness'. Is perhaps the human being holographic in nature, one part (for example, a cell or group of cells) containing something of the whole, even if in a less intricate manner? And are the numerous descriptions of early life that have been shared in psychotherapy sessions any more extraordinary than the now more accepted near-death experiences? 'I am round and smooth. I have no front or back or top or bottom.' Or 'I am everywhere at once. I feel with all of me. I am one big happening. I am a sort of circle filled with life.' Similar accounts occur again and again, arising spontaneously from the depths of the unconscious when this essential or primal consciousness is touched in some way. (As we increase the range of our self-awareness, we shall, I believe, need new words for distinguishing the different aspects of our consciousness – just as Eskimos have evolved a great many words for describing different states of snow.)

I have heard many such accounts of early life and witnessed the quality of energy from which they emerged, and they do not have the ring of mere images or dream experience. They are physically based experiences, felt in the body and rising to consciousness when someone is deeply in touch with their physical being. Descriptions of such experiences often include phrases like, 'I feel it right in every cell of my body'.

Dr Thomas Verny, an American researcher into prenatal life, has put forward the hypothesis that there exists some kind of organismic memory – memories laid down in individual cells. He states, 'This would allow even a single cell such as an ovum or a sperm to carry "memories", and would also provide a physiological basis for Jung's concept of the Collective Unconscious'. However, ex-materialist physicist Paul Davies is now even claiming that consciousness does not depend on any biological base at all for its recording of information. Such patterns can, in principle, be held by other substances of varying subtlety. It is no longer so 'way out' to hold that consciousness, in some sense, exists from conception onwards (or, in yet another sense, from before conception). I hold that human beings are never without consciousness of a kind.

What I Sense of My Own Beginnings

Over the years I have come to have a deeper and deeper sense of the quality of my own beginnings, and my intuition is that I did not want to incarnate at all: I wanted to bypass the physical world. Was I perhaps born in South Africa to justify, or give weight to, that position? My mother made a half-hearted attempt to abort me and it was fitting that I came into a reluctant womb – it mirrored my reluctance. My mother's energy and mine fitted together perfectly. Here I suggest 'connection theory' rather than a causal frame of reference. (I shall develop these ideas further in later chapters.) I don't believe that my mother caused my reluctance and frightened me off the world. What is relevant, if we would know ourselves as individuals, is how we connect with the world around us; how we fit into it and select from it and add to it.

So my position was initial reluctance, and this left its mark and was expressed in the shape of my feet, which have phenomenally high arches. I was pulling upwards and away from the ground; lost in a fantasy world and deeply introverted and idealistic. I wanted to 'keep my feet out of the shit', as an eminent psychotherapist once remarked. But once I accepted my humanness – my intimate marriage with my body – and accepted that for better or worse, for richer or for poorer, I was on this earth (and I remember vividly when I did so), I was rewarded with such an immediate experience of life energy that I have felt a sort of amazed joy ever since. In technical jargon, I 'grounded' myself, and it has been one of the great lessons of my life. However distressing were our family interactions, however appalling the political scene, I was simply glad to be alive.

My first conscious experience of my own power was when I was seven. (I am talking now of conscious awareness in the ordinarily accepted sense.) I was in the middle of a field, and I suddenly knew that it was pointless for me to wait for my mother to love me, or meet me in my world. She was never going to do that. I terrified her. But nothing could stop me from loving her. I could love her, and go out towards her and reach her in her world. I had the emotional equipment within me, just as I had physical organs that worked. That realization transformed my life.

I feel that I would be imposing on the privacy of my daughters if I were to write in any detail about my experience of mothering, but what I can share is that each conception was a completely different experience, as was each pregnancy, each birth, each face-to-face relationship after birth. And my two daughters grew up into very contrasting beings. Everyone remarks upon how different they are. So much for my say in the matter! Of course we have all sorts of enormously powerful influences on our children and responsibilities towards them, but I am talking about basic determining power over their essential quality of being.

No person is in a position to influence another person as profoundly as a mother her child, and yet I feel almost irrelevant *compared with their power to be themselves*. It seems to me that each drew from the spectrum of what I had to offer ('good' or 'bad'), to build their own psychological schema and life story in their own, special way. Things that I liked most about myself were not necessarily helpful to them: my faults, it seems, were sometimes just what they needed. The great mystery of human interaction. It seems to me ludicrous, trivializing, to pick out something that I did or said to them, or even some complex combination of events that involved us all in some powerful way, and name that as the *cause* of their character and behaviour. I spent years inventing plausible causal theories – I had a special talent for it. The only trouble was that I had to keep changing and adjusting them. It was very releasing to stop trying to understand my children and myself in that way, and to accept, with wonder, their unique responses to life and to me. If I am a starting point in my own right, and I experience that to be the case, then so are my children a starting point in their own right. I take neither blame nor credit for them.

The Impotence of the All-powerful Mother

If we attribute to mother the essential character-forming power over her child we, in fact, render *her* impotent as well as her infant. She can't get it right whatever she does or however she is, because if she is seen as *intrinsically* more powerful than her infant, then that infant is drawn to fuse with her or is driven to reject her, instead of growing up alongside her in his or her own right. And it seems that we are becoming resigned to this situation. Rejection has become a standard means of delineation. If mother is regarded as all-powerful, then every single thing that she says and does is given enormous weight and influence. She is trapped in an over-abundance of significance. What is more, there is nothing she can do to lighten her power because the very attempt to do so carries yet more power. She is rendered utterly powerless to be non-powerful. The more power she is given, the more the power to be a good mother, and nurture an autonomous being, is taken from her.

A priori, mother *cannot* make everything 'right' for her infant because she hasn't got that kind of determining, defining power anyway. She holds such power only for herself. She cannot mould another living entity, which is a source of energy in its own right, although she can be a far-reaching generator of conditioning if she is *believed* to be such a grand causal agent, and if the infant-in-us sticks with all those borrowed messages, internalizing and entrenching them in his or her non-conscious being. (I use the term 'non-conscious mind' to refer to an area of our psyche which we do not intend to make conscious. It is a store-house of material that we do not *want* to know, as opposed to that which we do not *yet* know.) It is this non-conscious mind that we must dare open to view if we would free our infant self into its true power – ensuring, at the same time, the possibility of full adulthood.

Claiming Our Initial Responses as Our Own

Once we let go of the search for an external cause to account for how we are and allow ourselves to connect with, and become aware of, our initial responses to life, we find that they make sense of all our living (and non-living) up to our present point in being. The experience floods our behaviour with meaning and relevance. It is not just intellectual insight, but a deep identification with our own discovery of ourselves. It is an experience of revelation. We are filled with a sense of homecoming, that sure sensation of getting to base as we let ourselves know our basic life position. We know the reality that we are born with energy and something of our own to give out. Is not the giving of our self to our mother our very first act?

We know also of our ability to select. We appropriate to ourselves from the environment what is fitting to our nature. What we take in from the universe expresses, and is a function of, our uniqueness just as much as what we put into the universe. That is the grace of individual selection. Once I am primary, then mother is secondary. (I refer, of course, to the whole 'I', the self.) This is the crucial reversal of emphasis. If I am primary, then all blame becomes irrelevant: it loses its 'juice', its 'fuel'. I may be deeply influenced by others and my social persona highly conditioned, but if I am, in essence, not caused by others but a self-generating system, then blaming falls away – it ceases to have a raison d'etre.

Before I go any further I had better deal with that troublesome concept, 'God'. I shall keep things as simple as possible. All meaning depends on a context, and so we are compelled to use a meta-concept of some kind to stand for the ultimate context. It is necessary to human thought. Such a concept cannot, in the end, be avoided. We also need to have a recognized mode of communicating with each other about the mystery of the Beyond, the acknowledged Unknowable, the Whole for ever beyond our understanding. Equally we seem to require a name which embraces our sense of the moving force both within us and without – directly experienced and yet pervading all things.

I conceive of 'God' as Original Consciousness, the Intelligent Principle, the Word, the masculine aspect of All-That-Is; I conceive of 'Goddess' as the Creative Process, Life, Manifestation, the feminine aspect of All-That-Is. Both aspects are equally involved in the unfolding of the material world. Together, as one, they are Love – a ceaseless outpouring energy that breathes the universe into increasingly consciousness being.

If I know myself as self-caused by the God-in-us, the divine at the core of all things, then I simply do not want to blame anyone or anything. Of course if we insist on keeping God strictly 'out there' and beyond us, then we can refine our victim state with super-blame. But if I recognize that I am indeed self-determined by the 'spirit within', then all blaming dissolves.

Freedom from blaming is an even greater gift than freedom from being blamed, and we can at any point in our lives collect this gift. It allows us to reclaim our energy and power as our own. The infant-in-us-all is indeed more powerful than 'mother' or 'other' because an infant experiences itself directly. The infant has direct access to itself – to life. The infant is all immediacy. The infant is raw consciousness free of concepts and words. The infant is the centre of the experienced universe and utterly focused on its being. And the infant is *someone* because an infant is whole spirit (we can't be half spirit) freshly and uniquely embodied. Have you ever experienced the aura of a new-born baby? Our 'isness' shines before we take our first suck of mother's milk. Our particular way of being has an immediate and profound impact on others from our first moment on. We are all sources of energy. If we deny this (the source energy – the self energy) then we become selfish, not selfless. We become suckers of others' energy, dependent and attached; no real give and take – poor breathers.

The fatal myth that we hold on to is that mother has all the power and we have none. We are victims. Of course, as freshly incarnated beings, we do become *biologically* dependent, for a time, on the particular vehicle of our developing life – on mother. No wonder she has an awesome place in our psyche. We need to be nested in the womb. Even though it is possible that if one womb failed us another would do equally well (after we had shrunk to nothingness once more and then exploded forth again into material process), we cannot avoid biological dependency on mother for a time.

The Myth of Total Dependency

Thus, there is a marked discrepancy between the status of our essence, which is indestructible, and our physical vulnerability. There is a sense in which, realistically, we are dependent, and this biological dependence needs to be acknowledged. However, instead of marking the vital distinction between the ontological status of our essence and the nature of our physically dependent developing self, we have allowed our experience of our dependence (fuelled, no doubt, by deep-seated cellular memory) to gobble up and overwhelm our consciousness of ourselves as a 'bounded singularity' and potent sourcepoint of life energy. We have well and truly chewed the necessary distinction into a mush, rendering ourselves a ready prey for the voracious Victim Archetype that we each, in some way or other, have come to express.

Could it be that the necessary distinction between our essence and our physical process is the truth that lies behind the false body/spirit or body/mind *split* in the thinking of our Western culture? Perhaps these dualistic habits of thinking only have such a hold on us because they borrow energy from the underlying truth (the necessity of making distinctions) which they have come to distort; a truth which has not yet been properly integrated into the workings of our psyche. They are grand and mighty mistakes, and possibly they are part of the disturbance that is bound to occur as energy gathers on the threshold of a new evolutionary leap. Distinction has been misunderstood as separation. And if we attempt to separate and isolate our physical process from our spiritual essence, as opposed to simply recognizing the distinction between them, then we enter into illusion; we start life from a false and unreal base. We can then imagine that we are *either* spirit *or* bio-process, and if we opt for bio-process then we require it to carry the load of our disowned spiritual essence. We can then identify our essence with our body, and thus act as if our *essence* is dependent on mother. As soon as we do this, we lay ourselves open to the energy of victimhood.

The Victim Archetype is a primal archetype; it arises from our repeated failure, at the primal level, both to distinguish and to claim our individual essence and our bio-process. If we reduce ourselves to soma then we also reduce our primary human state to one of total dependency and chronic victimhood. It is freedom and choice that then appear illusory and we have, indeed, forfeited our full humanity.

The victim position, from which victim attitudes and victim behaviour flow, is the most destructive of all modes of being; the most negating of all organizing principles of the human psyche, with far-reaching social and political implications. And yet it is the most common. It offers no remedy for experienced ills because blaming gets us nowhere; temporary relief, but the 'horrible world' with all its troubles continues unaltered. Victims call forth persecutors in all interactions undertaken from that position. Each mother (or significant 'other'), on some level, is made a monster, and to depend on a monster is a fearful plight indeed. How many mythical heroes we have invented to try and slay such monsters.

The human psyche, riddled with such fear, cannot evolve any further until it has divested itself of this myth. We must stop going back to mother (or, rather, *not* stop *at* going back to mother) and reclaim our essential infant power, if we are fully to know the source and organization of our being. We must go back to our very selves.

Chapter Four
Back to the Source

I believe that it is not just perversity that draws our energy so easily towards victimhood, but that our psychological vulnerability to the archetype arises because two precarious and momentous passages-of-being are coinciding and interweaving with each other. The first is the flip, at our conception, from timeless being into physical becoming in time and space. The second is the collective period of oscillation at the border between two evolutionary stages – oscillations that will continue until the new stage 'holds' and becomes the norm. And we are at the centre of this instability.

Having developed an ego (which, I propose, is what this latest stage of evolution has been about), human beings now have to learn how to integrate it and allow its rightful place and function within the Self (which will take us to the next stage of evolution). The transition stage, which we are in now, is about confusing self and ego. This confusion is most commonly expressed by treating the ego as if it were the whole self, and this equating and identifying of the ego with the self is the key to our difficulties at this time.

The Shock of Incarnation

I put forward the hypothesis that the notion of separateness has had to be increasingly emphasized by embodied consciousness over millennia (perhaps since the birth of language itself) in order to evolve the ego, with its power to differentiate; and this is such alien ground for the incarnating spirit, that knows only of oneness, that it gives rise to what I have come to call 'incarnation shock'.

I am proposing that at this stage of our evolution, we all start with a shock! The collective state of partial awareness into which we are born, the psychic climate of humanity riddled with its divisions, is so unappealing to spirit that it looks like embodiment in matter is a dreadful state to have taken on. We are shocked – in a state of shock – at the very point of entrance into the process of becoming a human being. It is extremely difficult for spirit to make the passage into a separation-orientated world, although this stage has been a necessary ambience for the development of the ego while it comes into its power to differentiate. (It is this ability to differentiate which, in time, enables the process of individuation and the emergence of a self-conscious universe – each individual, in its uniqueness, contributing to the conscious expression of the whole.)

Meanwhile, because human nature is still in the process of evolution and is going through a transition stage (and transition stages are by definition unstable), we are, collectively as a species, vulnerable and easily confused. In our state of shock at incarnation, do we perhaps confuse *biological* vulnerability and insecurity with *spiritual* vulnerability and insecurity? We act as if we could be entirely snuffed out by maternal imperfections or neglect, instead of confining our fear to the possibility of biological death.

Death belongs to our biology, and as such it is natural and can be naturally dealt with. Watch how animals manage it. They run, they fight, they struggle, and then suddenly surrender to it when the time comes. Zebras do not tremble in fear every time a lion passes on the off-chance that they may be tomorrow's dinner. (They sense when the lion has just eaten.) But human beings are different. Instead of leaving death a biological matter, our psyches latch on to it and treat it as an appalling threat to our whole being. We attach to a biological happening the full force and complexity of unowned psychic material. (This confusion also works in reverse, meaning that we later come to associate transitory psychological danger and change with the imagined finality of physical death.) Such attachment is likely to continue as long as the ego aspect of our psyche is dominant, because ego identifies with material objects and considers the self as a biological entity only. Thus we become victims of death; and act as if death is a persecutor. How very different is the repetitive, manipulative energy of victimhood from the clear 'once off' episode of exchange of life forms brought about by the engagement of prey and predator.

Chapter Four: Back to the Source

Thus, the psyche acts as if death will destroy it, our entire being, our very soul; and so lends this natural process the power of intense psychic distress. To take something natural, and inevitable, and regard it as an utter disaster is to blight our human landscape from the start, and encourage a state of evasion or melancholic resignation. Could this perhaps account for cot deaths? (Perhaps the infant tells itself, 'I might as well get this awful business of dying over right now – that is preferable to living with the terror of extinction'.) We need to leave death in its proper sphere. It is a biological happening, and our body knows well how to let go and be transformed from movement into apparent stillness. Our mother, and whatever is external to us, can only threaten our particular biological form, not our spirit, which simply is, and which can, perhaps, take up new biological form.

But we act as though our mother holds our very spirit in her hands to form and mould or reject and destroy. It is as if we abdicate our knowledge of our essential beingness, our knowledge of the indestructible element of each self, and focus instead on our biological fragility, loving and hating her for the power we assign to her. The whole point is that once we experience ourselves as primarily biological beings then we are, thereafter, *psychologically* vulnerable to mother. We come to believe that if she does not affirm us then we cannot be who we are meant to be – in the same way as we believe that if she does not feed us, then we cannot be who we are in the world. We add to our bio-fear (after all, mother does have the power to kill us physically) the full weight of our complex array of psychological fears; we merge the two. Thus, we imagine that she can also kill us on other levels – that she can wipe out our spirit. We must get her to love us, at all costs, in order to survive; and if we fail, then we must at least engage her guilt. And then we go on and have a second try at this with father, spending a lifetime, perhaps, yearning for his recognition, placing our sense of self at his disposal.

The paradox of the omnipotent infant-in-us is that our energy is actually diverted inappropriately on to another and so not given truly to self, although so bound up with *getting* for self. In our fear and weakness from having given away our power, we attempt to draw on another's power to get a sense of the power that we have abdicated. We place our power elsewhere and then, in our insecurity, we try to suck it all back. Our power becomes distorted into control rather than self-expression. (This kind of interaction can sometimes more easily be detected in marriage, or other partnerships, where it comes to full bloom.) Dependency and domination are two sides of the same coin.

But again, all this behaviour is not just an accidental quirk. We are not simply being perverse. Nor are we inevitably set for destruction.

A Necessary Bio-focus at the Point of Conception

Could it be that, during that crucial transition from one mode of being to another at conception, we undergo a necessary focus on the biological aspect of the self? The biological must call, must attract us into the experiment and adventure of life – lure us, almost, from our state of timeless equilibrium into one of instability and change. The accent of our awareness perhaps needs to be temporarily given over to the biological in order to enable that passage of incarnation. Do we then get stuck with this necessary concentration on the physical? This would hardly be surprising if we are also, as a species, in a state of evolutionary transition. There is just too much instability around. We are ready candidates for fixation.

However, our intrinsic ability as self-generating beings to take responsibility for ourselves can only be fulfilled – can only be made natural and become the norm – when there is a balance of awareness of spirit and body, rather than just this focus on the body. This is what is necessary to integrate the ego and bring to a close the debilitating and destructive divisions both within the psyche and without in the world; a world which we devise to mirror our inner conflicts, diversions and denials. As mentioned earlier, a divided psyche, at war with itself, cannot help but bring about a divided society and war among nations.

Awareness of self as both spirit and body is imperative if we are to integrate our egos within the larger self. This is what, I believe, the next stage of evolution is about. We can never give ego its fitting place in the psyche unless we achieve this balanced awareness. We need a more profound and comprehensive framework within which to cradle the insecure and fearful ego without denying the importance of the physical dimension to which it clings. If we are only aware of spirit, or only give credence and value to spirit, then we are liable to try and get rid of ego, and it will react with all the tricks at its disposal. We shall be overwhelmed with confusion as soon as we attempt to overcome, rather than utilize, a necessary part of our psychological apparatus.

The ego organizes reality in certain ways for good reason. If it has taken all these thousands of years to evolve the amazing complexity of a multi-layered consciousness, then what an abuse of life it is to try and abort and destroy an aspect of that consciousness. But if, on the other hand, we identify only with the body and say that the body and self are synonymous (I am only my body and my mind is only my brain), then ego will dominate, because ego has identified with body. If we are only aware of body, then we confuse ego with self and have to cope with life through ego-mediation alone – and we have all seen where that gets us. Until we extend our consciousness and invite ego to co-operate and play its part within a larger and more comprehensive framework, we are locked in this small, contained section of the self, and are ever vulnerable to insecurity and fear of death.

It would seem, therefore, that in order to integrate the ego, we have to achieve a balance of awareness between spirit and body, and for that to be possible we need to revert to our knowledge and memory of spirit almost immediately – in fact, as soon as our initial bio-focus has fulfilled its purpose, and the direction of life into the mode of matter has been established. But instead, we postpone this knowing, and sometimes for our entire biological span. What a paradox. It is the one thing – this memory of our wholeness – that could give us a security profound enough to enable our joyful participation in the mode of creative instability that is physical life.

Our Obsessive Avoidance of Death

So I see our present situation in the following way. Focused intently on the biological aspect of self at our incarnation, we have not known how to deal with our unowned psychic power. We have diverted it, distorted it, using it in the service of physical survival before all else. The resultant bio-survival obsession has made death a terror and a phobia. St Paul put it very succinctly: 'Evil comes from fear of death.' We, as ego-dominated beings, are always prone to confuse physical survival with psychic survival, and are thus driven to perform extraordinarily inappropriate actions in the name of physical survival – including abdicating our very humanity. We betray our loved ones, and grasp and grab and kill and torture. We build some societies which are scarcely fit to live in. Or we fanatically defend our families in order to achieve a form of survival through the next generation, defend our families in such hideous and divisive ways that we make a nonsense of what we are defending. Yet again we may identify with some sect, culture, nation or religion, and wage wars and devise monster weapons in the name of procuring the survival of that with which we have become identified. It is never spiritual values that we are so defending because they cannot be destroyed in this manner. Religious wars are either sectarian or political battles in religious guise; or they may arise from the loss of living contact with their source. expressing the depth of rage and pain and fear engendered by that loss. They carry the unspeakable intensity that springs from disturbance of our fundamental nature. Through our fear of death we create the conditions of death.

Our human arrangements make a very strange spectacle when we forget our indestructibility of spirit. Even if our immediate survival becomes assured, we are left empty and incomplete, and are prepared to exploit half the world in a vain attempt to fill our inner void with material goods: we consume as if we were indeed the starving masses that we wish to ignore. We ward off the face of death to come with pretty trinkets. It is not possible to be truly free and also treat death as an enemy. It was reported by those who survived Siberian prison camps that only when they lost the fear of death did they find their freedom – and, mysteriously. often seemed then to escape the death they no longer feared.

With knowledge of our spirit being, which is indestructible, both excessive avoidance of death and psychic focus on death eases, and the debilitating fear of death naturally falls away. Of course the word 'knowledge' all too often stands for a purely intellectual knowing. Such knowing on its own does not touch the level at which the fear of death strikes. We need to know with a fuller consciousness. Only then does our psyche detach itself from its preoccupation with death and free itself fittingly for life. With consciousness of spirit, we come into our innate 'animal' wisdom and are able to live at peace with our biological span, whatever that may happen to be. Like them, we shall in our own way also struggle and fight for life and then surrender when the time comes – when our time comes.

Once we are aware of our wholeness, of our being in spirit and body, then we can also meaningfully take responsibility for ourselves. Once we, as a species, have ready access to this balanced awareness from the beginning, once it becomes natural and a part of our nature, then mothers will be let off the hook, and at the fundamental level of psyche formation, victims will be no more. To depend on perfect (i.e. inhuman) mothers is to start at the wrong end. Whatever our omnipotent fantasies, we cannot make her as we want her to be any more than, later, we can make our partner or a friend what we want him or her to be. Nor can society produce perfect mothers (or even 'good enough' mothers) by means of social engineering or compulsory mass therapy. *Our true power does not lie in our ability to manipulate mother. It lies at the point of our direct access to the life force*; by claiming our own energy and 'whole-beingness' from the start – from the very beginning. If we have to wait for mothers to 'get it right', then we are lost indeed, and this transitional state of evolution will be spun out to our further pain and confusion.

A Temporary Shutter Mechanism to Establish the Direction of Life

The necessary bio-focus at incarnation, although it renders us vulnerable to an imbalance of awareness which in turn lays us open to ego's death phobia, does at least see us safely facing towards life on earth and gets us born. It is not just some terrible mistake, some pointless flaw. It establishes us in the direction of our biological process in space and time. Perhaps there will always need to be a brief blackout at incarnation; a brief eclipse of the consciousness of our wholeness in spirit at the moment of translation into matter – the mysterious profound moment of conception.

The movement from non-substance to substance, from a potential into an actualization which includes a fundamental *limitation*, is a strange journey; but with that instant of forgetfulness the focus towards matter is assured – as also is our commitment to becoming a part in the all-embracing whole. Once 'part-hood' is established and matter begins to take shape, once the space/time mode is fully underway, then it would also seem fitting that this temporary shutter should lift, and in so doing, apprehension of the whole and a sense of beingness in spirit would naturally reaffirm itself. And with it victimhood would cease.

Thus, our forgetting of spirit is not just an aberration. Perhaps at any stage of the development of our species, the passage of incarnation is so delicate that an initial forgetting, plus a biological bias, is necessary in order to establish the direction forward into time, following the arrow of time which will surely complete itself into eternity. For is not time curved as space is curved? Could it be that our entrance into material form is so finely tuned and highly unstable that we can easily slip backwards, instead of following the flow of life forwards into the process of physical and psychological development? It is only too easy to confuse our starting point with our finishing point because indeed, they are the same and yet vitally different. Life depends on knowing that difference. We are called to distinguish the virtually indistinguishable. Our taking on of material form marks this distinguishing process; the showing forth of what cannot be divided, but can only be brought to fullness of enjoyment through our distinction. The One made manifest. The One spelt out to take joy in. For this tremendous happening to occur, and be fulfilled, we must not confuse pre-conception with death. The arrow of time must be obeyed and lived. Perhaps a one-way valve system is required so that we pour our energy and our concentration into our bio-state to the exact point of no return.

The Extended Shutter and the Prolonged Eclipse of Our Awareness of Spirit

This one-way valve enables commitment to life on earth, which is later manifested as the will to survive. (Charles Darwin saw this as the basic life principle, but as I mentioned earlier, if it is lived as the basic, most fundamental principle then it betrays life; it is a necessary part of our human apparatus, but not the most fundamental.) This one-way valve or shutter mechanism enables commitment to life on earth, and gives us a survival *preference*. But if it is extended, blocking out awareness of our wholeness in spirit for too long, it then unbalances and diverts the psyche. Here is the dilemma. And a small irregularity at this vital starting point of our rapid biological development has enormous and far-reaching consequences, just as an infinitesimal alteration in speed or temperature in the first micro-second of the Big Bang would result in an utterly different universe.

I put forward the possibility that the more evolved human being will have a shutter mechanism which operates just long enough for us to get into the bio-flow, but not so long as to become bio-obsessed and thus terrified of death. If we start life with a terror of death, then we are liable to be hooked on mother until we die. We cannot easily move beyond infanthood.

So I propose that the present elongated eclipse of the light of spirit (an eclipse, in itself, fitting for the actual moment of incarnation in order to establish the direction of the life flow) is a mere phase in the evolutionary process. The shutter has had to be fairly substantial while we, as a species, were developing the ego, because the preoccupation with separation was so shocking for spirit, and thus the pull backwards against the arrow of time, against the direction of life, all too compelling. As I said earlier, it has been extremely difficult for spirit to make the passage into that separation-orientated world which has, nevertheless, been necessary for the process of differentiation and individuation to become possible – all working towards a self-aware universe.

But now the ego is established, now that this element of the equipment of individuation is available to us, the ego is ready to be properly integrated within the self. As a species, we are poised, waiting for just such an integration of our psyche. In fact, we are desperately needing to 'place' our overworked ego within a fully functioning self so that it can no longer go on inflating as unfitting energy is pumped into it, nor deflating, in horror, at all that is expected of it.

Now that the ego is here, the prolonged shutter is no longer underpinned by any evolutionary necessity, and our awareness therefore has the power to shorten and refine it. Conscious awareness is extraordinarily potent when it goes with the stream of life. And it is just because the results of the extended shutter are so devastating that our awareness of the process is urgently required. Without this expansion of awareness, we will continue to be caught in the effects of our present outdated situation, becoming, as we do so, an effect ourselves – a victim.

Physical Dependence and Annihilation Terror

The prolonged shutter renders the infant ignorant of the true state of its security: the indestructibility of spirit and its assured relation to the whole·. If we really knew this truth, then we would be secure. Freedom from fear of death is the evolved state that we need to attain. But meanwhile, focused only on its biological reality, the infant feels utterly dependent on mother instead of being dependent on mother in one mode of being only. *It is physically dependent at that very point when physicality is dominating its awareness.* So the first time that mother fails, or frustrates the infant, fear sets in. When this is repeated, terror of complete annihilation develops because the possibility of physical death, for the physically orientated, is equated with absolute destruction.

Here we come to an absolutely fundamental point, one that lies at the heart of psychopathology – namely, that this error, this impossibility, gives rise to a feeling (the fear of the absolute destruction of our whole being) that the human organism was never designed to process. All other feelings can be dealt with if they are allowed to flow through the body. But once the body has contracted against annihilation-terror, it loses its flexibility and can no longer deal appropriately with other, inevitable, natural and fitting emotions. In other words, our whole system becomes furred up, jammed, and eventually cannot

Chapter Four: Back to the Source

help but be an inadequate vehicle for the movements and expression of the psyche. We become trauma-prone. Traumata arise not so much from painful happenings themselves but from our blocking against those feelings that are provoked by such happenings. Repressing the memory of them, we forgo access to their completion at a later date.

The Prevalence of the Defended Personality: Regarding Feelings as Enemies

Once we are in a continual state of constriction in order to keep the ultra-charge of annihilation-terror at bay, then any powerful emotion will seem unmanageable, unable to be processed or cleared, and therefore overwhelming and dangerous. The body loses its sense that it is natural to let feelings flow through it: we are robbed of the basic awareness that it is good to be a live, sentient being, adapted to respond to a varied, changing and challenging world. Ordinary feelings begin to be experienced as frightening pressures; too powerful, too charged to allow through our ever-constricting and constricted emotional channels. And so feelings themselves become enemies. We start to protect ourselves from them, to guard against them. We are divided against ourselves and the neurotic personality comes into being. Forgetting our ultimate and essential wholeness for too long, we distort the whole entity which we were born to live. And so our distorted bodies, our distorted postures and breathing patterns, our distorted perceptions and interactions, rising from this early error, this annihilation-terror, create a world that justifies the blockages that it is built on: a world against which we must defend ourselves. And once locked in a defensive mode of being, we experience ever-less choice, and a mounting need to control.

All this spells disaster, especially if we see the situation non-dynamically, as a fixed flaw in human nature. After all, is not the blocked personality universal? Who does not fight against at least some of their feelings? Are not we indeed trained to do so as part of the process of becoming an adult? Are there not 'bad' feelings that we had better forbid and stamp on before they even begin to rise towards expression? And so, of course, we are all chronically tense. Is this not our human condition? We believe that we must be continually on guard against our 'lower nature'.

Sigmund Freud spelt it out for us: the dark and powerful Id, our suspect instinctual energy, must be called to order by the rational mind, the ego, which unfortunately is not strong enough for the purpose, even when supported by the offerings of the superego: guilt, idealism and the daunting threat of judgement and punishment to come. The concept of superego is, I believe, an attempt (but unfortunately a limiting one) to account for our profound sense that we have a Higher Self – an infinite self. It is a concept that can all too easily degrade this aspect of the self, reducing it to warder and punisher. The troublesome life-force simply will not be so contained and thus leaks out sideways. If pressed down too tightly, it will explode. No wonder Freud later posited Thanatos, the death instinct. The best that can be hoped for is a compromise. It seems that we have sentenced ourselves to a ceaseless battle between conflicting energies, a psyche at war and divided against itself. The defensive personality becomes the distorted path to social responsibility and the mistaken image of adulthood.

If we continue only to acknowledge the finite aspect of the self, and try to keep the infinite aspect of our nature squashed within the finite, then we condemn ourselves to be hopelessly out of balance and thus permanently unwell. Neurosis is, alas, the norm in most societies. We are forever haunted by the underlying despair of the imprisoned and by the unsatisfied longing for freedom: freedom to be our complete selves. Real transformation, and thus the next stage of our evolution, is utterly blocked if we adhere to this limiting view of the workings of our psyche.

So, too, is the notion of self-responsibility rendered vacuous and ineffectual. We mistakenly translate the deep yearning for our wholeness into a belief that we can only find that completeness in some special 'other'. Romantic love is the prevailing mythical paradise on earth sought by the infant-in-us-all – the 'grown-up' version of the ecstasy of the womb. We long to find and enter that capsule of mirrored self-absorption, safely oblivious to the rest of the world. There is, of course, the extraordinary anomaly of open-hearted saints and open-minded geniuses, but the rest of us give ourselves to our defences and blockages, our escape mechanisms and avoidances, accepting that human nature 'just seems to be this way'.

The Possibility of Transformation: Conscious Participation in Our Own Completion

We have a choice. We can see our human predicament as a fatal, fixed flaw; or we can see it as part of a living, moving, unfinished process that, if consciously entered into and participated in, could be transformed. A willing consciousness is what is needed. And trust that life itself is the perfect designer, the perfect artist.

It is not just that any creative endeavour is likely to reach a sticky patch, and needs faith in its initial thrust to see it through to its completion, but that the greatest art is often born at such times. Divine creativity is vividly manifested when its creatures are themselves required to participate creatively in their own fulfilment. The means fit the end. Each of us, by coming into an awareness of spirit and taking responsibility for our wholeness now, will give evidence of, and thus help bring into being, a natural state of full responsibility and basic security for our entire species. Just as there comes a time in the evolutionary process when we have the power to interrupt and hold back that process by our refusal of awareness, so also, at that same point, we have the power to release and enhance its development through increasing our awareness. And have we not now come to this point? The fact that the very survival of our species depends on a more comprehensive consciousness indicates that this could indeed be so. Is it perhaps entailed in the evolutionary process that at some stage, certain constituents within it become active participants consciously developing its course? Is not this all part of the evolution of a self-conscious universe? We have to find ways of reducing the length and strength of that initial shutter: that mechanism of original repression – the repression of our origin. Once we do this, as a species we will remember, *and remember well before we are required to be separate from mother*, the reassuring memory of our oneness in spirit: a memory which, during this recent phase of ego development, has been too tantalizing to bear. We need to seek ways of refining that shutter until it fulfils its designed purpose, until it merely sets us in the direction of life. And now that its elongation has outlived its evolutionary necessity, it is very malleable to our awareness.

If we do indeed find these ways (and I shall be exploring these possibilities more fully in later chapters), then our essential indestructibility and state of wholeness will be remembered almost immediately, and infant annihilation-terror will be no more. Fear, anger, resentment and disappointment arising from human mothering are manageable and natural emotions which can flow through the body and thus bring us no harm. We shall no longer be traumatized and caught up in repeating our past hurts. We shall no longer need to misuse the flexible mechanism of emotional *regulation* by turning it into a blocking device against experiencing our feelings – feelings that need but to complete themselves.

The Use and Misuse of Our Mechanism of Emotional Regulation

This mechanism of emotional regulation gives us the sophisticated ability to contain the expression of emotion when necessary. With its aid, we can both accept and allow our feelings and be in charge of the way we express them. It is the tool of choice. Timing is often crucial to the attainment of satisfying interchange with others. To use a very obvious example: we can suspend our fear when we have to deal with a child who has a gaping wound, or when something catches on fire. Our attention at such a moment needs to be given to action. Later, after taking the appropriate action, it is necessary to allow the suspended (or contained) fear to move through the body – to let ourselves shake or cry or moan, to talk about the experience with others, and even perhaps to dream about the experience until the energy of that fear is fully discharged. Or to cite another example: if we know that it would be unproductive to express the full extent of our anger at a given moment, that it would only exacerbate the withdrawal of the other person when we wish to stay in contact with them, then we can regulate the level of emotional expression and clear the remainder of that energy at another time or in other ways. We may allow it to transform into humour, for instance. On the other hand, if the presence of our anger is blocking the very contact we desire, then it may well be more creative to express it directly and live out the dynamic that may flow from such expression.

The emotional cycle is only complete when the body has returned to a state of equilibrium. For that to be possible, it is necessary that we accept the feeling *whatever* it may be, and regardless of whether we choose to express it or contain it; that we do not judge it. In fact, it is enormously important that we learn to let go of our habit of making judgements about feelings, and approach them as neither good nor bad, right nor wrong; they simply are what they are. It is our actions, not our feelings, that require such assessment. Guilt about having a feeling prevents relaxation after expression, and traps the emotional remnants in the body tissues. In fact, the more we judge a feeling as bad, the more we prolong its influence on us and on others. But what is of even more import, guilt can cloud our actual awareness of a feeling. The more vehemently we forbid the occurrence of a murderous feeling, the more likely we are to commit a murder – the more likely we are to perform a violent act of some sort. We cannot be in charge of what we refuse to acknowledge. Forbidden feelings can burst into regrettable actions. We would do well to see ourselves as beautifully designed feeling beings capable of living through stress and regulating and processing the full range of human emotions.

However, we convert this valuable regulative capability into an automatic blocking device, and as a result we drastically disturb our human functioning, for we obstruct the very flow of life within us. We hinder the movement of 'positive' feelings as well as 'negative' ones; we impede pleasurable sensations and feelings of excitement and joy as well as our anger, grief and fear. Our capacity for emotional regulation gives us a flexibility in our social responses, and allows us to match expression of emotion with the unique context of the living moment. It enables us to be responsible in our personal interactions and thus gives us greater freedom to create the relationships that we need. We are not at the mercy of our feelings – unless we deny them or judge them. It is tragic that the very ability that gives us added freedom and subtlety of expression is converted into an habitual blocking mechanism that does far more damage than just limit us. It turns us into defended and defensive beings. In refusing our own energy we are not only divided against ourselves, but are forced to use yet more energy to achieve this refusal. A forbidden feeling does not just 'go away'; it is an energetic event. Denial costs us far more than we realize. We trap what is unacceptable to us deep within our being, and then wonder why we are filled with poison, why we are fatigued. We cheat ourselves of the pleasure and the joy that could be ours. What a terrible waste of life. What a crucial misuse of our amazing resources. Our profligate use of energy in the world outside us is a reflection of this ceaseless inner wastage. We have been equally unaware of both.

Acknowledging Spirit and Releasing the Template of Repression

Repression is simply unnecessary once we have let go of that first and most crucial repression, that primal repression at incarnation, and thus allowed the vital memory and *experience* of spirit which carries an immediate knowledge of the indestructibility of our essential being. It is that template of all later repression that we so urgently need to acknowledge, along with the template of all fear – annihilation-terror – which naturally begins to dissolve once we reclaim our being-in-spirit. All lesser fears and repressions stem from them. We would not compulsively need to forget, and use our energy to keep at bay, emotions that were no longer overwhelmingly disturbing to us. No feeling would be experienced as too charged to bear. We would not, therefore, involuntarily mobilise against the more powerful movements within our being.

Often the only highly charged energy which we allow to escape through our well-developed blocking devices is sexual energy. The species must continue. Much of the rich variety of libidinous and creative expression open to human beings tends to be sublimated into sexual activity of some kind. The aggression and violence which sometimes accompanies this desperate release has led us to believe that sex and power over others are the motivating force of the human race. And does not this very combination throw up the victim/persecutor dynamic in its most obvious form? Surely here, at least, we have real victims? Once sexual energy is split off from spirit, we are at our closest to losing our humanity.

As we know from experience, neurosis does not fall away simply through finding a means of sexual expression, or even by achieving a good sexual relationship. Neurotic organization loses its grip only when annihilation is recognised as an impossibility; when we reach full acceptance of our feelings and thoughts and allow all manner of inner energetic movements to be processed through our body and the layers of our psyche. We free neurotic habits through an openness to our whole self – from infinite spirit to a little feeling of embarrassment – utilizing our mechanism of emotional regulation which enables choice of expression and responsible social interaction, rather than deforming it into a means of blockade in an internal war. Because repressed sexuality is the energy that most often breaks through even the strongest of defences, we neo-Freudians imagine it is both the cause and the solution of our problems. Certain symptoms may be ameliorated by sexual expression, and pleasures gained, but the personality does not become whole unless the whole person is expressed: all aspects of our being need to be acknowledged and valued.

The State of Wholeness and Libidinous Well-being

We have almost completely lost touch with the grace of our initial sexuality. Our propensity to block our feelings not only impedes the passage through our body of all our natural emotions, it also interrupts that very subtle circulation of the energy of the libido – the expansive flow of well-being. This flow is encouraged by physical contact and touch, by contiguity with flesh. It resonates with, and so reminds us of, the continuity of spirit. It re-minds us. It helps us remember ourselves, our true selves – re-member into wholeness. It is exquisite to experience these subtle libidinous streamings through the body. They bring a deep sense of well-being – both with self and the world. As we allow their movement we know, in some non-verbal fashion, 'I am the river. I need no bridge.' This can be seen as our cosmic sexuality; the sweet, pleasurable, flowing stream of life that nourishes every cell of our body – that relaxes every muscle – and invokes an unquestioned security as it lets us know that all is well in the biological mode of being. It is not surprising that so many of the mystics use sexual imagery when attempting to communicate the quality of the human experience of oneness with All-That-Is.

This libidinous circuit would tend to be most continuously activated in the womb. Is it, perhaps, a natural aid to see us through the necessary 'shutter period' while we establish our commitment to biological being? The warm circuit to keep us going through the time of the cold waters of Lethe? Does the potential to become full adults of our species lie in remembering our wholeness well in time for our birth? As I was saying earlier, new research indicates that the foetus has a brain capable of supporting self-awareness and memory from the seventh month onwards. Our physical completion and knowledge of our spiritual wholeness would then coincide in an integrated readiness-to-be-in-the-world. If so, then we should indeed be born into wholeness or 'redeemed': born into wholesomeness, not 'sin'. Mother could be simply mother, and no persecutor, because we would be no victim.

Chapter Five
Self-Concept and Meaning

If we are to claim our original power and wholeness, thereby freeing both ourselves and mother, and removing that fundamental misapprehension which feeds fear and hate of the feminine as well as our victim state, then we must go back to our very selves. But what is involved in this process?

We first have to know what we mean by a self. We also need to clarify how we experience our self-being in our daily lives. This is an exploration of vital importance because our concept of self – of what we conceive a self to be – dominates our whole system of meanings and thus fashions our way of being in the world.

Approaching the Self through a Hierarchical Structure of Meaning

In our Western culture, concepts of the self have drawn on the prevailing combination of dualistic, moralistic and hierarchical thought forms; crudely speaking, we see ourselves as having a higher and a lower nature. Freud, of course, devised a more sophisticated version of self when he portrayed a dynamic interplay between the forces of Id, Ego and Super-ego. Although his concept of the movement and repression of energy within the psyche has made an enormous contribution towards our appreciation of the life and complexity of our internal world, he still left us with a depressing legacy – the concept of a self necessarily divided, difficult and defensive. Shockingly bold and innovative at the time, such a notion nevertheless reflects the patriarchal and hierarchical thinking of his day.

This hierarchical way of seeing ourselves and our world is still with us, and has been given expression in a non-moralistic mode by social psychologists such as Harry Stack Sullivan. Models have been devised to give a hierarchical order to those contexts which give meaning to our behaviour and experience. Although archetypes have been placed at the top of such hierarchical systems and have been considered the prime generators of meaning and thus the principal organizers of our experience, self-concept is a close rival for this position. These top levels hold the power to order all lower levels – all our attitudes and ideas, the dynamics of our relationships, our feelings and thoughts, our choices, actions and decisions, our speech acts and body language. If this is so, then only that which challenges our archetypal allegiances, and which calls into doubt and stretches our concept of self, can really alter our behaviour, reverberating through all the lower levels of our system of meanings.

The Implications of an Ego-based Concept of Self

It is the self-concept which equates self with ego that is the most common and crippling context of meaning in our present culture, and its limiting nature is disguised by the reverence we pay to the purely rational mind. If we base our notion of self solely on the ego, then we cannot help but see such a self as an isolated unit, for the very function and purpose of ego is to differentiate the world into definite objects and make abstractions out of that world. It is designed to define and categorize; to deal with an outer world of discrete entities and an inner world of discrete concepts. With this important ability we come to give ourselves definite boundaries so that we can take responsibility for ourselves as individual entities. We define our thoughts and feelings as ours – that is, if we are functioning properly. But the danger is that when ego consciousness turns back on itself in reflective mode, it treats *itself* as a discrete object; it thus separates itself from the rest of the self. In its eagerness to define the world it has defined itself in a similar manner – it has approached the psyche as a material entity and attempted to divide it into bits, ending up locked in itself. Becoming a fragment of self instead of a function of self, the ego then perceives all other selves in a similarly fragmented way; it can only recognize others as egos. In this state of fragmentation, we cannot help but feel disconnected from each other; the shared levels of subtle interconnectedness are no longer available to our awareness. Once isolated in this way we shall naturally perceive interaction in terms of competition with other isolated units, or bounded groups of such units. We shall be doomed to perpetual, chronic insecurity, dependent on those very others whom we also regard as rivals (if not downright enemies), and whom we shall, understandably, have difficulty in trusting. It is a disastrous state of affairs.

It is hardly surprising that we then long to find someone of our 'own' from among the vast alien herd – we long to mark and lay claim on a particular person or group, and so ease our appalling sense of isolation, deprivation and lack.

Once we conceive the ego as the essential self, then we are caught in the doomed choice between dependence and independence: between dependence on some special other whom we try and keep as 'ours'; or lofty independence, imagining that we don't really need anyone and can make it on our own. An ego-based self cannot experience, and therefore cannot enjoy, the richness of our interdependence. We human beings deeply need contact with each other on all levels of our being – physical, emotional, intellectual and spiritual – as well as requiring the obvious practical modes of co-operation necessary for survival. The movement we need to make is not from dependence to independence, but from dependence on one particular 'other' to a life of conscious interdependence.

But if we remain entrenched in our egotistical view of the self, then co-operation with fellow human beings will always be a taxing and uphill struggle. We shall always feel unlovable and be unable to love others; we shall always fear rejection and be easily offended and humiliated, on both a personal and national level. We shall be quick to flare into violence in order to try and grasp the power that eludes us, or to wreak revenge on others in the ceaseless battle for control of the uncontrollable. Such a diminished self will always blame others and external circumstances, lacking any sense of being in charge of her (or his) own life, even though she fights to gain control of the world through any manipulative means she can devise. Endless, seemingly 'inexplicable' self-defeating behaviours are bound to arise. If the ego is puffed up to take the place of the whole self, when in reality it is only an aspect of self, then we are easily deflated and prone to collapse, or else given over to obstinate rigidity. We are frightened, proud, dependent, grasping because we have no sustaining rooting in the soil of our collective source of being, a source which is only known through those aspects of self other than the ego.

Although the power of living consciousness and of full being cannot be annulled, the most fundamental of difficulties arises when we condone the dictatorship of the ego – when we misuse our ego consciousness to deny all other aspects of consciousness, and treat the self as if it were only a material object. If only we could realize what violence we do to reality when we conceive of ourselves as separate, externally interacting units in a mechanical universe – the 'building block' model with its separate parts accumulating into the whole which can then be defined only in terms of those parts. It is not just a philosophical mistake; its repercussions are enormous. We can never find solutions to our political, social and economic problems as long as society is experienced as a vast conglomerate of competing entities each divided from the other. What is more, there can never be a place for the full self in such a universe. If we hold to the above belief system, then our conception of self is bound to *remain* limited to that of pure ego and held in that distortion. Real transformation of our present social arrangements will not be an option. The United Nations will continue to struggle against the odds, and no new order will emerge.

Perhaps it is just because the ego has reached the peak of its own evolution that it assumes the role of young upstart dictator over the rest of consciousness, which is yet to manifest fully in its vast and intricate richness. Could it be that it also suffers from the insecurity of the newly evolved (relatively speaking), and is therefore reluctant to forego the focal position which it necessarily had while in the process of coming into being? Whatever the reason, the newly formed ego seems determined to remain in the saddle of consciousness and keep a grip on the reins of awareness, refusing to take a back seat when appropriate. (It is possible to conceive of the ego in these personalized terms just because we have each become so thoroughly identified, as a person, with this function of consciousness.)

For as long as we continue as a species to remain *centred* in ego consciousness, then we shall be inhibited from admitting to the rest of the self (except at those awkward moments when our rationality slips, and we are deeply moved or touched by love or by beauty, and unaccountably filled with awe and gratitude). Our much-needed integration will elude us. The great danger is that the ego is quick to discard what cannot fit into its mode of thinking. It is thus drawn to deny the non-linear, unless it can be safely placed in the category of abstract thought systems such as mathematics.

The ego is at a loss in the presence of multi-dimensional levels of being, deskilled and confused. Most significantly, it cannot admit the non-linear nature of the self without being thrown out of the saddle. And it cannot conceive of spirit at all – the indivisible, the infinite, the timeless 'isness' at the core of all life. The ego must, by its very nature and function, bypass what cannot be differentiated, categorized and named, or else hand over consciousness to another aspect of self – the very thing that it is so reluctant to do. Contemplating a reality of essential interconnectedness and interpenetration blows its operational system and renders it non-functional.

If we treat our ego consciousness as our whole consciousness rather than as an aspect of consciousness, then we confine ourselves within a linear, surface view of reality and so do not connect with material that is not amenable to this mode of experience. We blindly and unknowingly attempt to live only 'the tip of the iceberg'. Furthermore, if we refrain from recognizing our multi-dimensional nature, then our ego is left to hi-jack our reflective capacity. If we reflect only on the domain of ego, and utilize only the skills of ego, we allow of no other aspect of self to which we can relate. We are thus in danger of forming a reflexive loop – an ego-referring loop – which merely perpetuates our self-limitation, rather than allowing a self-referring loop which refers to the whole self and thereby builds a self-generative loop – which is the very spring of evolutionary form.

The great mystic traditions of the East perhaps developed as a balance to the general thrust of ego during this last stage of human evolution. They testify to the reality of human experience beyond the confines of the ego – a great offering on behalf of the entire species. However, it seems it is only possible to live such wisdom in monasteries or special settings suitable for the meditative life. The structure, ritual and regular daily rhythm of such an existence partially substitutes, or stands in, for the ego structures of those in the community: such structure holds the psyche together, and creates boundaries, leaving the mind free to focus on the timeless preoccupation of watching itself in stillness and emptiness until serene illumination is reached.

Certain of the disciplines involved in Western contemplative life likewise fulfil some of the positive functions of the ego, so that the ego itself can rest, can relax its hold over the psyche which is then released to extend its consciousness, and apprehend that infinite and boundless aspect of Reality that underpins and permeates all existence. But ego is only suspended, or partially suspended. It always re-emerges. It can only be put to one side within a highly structured and disciplined setting and, as a species, we are not designed to live that way.

Although it can be deeply nourishing to us as individuals to lay aside times of quietness in which we deliberately let go of ego, it does not mean that we should live daily life without the ego, or that something is wrong or inferior about ego consciousness. Discarding the ego, as is attempted in much religious thinking and practice, is hardly an answer. Not only is such a project perceived as utter negation for ego-dominated beings (which includes most of us at this present stage of our collective psychological development), and therefore naturally viewed with suspicion and simply avoided, but anyway the ego does have its part to play as an important aspect of self: it is not just an aberration. It is the *dictatorship* of the ego that we must relinquish, not the ego itself. As human beings cannot negotiate their way in the world without ego consciousness, it is pointless to pretend it to be expendable.

Merely to undermine the place of the ego is counter-productive because it is a weak ego that is burdensome, always requiring to be propped up; a weak ego absorbs energy. Also, as we tend to project unowned parts of ourselves on to others and the world, the denial of ego could, paradoxically, only further reinforce our perception of fragmentation. The 'egoless' either become psychotic and know no boundaries at all or, in the denial of ego in themselves, are liable to place on the world a false emphasis on factions, conflicts and divisions, viewing their society with an unbalanced harshness. Such a world, for the would-be egoless inhabitants of it, *must* be transcended. Life is seen in terms of escape from matter (which, of course, has been stripped of meaning and rendered unreal by its fragmentation and dissociation from spirit).

Meanwhile, those who cannot manage this fantasy of 'rising above it all' are left to grasp bravely and tenaciously to specific pieces of reality – as expressed in our consumerism. Society is thus further split between those who are 'spiritual' and those who are 'materialists'. The ones given to ego denial dub the only world known to all those 'other' egos, the material dimension, as mere illusion – a kind of penance or life sentence. If we judge physical life as an unfortunate low-grade form of being, then we are hardly likely to learn to live it with grace; to know it as an amazing venture that we have yet to complete.

When our self-concept is synonymous with ego, or is only a socially defined image or role, and as such is given a high-level position as a generator of meaning, then many episodes in our life that *could* be enriching will be experienced as threatening and humiliating. These happenings then tend to shake our fragile sense of security, rather than stimulate conscious change. Such challenges are only creative if contained within a more comprehensive, flexible and living conceptual framework than any that a purely ego-based self-concept, transitory self-image or mere social role can afford. Panic rather than transformation is liable to take place, followed by a desperate search for reinstatement of the status quo.

An ego-dominated psyche will always be energetically conservative. (However, as the ego's range of concern is very local and superficial, it is hardly surprising that our species has, at the same time, been so slow to take the necessary steps in order to conserve the planet.) A relatively minor episode can trigger alarm, can disturb our whole ephemeral foundation of meaning and, therefore, our whole way of being in the world. We have settled for too flimsy a construction, a poor psychic 'home', a minimal pseudo-self to live in, and with, and from. Preoccupation with how to defend such a 'home' is bound to follow, with defensive responses becoming 'natural'.

The more profound the self-concept, the more likely it is that reverberations from various episodes or relationships can be accepted and 'placed' and then allowed to flow at less significant levels. They don't necessarily infiltrate all levels of meaning *unless we consciously choose to perceive them as a challenge that can facilitate further creative change.* During some painful or tricky interchange we can tell ourselves, 'That's how he sees me'. Held safely within a full experience of our self we can also allow the other their experience and reality. A secure self can discriminate between valuable feedback, destructive attack or undermining indulgence. A secure person can accept, and even welcome, the richness of differing perspectives and viewpoints. But an ego-based self-concept quickly becomes a victim self-concept.

How can anyone find themselves, trust themselves, truly express themselves, let alone love themselves or anyone else, when operating from a fundamentally defensive and competitive position? Such a belief guarantees an impoverished base for our evolving human race; it is bound to undermine psychological growth and turn it into an extraordinary struggle and a rare phenomenon. It says a lot for our inventive resilience that we have survived at all, albeit in a stunted fashion. But the cost is enormous and no longer holds any necessity. Now that the ego has been fully developed and its skills perfected, it no longer need be the focal point of our consciousness. It is ripe for integration into a larger self.

The Relationship between Our Concept of Self and Our Concept of God

It is easy to understand why those with a purely ego-based concept of self, or attached to a mere image of self or social role, will either have to make do with the lean philosophy of reductionist materialism, or else take on (or even, perhaps, tack on) a belief in a purely external God. Their whole way of seeing and being squeezes out the presence of 'God within'. There is no room in such a minimal view of personhood to include the divine. This objectified God, who has to remain forever banished to the beyond, is nevertheless a necessity if they are to get some recourse to a more effective and stable high-order level of meaning. He is also their only access to any kind of personalized meta-view. But they are destined to be ever searching for ways to bridge the gap between their fragile selves and this God who resides outside their mode of being. (They may pay lip-service to the immanent side of His nature, but it can only remain pure theology for an ego-based self.) And so this awesome concept, which has no place in a shrunken inner world, naturally has to be 'individualized' to help ease the abysmal gulf between their conception of themselves and their conception of Him. The logically necessary meta-concept has to be humanized because the aspects of self that can apprehend other orders of Being are not being activated. He becomes the kind of Father God that serves the needs of our infant psychic state and yet-to-emerge self. And because ego-selves are not fit to be His sons and daughters, we search for special (or even unique) instances of Sonship, setting such people apart from the *kind* of beings that we perceive ourselves to be.

So we look only outwards for wisdom, to ancient prophets and living gurus, believing that true wisdom always must, necessarily, lie in others. We set up a need for those larger and freer than our constricted selves. It is not difficult to see why religions which worshipped one, sure, externalized God, whose word was revealed by a Son or special agent of truth in human form, were essential during the long period of our human story while the ego was being developed as an aspect of the self. The cultures of the West have cradled the development of ego within the powerful ambience of a belief in a separate God.

For the less individually orientated culture of the East, such a personalized monotheism has not held dominance. Finding ways of detaching the mind from the material plane, and the desire to merge into a cosmic oneness while still in physical form, is their expression, it seems, of our general human reluctance to live out our full selfhood and human-beingness. The deep ambivalence which people of Eastern traditions appear to feel about being on earth – their view of the physical space/time mode as only illusion rather than as one aspect in the infinite continuum of a greater Reality – has brought out an emphasis on many incarnations. A belief in reincarnation is part of everyday thinking in the East. Somehow they know that ultimately we, as human beings, must come to terms with this world. Could it be that until they, in their own way, see life on earth as an opportunity to serve and express the greater Reality, rather than a self-induced karmic punishment, their social and political functioning will perpetuate their experience of this world as a place principally of suffering? Their greater acceptance of death is won, it seems, at the all-too-heavy price of devaluing the physical aspect of human life.

On the other hand we, in the West, who have provided the nursery for the developing ego, hold on to this physical dimension for all we are worth, and count our senses as the only messengers to tell us what is real. We feel intensely about our 'one and only' incarnation, and grab at all we can, while we can. We are thus spiritually deprived, whereas the peoples of the East are materially deprived. We are involved in attachment while they are involved in detachment. Our peopled globe is like some great split brain, the left hemisphere severed from the right hemisphere so that neither can aid and complement the other and thus enable us to come into completion as a species.

The Civilization of the Split Psyche: The Challenge to Become Whole

In order to indicate something of our human condition, I am choosing to make bold generalizations and use the crudest of brush strokes so that we may view ourselves on a broad canvas. As the ego has been valued and nourished within our Western culture, I believe it is also fitting that we of the West endeavour to recognize the true place of ego in the functioning of the whole self. The people of the East have had other aspects of self in their keeping; they have honoured the eternal presence of spirit and the universal living principle of the Tao. In the words of E.M. Forster, 'If we could but connect'. If the marvellous collective mind of our species could but connect, now that the necessary time of separation-focus is over. Our ego has been born, nested, nourished, and is ready to function appropriately within the larger self; that many-layered self which we must now remember and reclaim as who we truly are. A great re-membering is due.

As I mentioned earlier, it is pointless to entertain the myth that the ego can be eradicated. The ego is an established part of the human psyche, neither accidental nor incidental, although it should never become central or be thought of as fundamental. And so it will not

Chapter Five: Self-Concept and Meaning

help to try and dismiss the ego, or to punish ourselves for its misplaced activities. Not only does a weak ego dominate more than a healthy one, but is not this only another form of blaming? I suggest we call the antics of the ego a 'blind' self-referring loop which, as soon as we acknowledge the whole self, we need perpetuate no longer.

We in the West have allowed our ego to over-reach itself in frenetic activity because of our difficulty in remembering, right now at any given moment, our grounding in spirit. We have, at this time, nothing very substantial, spiritually speaking, with which to balance or offset the workings of our ego. For the most part we have not been able to draw on our religions at this vital point in our psychic development because the actual structure of these religions still mirrors and serves the needs of the ego-based, victim self-concept. And given our propensity for compartmentalizing and specialization, we have developed very little spirituality outside of the religious domain. We need either to tap the *source* of our religions once more, or else open ourselves to the wisdom of other and ancient cultures, making our own distillations of their offerings, before those cultures lose themselves in the energy of 'ego imperialism' and get flooded by outdated and dressed-up importations of materialism.

One would expect that those of us in societies which put a high priority on choice would be most ready to release ourselves from the Victim Archetype. Surely we should be alerted by the dichotomy between our conscious belief in our ability to choose (enshrined in our democratic institutions) and our propensity to blame and feel victimized and powerless. Have we not fought wars in the name of preserving our right to choose? We should be able to embrace a non-victim self-concept more easily than are those who have long been accustomed to very rigid social patterns or excessively authoritarian and repressive political regimes. One would expect us to be more aware of challenges to our victim viewpoint and more open to pick up on and deal with anomalies in our victim reading of situations. We should increasingly be faced with the decision to rethink that all-too-common utterance, 'I can't help it'. This could lead us, in turn, to look at familiar situations afresh, and discover new possible ways in which we could act.

On the other hand, if we refuse to let go of our victim

self-concept, can we really consider the declaration 'I want to change' to be authentic? The statement could even be used as a cover to keep the old self-concept intact – 'Of course I want to change, but I can't'. If so-called 'free' and relatively liberal societies do not take a lead in dismantling the hold of the Victim Archetype and victim self-concept, then our culture truly demonstrates how very serious are the consequences of its dualistic thought structures. We are, in truth, only living from our 'heads', and our rational 'grown-up' principles have little connection, and thus influence, on the gut feelings of our infant selves we are so busy trying to control.

How Dualism Serves the Victim Self-concept and Thus Engagement with the Victim Archetype

The artificial dichotomy between spirit and body, mind and matter, intellect and feeling, has taken its toll. When we sever complementary unities, when we split asunder that which is evolved to function as a living whole, we scatter our powers and then naturally experience ourselves as victims. We endeavour to function as human beings with only part of who we are. If choice is confined to a separate domain of the purely material, then it seems that it runs rampant in the service of our addictive consumerism. But material goods can never satisfy the internal pit of emptiness that we create when we attempt to negate the whole selves which we were born to be. The intrinsic power of self-generation – greatly accentuated when organisms are complex multi-dimensional entities because then, the capacity is gained to make significant and creative choices from the deepest and most subtle levels of being – this natural human power is sadly interrupted by artificial demarcations forged within the psyche, and then imposed on the world around us. With the internal divisions held rigidly in place, choice is reserved for the trivial and even becomes a diversion; the victim self-concept is held intact; and so the Victim Archetype still reigns supreme.

Now only certain concepts of self admit to, and thus open us to an awareness of, our engagement with a particular archetype – thus affording the opportunity and choice of gradual but increasing disengagement – while other self-concepts encourage us to stay so engaged. Our concept of what a self is thus has an enormous impact on our reality. The self-concepts which we employ either aid the discovery of our self, enhancing the likelihood of experiencing what it means to be a whole and undivided being capable of making choices, or play a part in veiling our knowledge of self. Given the prevalence of an ego-based self-concept (whatever our self-image may happen to be), we fight for our right to be a victim. We want to be told, 'Of course there was no possible way that you could have dealt differently with that situation' (which is very different from compassionate understanding of how it is that we have acted as we have). It feels impossible to forego such a 'natural' and familiar position. Would not our whole world topple without it – if we had to face that we could have created a very different life for ourselves? How dare anyone suggest that being helpless is not fundamental to our human condition. And of course, if we hold to our right to be victims, we hold, too, to our 'right' to be victimized – although we are unlikely to conceive of our activities in these terms. 'I *have* to do this or he'll be upset. I have no choice.' Such statements punctuate all our lives. As victims, we all know victimhood is something that we cannot help.

It is no use evading the fact that being a victim has come to *feel* like it is a hard reality of human life. This is only to be expected if we entertain a self-concept which renders us so available to the organizing energy of the Victim Archetype. We need to acknowledge the hold of this archetype on our collective psyche. In an important sense we *are* born into victimhood, and the victim/persecutor/rescuer dynamic is the agreed mode of interaction at this stage of our development. We have to accept that the victim in us cannot easily be dismissed. To turn our victim energy on its head and blame ourselves for being victims will only trap us in a downward spiral of non-development.

Acknowledgment of our vulnerability to the Victim Archetype – recognition of its all-pervasive presence in our lives – is the most creative step towards transformation that we can make. It is only through a compassionate and understanding *acceptance* of the self which we have split into bits that we can allow the process of integration to take place; and only such integration can relieve us of our acute vulnerability to the Victim Archetype.

A word about archetypes. Although archetypes have usually been given the status of *a priori* psychic constructs, I nevertheless consider them as contingent or *possible* organizing structures of the human psyche; and I contend that the range of these collective forces is vast and unfixed and ever-evolving. Just knowing that our psyches *could* operate in accordance with a different organization, and are as fitted to do so, can lift the present lid on our imaginations and allow glimpses and tastes of a more free and joyful way to be in the world.

The pull to be victims will perhaps always be with us; but if we begin to integrate our split psyches and let ego ease its dominating hold on our consciousness, then we can increasingly open ourselves to the experience of how we can also *not* be a victim. Thereafter, we at least have evolved a choice – we can be a victim or we can not be a victim – and thus we reveal our release from automatic adherence to the Victim Archetype: we no longer simply let this particular organizer of the psyche programme us. We know that we are able, if willing, to create a different reality for ourselves. It may take many years to clear the hold of the victim in us, but what is required right now is that we know it can be done. This knowledge will set in motion the transformative undermining of that fixed allegiance to the archetype which, at present, makes it the ruler of our psyche and thus of our interactions in the world. It will also ensure its eventual relegation to being but one amongst many possible organizing structures of human meaning.

A divided psyche can never hope to disengage from archetypal energies; it can only be at the mercy of them. But once we move beyond dualistic thought structures, once we realize that we have been attempting to live life from one section of our psyche only and begin to claim a fuller notion and experience of self, then we can begin to let go of our involvement with a particular archetype and allow connection with new and more rewarding organizers of our meaning. An increasingly conscious self can actively disengage from the structuring energy of the Victim Archetype, and connect instead with that of the Archetype of Self-Generation (for instance), thus allowing a very different organizing force within the psyche to empower the construction of a more fulfilling human reality.

A fittingly comprehensive concept of self could also, in time, perhaps allow us to drop self-image and identification with roles (along with their attendant insecurities) altogether from our system of meanings. We could then deal with the level of episodes more directly and economically – uncluttered by projections – and move *with* life, as it unfolds in the present, with a greater grace.

The Implications of a Self-concept Based on Spirit

It may be clearer by now what I meant when I stated in earlier chapters that the self is primary; that 'it all starts with the self'. I contend that how we conceive of the self is one of the most powerful ways in which we determine our lives. If that is so, then it is absolutely essential that we know of self, and know ourselves. As I have already indicated, only certain concepts of self facilitate the process of transformation or true creativity – let alone encompass the possibility of gaining freedom from archetypal powers. Indeed, only certain views about self give us the sense that we have the ability to choose at all, or have real power to act – that is how fundamental our self-concept is in determining our experience. (The philosophical problem of free will can be seen as a pseudo problem which only arises when we identify the ego as the self.) Self is the core and medium of our experienced reality. The notion of a multi-dimensional self affirms the level of operation where boundaries are necessary and appropriate limits set, while also inviting recognition of the infinite. We can thus know the self as an access point to All-That-Is, as well as a unique expression of All-That-Is. We only place centrality on to external objects or systems if we are operating from a diminished view of self.

A concept of self which embraces the dimension of spirit, and leads us into a living knowledge of our being in spirit, is the most potent means we have of consciously organizing our meaning and creating our experience. Knowing that each self contains direct access to the infinite (not the Infinite Itself, as that, of course, cannot be contained), we know, too, that we can generate our own meaning – that is, if we dare be our full selves. Meaning relies on a context, and can only be defined by including its context; and for that reason, the meaning of meaning itself can never be captured in a definition. The self that knows spirit, however, carries the context of its meaning within itself;

a context comprehensive enough for any human eventuality because it is no less than Infinite Beingness. The self's meta-levels of apprehension lie within the ever-unfolding layers of subtlety that give form to each self. The biological aspect of our being is context dependent (ultimately dependent on mother earth, not one particular person), but the spirit in us, by its very nature, carries its own context and creates meaning. As part of that activity, it will draw on culture and environment, but there is ultimately no infinite regress problem to human meaning (which cannot help but transcend the verbal) when a self is the very access point to the Infinite Itself: the context of all contexts.

I believe that the only satisfactory foundation for the self is recognition of our spiritual essence; that essential beingness of each individual – the timeless aspect that lies beyond our three-dimensional picture of reality and our linear mode of thought. We can obscure and blur, resist and divert the expression of spirit in ourselves, but spirit itself is not subject to destruction. Only with a security of this nature, which alone can relieve us of the underlying fear of annihilation which ego suffers, are we likely to give the larger share of our energy to life rather than to defence and resistance; and only then are we geared *for* life. We can then experience our will-to-be, and know that the moving force within each individual is one with the moving force in the universe itself.

However, at this point in our evolution the bulk of our energy is caught in holding rather than being given to expression; it is seldom allowed the freedom to go with the movement of life in us. It is worth imagining what it would be like if the balance were reversed, as indeed seems to be the case with all other creatures, and we began operating with a greater proportion of our extraordinary potential as a species. Why should it seem strange that humans simply function well? This would indeed be possible if we disengaged from the Victim Archetype – if we let go of our bias towards dependence, attachment and blame – and such a release rests on the recognition of spirit as the creative core of our being. Moreover, is not spiritual energy, in its amazing subtlety and power, the only quality of energy capable of generating all the complexities of *known* human experience and the intricacies of human thought and interaction as they even now daily occur? Nothing less than spirit, as the ground of our being, is of a nature profound enough to account for, let alone fulfil, our lived human-beingness.

We cannot hope to explain the way we manifestly and explicitly behave without some concept of spirit. And I do not now only refer to acts of sainthood or heroism, but to the shadow aspect of our dealings with life. We are left stunned by much human behaviour and quickly dissociate ourselves from it by saying, 'How *could* anyone do such a thing?', or '*We* just want peace. What is the matter with them?' Spirit generates the unlimited aspect of our nature, and this is shown with horrifying clarity in our modes of destruction. No action is too awful to perform in the name of defence. We can cut up babies and devise slow tortures for each other once we have decided who the enemy is. If our creativity has no limit or set boundary or decent cut-off point, so, too, with our destructiveness. And that ingenious destructive power reigns – by utilizing our psycho-physical modes of blocking and complex systems of denial – when our energy is turned against ourselves. We then become intrinsically defended beings, and our array of ever-developing psychic manoeuvres to keep ourselves 'safe' (paralleled by the extraordinary lengths, both brilliant and foolish, to which we are prepared to go in order to achieve national 'security') is evidence of the reverse side of our creative urge. But with a direct and living knowledge of spirit, we have access to a security so profound that we no longer need give so much attention to distorting our powers; that turning against our own energy and displacing unwanted aspects of ourselves on to others need not take place, and we can release ourselves into the process of fulfilment and completion.

We Are One Body

However, we are equally 'body', even though spirit is primary and prior to body. It is our physical form which marks us as human rather than some other kind of spiritual entity. And once we have incarnated, is it not our business to be fully human and not pretend or attempt to be another sort of being? Of course we retain elements from our rich heritage of mineral, plant and animal life, and perhaps even have a special relationship with energies from other unseen subtle realms of being; but we have ended up as human, and our purpose is to be human. Only with a balanced awareness of spirit and body are human relationships rendered fully human(e).

We each are a single body, and we all share in one and the same kind of body. Each body is both unique and distinct, and yet we also have common needs and feelings. And we all, without exception, need bread to eat and water to drink as well as food for our embodied spirit. We all feel hunger, joy, pain, sadness, pleasure, anger, grief, compassion. All peoples laugh and cry and dance and sing. And if we do not, then we are denying our 'oneness in body'. We are denying that grounding in our shared Mother – Nature herself. We are one in spirit (which cannot be divided, although it does manifest and express itself in diversity), and we are in one body (which defines the aspect of the universe for which we alone are responsible, as well as marking what we all share as human beings). Our body gives us our material boundaries and recognizable shape. We each need to honour both our own bodies and that of other human beings. Our body holds and contains and gives a form to our energy so that we can live out a special aspect of the Whole – of All-That-Is. There is no sense in which our body is inferior to our spirit. It is the distinctly human expression of spirit and the vehicle for making spirit manifest. Body is in a continuum with spirit; the dense and defined end of the human spectrum, a spectrum which increases in subtlety and goes on to infinity.

However, the drawback in describing and understanding the self through contemplation of spirit and body is that these two aspects of self have for centuries been torn asunder, and are still carried within a moralistic ordering of higher and lower in our collective 'civilized' memory. It is thus almost impossible to free ourselves of this habit. It is revealed in the way in which we try and 'prove' spirit or spiritual power by tampering with the physical; defeating the laws of physics is seen as an ultimate demonstration of the superiority of the spirit over matter. (Perhaps it is because such laws are regarded as the most powerful expression of the physical domain although, of course, they are not themselves physical.)

Miracles and scepticism go hand in hand in dualistic hierarchical civilizations. Instead of respecting both body and spirit, and allowing each aspect to contribute in its own way to the whole being that we are – and the whole universe that we live in – we set them against each other in a contest of strength, and try and force a choice between them. We go for 'mind over matter' rather than letting mind deal with mind. It is our fixed systems of thought and the resulting destructive patterns of behaviour that could do with some bending, rather than metal spoons. It is the rigidity of mind that we need to look to, not the natural resistance of mass. I personally feel uneasy when we focus our human resources and ingenuity on striving to change what *is* (as with genetic engineering), rather than use our creative impulse to change and develop our *conception* of what is. The power of the mind lies in the immense potential it has to alter *itself*, its own structures and operations, and thus our mode of expression and experience of the world.

The Limitations and Dangers of Hierarchical Models for Understanding the Self

As hierarchical models are conceived of on a vertical plane, they are all too likely to be mapped on to the vertical, upright body of us human beings – and to ill effect. The fact that this mapping is done unconsciously only increases the power of its influence. The model lends itself to our regarding the head, and therefore the intellect, as more important than the heart or feelings, still more important than the sexual area of the pelvis, and vastly more important than our feet which touch and connect with the earth. This model and this mapping process fit all too neatly with our entrenched dualistic structures of thought – which is hardly surprising, as its origins lie in such thought. It presents us with a convenient divide between our higher nature above the waist and our lower nature below it. A moralistic split is set up between heaven, spirit, intellect, agape and 'good' heartfelt feelings represented by the top half of our body; and earth, physicality, sensuality, lust and 'bad' feelings such as anger associated with the lower half of our body.

Hierarchical models can thus be disadvantageous when used as an approach to the self, because any grading into 'higher' and 'lower' invites judgemental comparison and a need then to separate what is deemed good and what bad. In many contexts, the terms 'higher' and 'lower' have become almost synonymous with 'better' and 'worse'. Such a model, and the whole way of thinking that it provokes and promotes, lends itself to division and convenient cut-off points. Just because the lower levels are, by definition, regarded as less important or powerful, they can only too easily be dismissed altogether as of no significance. We can fall into imagining that we can dispense with such levels – especially when we judge them to be intrinsically inferior or troublesome. Terms like 'primitive', 'animal instincts', 'baser urges' are all too often used in a pejorative way. In fact, anything outside the control or understanding of the favoured rational ego tends to be approached with suspicion and regarded as 'uncivilized'. It is a totally alien model for an organism which only functions and flourishes as a whole entity.

Although some 'parts' are not essential (an arm, for instance), the human organism is nevertheless impaired if an arm is removed. To treat the whole lower area of the body, in some abstract way, as a kind of appendage, or to entertain the more serious fantasy that we can operate perfectly well by simply paying no attention to our physical animal nature and certain categories of feeling, are both fairly frequent forms of psychological dissociation. It seems to me that the hierarchical mode of thought encourages such divisions, judgements and dismissals. It has also given credence to the destructive separation and polarization of feminine and masculine qualities, affording them a different status, and has thus served patriarchy all too well. It has influenced our attitudes and behaviour in untold ways which are still in the process of emerging into the field of our awareness.

Change as an Inevitable Threat to the System

Perhaps the greatest drawback to using models of a hierarchical nature, however, is that they do not easily allow for change; they favour the homeostatic principle, not the transformative one. Such systems tend to hold the status quo in place, especially if the upper levels are 'invisible' and do not come within the arena of our conscious attention. It is hardly surprising, then, that the entwined high-order contexts of Victim Archetype and victim self-concept tend to rule

Chapter Five: Self-Concept and Meaning

our interactions. The destructive force of a self-concept based on the Victim Archetype contaminates all our experience; all our beliefs and attitudes and ideas, the quality of our relationships, our feelings and thoughts, our choices and decisions and actions, making change unlikely. Only when life throws up a very marked and unusual dissonance between the ordered levels in the hierarchy of meanings can the system be disrupted and change then occur; only then can a lower level gain some power and be experienced as the context which gives meaning to a higher one.

Change, growth and development, therefore, rely on insistent disturbance of the established order. This is the one way in which those higher levels of psychic organization can give way for new patterns of interaction. Experience of trivial choices between material objects does not often challenge the higher-level Victim Archetype or victim self-concept; but if we experience that we can choose not to feel rejected, or defeated, then our victim self-concept is certainly called into question. What is more, each time we refuse to be a victim for another, or a persecutor or rescuer, we bring about a dissonance in *their* system of meanings. If this misfit in mode of relationship is repeated, then we engender creative dissonance in their experience. Because a different dynamic emerges in these episodes, a new quality of interaction, they may be moved to make a decision to redefine their self-concept, rather than discount the episodes. The trouble is that we all-too-easily remain split in the contradiction that such dissonance affords and enter a state of confusion, or divide our experience into separate compartments in order to try and live out the contradiction. In so doing, we violate our organismic nature and have to call on ever-more rigidity.

A fixed or set hierarchical system is anti-life; it does not allow for the movement of life or fit our ever-changing reality. We therefore urgently need disturbance of our systems of meanings in order to generate the asking of new questions. We need to see that something is amiss and that the old order of meaning cannot hold. But the problem is that reliance on dissonance is hardly an effective vehicle of change. We have a deep aversion to the disturbance of our systems of order and yet, in any hierarchical approach to the understanding and perception of self, we are required to welcome such disturbance and give it *prime* importance. For any change to occur, it is necessary that we respect and give special attention to that which threatens our present order, not regarding it as some kind of aberration even though it is naturally experienced as such. Learning is thus an atypical and stilted procedure; and change can only occur through an exception to the rule, through happenings that are conceived as 'against' the system of ordered levels, rather than being accepted as the natural mode of all life.

It would hardly come as a surprise, then, if we were habitually to refuse to give our attention to the vital information that could bring about change when acceptance of it can do no other than undermine our present ordering of meanings. And if we do refuse the information that dissonance between the hierarchical levels throws up, then we enter ever-deeper confusion and divisions within the self. This is what occurs when a two-tier contradictory message is used in an interchange; the 'double bind'. It demands a reorganization of meaning, but far from promoting change, it has a blocking effect. R.D. Laing maintained that the very purpose of this phenomenon is to cause confusion and prevent clear communication between people. The relationship remains exactly where it is. The status quo is upheld.

If an openness to the *breakdown* of the self's system of ordering meaning is the only means of change, then the future of our species does not look hopeful. A hierarchical model for understanding the operations of the self reveals how utterly transforming it would be if we *did* choose to take on a new high-order context of meaning; but such a decision can only be reached by means of a process that is bound to stimulate our resistance and fear because it poses a threat to the whole way the system is *supposed* to work. We are far more likely, when faced with disturbance of our system of meanings, to withdraw, contract and flee into unconsciousness than we are to wake up, or let go into expansion. The probability is that it would take many momentous episodes, all unwelcome because contrary to our cherished belief system, to shake our present self-concept or the archetype holding sway at the top of the hierarchical structure of meaning. Such dissonance is likely to be denied or avoided, and the old patterns of interaction thus left intact.

So how do we get to take on a new high-order context? That is the crucial question. It is not difficult to see that if we did seriously explore and embrace a new self-concept, and try out the belief that we are not a mere victim of circumstance, for instance, then we would begin to experience more and more choice – and different kinds of choice. The feedback system of new experience reinforces the new belief, and the new belief vitalizes and gives birth to new experience. After a time, we would begin to define our relationships in different ways. And if we could somehow manage to clarify and suspend our old life-scripts (such as 'I cannot get close to anyone or I shall betray mother'), then we might act in different ways and, eventually, novel happenings or episodes would begin to emerge. Even a change of self-image (which would naturally come far lower in the hierarchy than our concept of what we are as a self) could engender an expectation that we are well liked and so free us to interpret as humour what before would have made us defensive, or enable us to receive a compliment with warmth and openness, as opposed to discounting it with irritation in the fear that we are merely being flattered.

The hierarchical approach clearly illustrates that the less force a context has to generate meaning (i.e. the lower it is in the hierarchy), the more amenable it is to change – it poses less threat to the system. In other words, the less-effective level is the easiest to change. And yet we have the growing sense, at a collective level, that change of a *profound* nature is essential if we are to survive as a species; that change must occur at a level that carries real power. But the higher the level, the greater is the dissonance and disturbance, and thus the likelihood of us defending against it; and the greater the potency, the greater the resistance. And it is no good simply adopting a new high-order position with the rational mind. If it is not lodged deep in the psyche, we are merely entertaining ourselves with a fantasy or escaping into empty idealism. How do we reach an openness to change at a level that carries sufficient significance – that carries the necessary transforming force? We drop the hierarchical way of viewing the self.

To free ourselves from the stultification inherent in this kind of cognitive ordering, it can be helpful to look at the self freshly through the structure of a different understanding of the human psyche; through the living experience of another culture. I should like to use the very earthy and practical model of the self evolved by the American Indian peoples. Only if grounded in a truly fitting self-concept, one that fits our human-beingness in its fullness, can we become well as a species and, indeed, be welcome on earth.

Chapter Six
The Circle of Self

I felt real joy when I came across the Medicine Wheel, as it seemed to offer not only a fresh, non-linear, non-dualistic, non-hierarchical way of seeing the self, but also provided a structure which has helped me to organize my thinking on related issues which have long been of deep concern to me. It afforded me the opportunity to approach the age-old opposition between free will and determinism in a new and releasing way. I will draw on this model over the next three chapters.

Carl Jung stated that the circle was the symbol of individuation, that it expressed self-integration and the coming into our wholeness as an individual. In our culture, individuation is understood as a state of psychological maturity – something that we eventually hope to attain. The American Indian peoples start with a circle. They approach the self through the idea of the circle and know of self by moving through that circle. And they gather together in sacred circles, in which there is no privileged position, in order to learn about self and to honour the self. All are equal and all are connected in a circle, and any point can be the starting point. When we form a circle, each member of that circle has a different angle on the central reality that they share, and all these viewpoints are equally important, equally valid. All have something unique to offer and add to the richness of the whole. There is always something that other members of the circle can see that we cannot see.

The formation of a circle is an expression of the non-linear nature both of the self and of all interchanges between selves. Interaction between people, however it may later be described and reported and made to fit the structure of our language, is never linear. Continuous and circular actions and responses occur simultaneously on various levels, in both the internal world of thought and imagination, and in external mode through the body language of facial expression, tone of voice, eye movements, gestures and postures, as well as through the complex multiple meanings that flow from the arrangement of the words we use. All these levels are co-present and operating together to weave a human happening which we agree to give a relatively discrete shape. If we wish to mark a happening as especially significant, or as sacred, some form of ceremony or ritual is often used.

Perhaps the simplest, most ancient and most powerful of all rituals is this coming together and making a circle. Some among the American Indian peoples then take a stick to which a feather has been attached, the feather speaking to them of air, heaven and spirit which is ever connected to the body of the earth into which the stick is pierced. The ceremony has thus begun, and the creators of the circle pass over an invisible threshold and enter a state of focused attention. The placing of the feathered stick in the ground represents the interpenetration of all dimensions: the union of the infinite and finite, spirit and body, heaven and earth, timelessness and time. It becomes the pivot of the present, acknowledging the magical power of 'this' moment, 'this' particular place, 'this' singular group of unique human beings – a nodal point within the ever-moving dance of the universe.

The 'Shields' of Self Reflection

The American Indian peoples speak of their teachings as being carried by 'Shields'. This can have unfortunate connotations for us in our culture; we associate the word with war, battle and defensiveness. But the Indian peoples treat the shield, in this context, as we would a mirror – a shiny surface that reflects back to us our selves. If we would learn of the world, we must first look at ourselves, and see ourselves.

All learning starts with the self. All wisdom is based on awareness of self, which thus allows the clear seeing of others and the world around us. This may be misunderstood in our egocentric culture. We have so habitually equated ego with self that we can all too easily confuse the process of being centred in the self with narcissism, or with an unhealthy and exclusive introversion. But for the American Indian peoples there is no real division between inner and outer, subject and object, self and the universe. Dualism has no place in the circle of life. Experience is not split up into separate categories. It is understood as one happening; and that which is internal and that which is external to the self are like two sides of one coin. Thus, they believe that anything that we meet as we walk through life can be a mirror to show us who we are. They trust in the synchronicity of the universe, and that we shall encounter whatever it is that we need to learn if we do but dare to see, to select. They approach the world in its particularity rather than in generalities and abstractions: they speak of the spirit of this particular tree, this stone, this bird – a mode of awareness which affords an immediate and meaningful connection within a living homogeneous universe.

And so if an American Indian wishes to undertake a vision quest in search of her- or himself, and goes to the shaman to ask, 'How shall I attain wisdom?', the shaman will simply point to the wilderness and say, 'Go, and there you will find yourself'. The world is full of continually changing mirrors reflecting our truth to us; we need but be alert, open and receptive. Wisdom is gained by recognizing the rich feedback that the world is ever-generous in giving us, and in this way we come to see ourselves in all our fullness. This deeply personal relationship to the universe recognizes the reality of our interdependence in both a profound and very practical way.

Given that the shield is a mirror, we can appreciate how important it is that we do not hug it tightly to us in order merely to protect ourselves from the world or hold the world at bay. For the shield to be our teacher, it needs to be held lightly and at a little distance from us. If we take up a purely defensive stance, if we pose ourselves against the world, then we see nothing. We see neither ourselves nor the world. Instead, we project certain unseen aspects of ourselves on to the world and then defend ourselves against what we perceive as external and alien to us. We then make a hard and blinding divide between perceiver and perceived, and thus lose our gift of human perception.

There are four basic shields or reflectors of our human beingness, and these are named after the four directions of the globe on which we live – South, North, West and East. Each of these directions has a rich psychic meaning and yet is also an aspect of everyday, ordinary living. We need to know the special quality and energy of these directions on the psychological level if we would find our way around our internal space, just as we need to know them on the physical level if we wish to orientate ourselves for practical purposes in our exterior space.

Moving through the Medicine Wheel: The Four Directions Expressing Different Aspects of the Psyche

Here we have the circle once again. The four directions, or rather our movement through these key aspects of our human-beingness, make up the Medicine Wheel – the wheel of healing. In fact, the eight cardinal directions – south, south-west, west, north-west, north, north-east, east and south-east – are mapped on to this wheel; but for the sake of simplicity I am going to focus on the four most fundamental directions of being.

The beauty of this approach to the psyche is that all four directions are not only of equal status but can only be seen and known as a whole system; they make no sense unless they are in relationship with each other. The North without the South is utterly meaningless. (It is interesting that the north pole of a magnet can never be separated from its south pole. If a magnet is divided in two, each half still exhibits both poles.) The self is seen as a complex interweaving of energies that naturally form a particular whole – a circle (or sphere). What is more, North can become South from another position, or what was West can become East from a new standpoint, and yet neither is confused with the other – at any given moment, they express a valid and valuable distinction specific to a particular context. They are also all co-present, whatever direction we may be facing. They never disappear or lose their force or relevance. The four directions of South, North, West, East are utterly interdependent yet clear, unfixed yet distinct. They are ever-moving but do not merge or fuse together. They beautifully express the nature of the psyche.

Moreover, there is no moralism involved. No direction can possibly be judged better or more powerful than another, no direction is higher, or lower, or more or less necessary. As a model, the wheel of the four directions offers a way of viewing the self which encourages

Chapter Six: The Circle of Self

full acceptance of all aspects of our being. It is easier to love such a self. What is more, wholeness feels natural – not something to be attained after a long hard struggle. Such a self is either whole or it makes no sense – is a nonsense.

We start as a whole circle and then learn ever more about our inner, moving, distinct directions of energy. Wholeness, or healing, is not a matter of attaining what we never had, but a matter of balancing what was always intrinsic to us. If our energies are out of balance, then we are a poorly functioning organism, but still an organism; and if they are in balance, then we live in good health and humour. But we are always changing, as life is always changing, and so we continually need to enter the medicine wheel and check our state of balance or imbalance; sense in which direction our energy is stuck, recognize what directions we are reluctant to engage, notice whence we always flee or to which direction we are easily drawn and all too ready to place our attention, to the exclusion of the other directions. For we need to partake of each direction to be the whole individuated person, the circle, we were born to be. I like to see each self as a ball of energy, with no absolute dividing edge, pivoting around a unique point of infinity and held as a whole by an untiring attraction to the central core of our being.

If we imagine the self as a sphere, which contains the whole embodied life of the individual, then we are freed from the sequential, developmental model of linear stages and steps with the resulting in-built view that some people are 'further ahead' than others. It is a way of conceiving of the self in its temporal entirety, the sphere generating the energy of the future self as well as the past – all is accessible and nothing is lost. At any point we can key into the damaged areas or distorted messages of the psyche, just as we can, at any point, move away from them and into richer ground. Nothing the self has lived 'goes away', but also nothing need be fixed; we don't have to remain held by debilitating aspects of our experience; and when we return to them – as we are bound to do – we have not slipped right back to square one (with the disheartening prospect of struggling through the same old stages until we get back to our newly found positive stance).

The mature self is the self that has spurned no part of itself while engaged in exploring and recognizing and claiming the most creative and satisfying features that ceaselessly unfold from within this globe of inner life – this globe which affords an infinite multitude of possible perspectives. The mature self has learnt how to move through its damaged areas (which may well be experienced acutely each time they are visited) and allow ever-new angles of perception, as well as being able to access valuable old lessons and the wisdom of its lived experience.

The Dark and the Light Mirror

Each direction has what the American Indians call a 'dark' and a 'light' mirror. The light and the dark always go together, and therefore each aspect of our psyche has its light and its dark side. It is a sensitive and yet very practical way of dealing with our 'Shadow'. Rather than all our less delightful or positively repellent qualities being lumped together in one intimidating archetype (which understandably makes their assimilation and integration a very daunting endeavour), different aspects of our shadow emerge in manageable form, and always in relation to a light aspect. We can pin-point the exact quality and workings of the dark aspect within a living situation, in its context, meeting it rather than rejecting it. It is regarded merely as a mirror to be looked at and learned from. It is only 'bad' if it remains unseen; it only has harmful effects if we refuse to give it the light, the attention, of our consciousness. It is accepted that the dark side is bound to be there, and is not some terrible weakness or flaw in our nature. It is not approached as a fault, but as an aspect of self which calls for our awareness.

So the dark side is always looked for rather than kept hidden or rejected. In the same way as is any light aspect, it is treated simply as a part of the self. However, it is sometimes called an enemy, for it requires our alertness, and each of the four directions has a particular enemy which calls for our attention. But for the American Indian peoples, 'enemy' also implies respect and a challenge. The name marks a psychological state that we must not avoid or ignore; we must know and meet its power. The term 'warrior' is also used in this positive sense, but can easily be misunderstood in our culture. It is important not to make a false mapping across from our notions and methods of warfare, especially as these are based on maintaining a rift between contenders in any battle. (The extreme end of this spectrum is the complete lack of living contact between those endeavouring to wage nuclear warfare. Such an 'approach' towards an enemy brings only destruction and devastation.)

Balancing the Powers of the Four Directions

I should like to unfold in more detail the nature of each of the four basic directions. They could be understood in terms of archetypes, regarded as basic, given configurations of psychic energy that organize our attitudes and behaviour. They are certainly seen as 'places' or positions within the psyche which carry a distinctive quality of energy. The power of the South is called on, or the powers of the East evoked, in accordance with what may seem appropriate at any specific moment or in any particular situation. However, although it may be necessary, in the process of balancing our state of being (or, indeed, the community's state of being), to give special emphasis to one or two directions, the medicine wheel, once entered, must always be completed. This is intrinsic to the healing process. We must at least touch on each direction of our being, recognizing each aspect of self as well as fulfilling our commitment to the whole of our self. We must move around the entire circle and pay attention to how we relate to each direction.

We may often get surprises. Each time that we enter this wheel of life, it is a different experience, because *we* are always different. In spite of our blockages, we are always on the move in some way or another. Life cannot stand still. We approach those same reliable directions – South, North, West and East – from a different context, from a new perspective, and with altered needs. We also bring to them an ever-deepening awareness and appreciation of their qualities and their place in the working of our lives. As all energy is in continual movement, it follows that the balancing of our energies is a continual process. We enter the wheel and complete it, re-enter it and complete it, ever growing into the fullness of our self. We thus extend our experience of our potential both as human beings and as individuals, gradually bringing more of our hidden humanity into the light of lived reality.

The Direction of the South

It is appropriate to enter the wheel from the South. The South is the place of our 'Child Substance Shield', and as such it reflects to us everything that we need to learn about our actual, personal, substantiated childhood, as well as offering us the opportunity to connect with our living and ever-present 'child' energy. Starting in the South also reminds us that we need to approach life freshly, as a 'beginner'; that in a sense, we are always at the beginning, and that there is the possibility of a new beginning at any point in our lives.

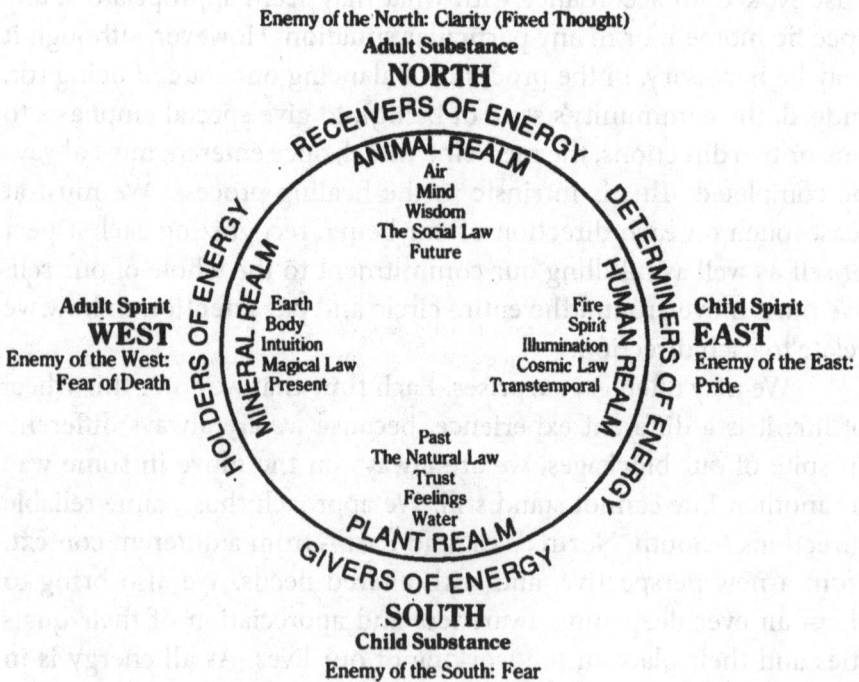

The Circle of Self

The quality of each of the four directions is expressed by one of the four elements – Earth, Water, Air and Fire; and it is the South which carries the energy of the Water element. The aspect of our human-beingness that it addresses is that of feelings, which need to flow as water flows. They need to move freely through our bodies, and

Chapter Six: The Circle of Self

not become the trapped stagnant pools of repression or the sludgy swamps of our resistance to change. Feelings can be contained, as water is contained, in beautiful lakes; but if powerfully racing torrents are dammed up by immense barriers, forbidding their movement, then fearful flooding and destructive violent action can result. The more we let ourselves experience the nature of water, the more we understand the nature of feelings. So in the South, we contemplate all the qualities of water – not only its movement and flow but its freshness and transparency, its receptivity and flexibility, and its life-giving nature. Is it not essential to all life?

So, too, are feelings vital to our human living. Water quenches our thirst and sustains us. It also cleans and purifies us. Any clearly expressed feeling is a 'clean' feeling, and allows for clear, 'unsticky' interactions. Water has long been used in rituals of initiation and purification as well as being a practical, everyday agent of cleanliness and refreshment.

The time orientation of the South is the Past. Here, we 'purify' the past: recognize, and unblock, and allow old repressed feelings to take their course and complete their cycle. It is in the South that we come to terms with our past – claiming it as ours, and freeing ourselves from its unnecessary constraints, its outdated modes and set patterns. We look freshly at our childhood traumas so that our energy no longer gets stuck at those painful spots. We use the mirror of the South to move from the victim child, the manipulative and over-adapted child, into our free and spontaneous child.

The special quality of the South is Trust – trust in life, in ourselves. This means trusting our natural responses, our preferences; allowing ourselves to be truly who we are. With trust of self, secure in being who we are, we can also give our trust to others, and not automatically take up a defensive attitude in our relationships.

Our Southern self generates our power of giving. It is associated with the Plant Realm, and plants are seen as 'The Givers of Energy'. They give us their beauty, they give us oxygen, they give us our food and shelter and furniture and tools. So, also, the child-in-us is seen as the giver of energy (and yet we so often regard children as the exhausting 'takers of energy' in our culture). We start life as a giver of energy, a source of energy. We are natural givers if we trust ourselves and believe in ourselves – if we let go of our old need to blame others and control them.

To turn now to the dark mirror: the 'enemy' of the South is Fear. It robs the child of its trust, responsiveness, joy and playfulness, its spontaneity. And past fears remain our enemies unless we have visited the South enough times to recognize them and release them, letting the fear flow out of our system as water flows out of a vessel. The most serious challenge posed by this enemy is that it can cheat all our other feelings of their flowing quality. It can lead us to constrict and block their movement, as we fearfully tense our bodies and limit our breath, and in so doing we end up only half living our lives. If fear dominates our being, then we betray our child self, born to be a giver of energy to the world, not to hold it at bay.

The Indian peoples speak of the 'sieve of fear'. I imagine that it means letting our fear flow through the permeable sieve of the body, the only remaining 'bits', or instances, being those that are substantial, requiring us to deal with them in some way. For fear is given us as a natural protection. There are things it is fitting to fear. Fear is a very rapidly moving energy; certain hormones are released which bring us into a state of highly charged awareness; and we can then gather our powers to act promptly and appropriately with whatever may endanger us. Once the danger is over, or seen not to be a danger after all, then the energy of fear needs to complete its cycle so that we can relax and return to a state of equilibrium once more – ready to respond freshly to whatever may next occur. But instead, we forget the 'sieve of fear' and hold on to it, store it, and return many times to our 'cauldron of fear' to give it a stir, to make sure it is still simmering. Every now and again, we may even feel driven to get it bubbling really fiercely. We feel the charge of energy once again, but do not release and clear it. This habit is a refusal of the flowing quality of the South as well as an avoidance of the core attribute of this direction – Trust. In this way we give ourselves over to the enemy, Fear, and let ourselves be ruled rather than alerted by it.

The South is also the place of the 'Natural Law'. The child of the South is a lover of nature – at home on the earth. If we would but follow the law of our bodies, if we honoured its intrinsic design, then we would allow feelings their rightful passage through our being. We would not permanently trap our fear within us and thus trap ourselves in fear, misusing fear to trap other feelings – even those we most long to experience.

Each direction on the wheel is also marked by an animal. This is not a symbol so much as a 'companion image', drawn from their contact with the spirit of the animal. It is as alive as the actual physical animal; a charged field of energy which continually stimulates intuitive understanding. The animal of the direction is not an abstract entity of the intellect that calls forth interpretations, but a source of direct knowing through our own animal nature.

The animal of the South is the Mouse; small, playful, energetic, resourceful, fast moving and far from timid. It is interesting how often fear is evoked by the spontaneous unpredictable movements of this little creature. The Snake is also sometimes considered the animal of South. Does it not exhibit pure and effortless flow in its movement? And it sheds many skins as it grows, just as we need to shed our psychic skins – those old patterns and decisions which no longer fit our present reality. The snake doesn't hold on to its past; it lets it go. No wonder it is a symbol of wisdom and of healing in many cultures. (Heal the child-in-us and we are whole.) The snake also indicates the power of the child: the uncoiling of life energy. It carries, too, a reminder of venom and poison, even in the very young, when we misdirect that energy and relate defensively to one another. In the South we find and live our Mouse self or our Snake self; our vulnerability and our power.

A further thought in the mode of our own culture: just because since ancient times, the snake has been so rich in symbolic meaning for such a wide range of different peoples, does it perhaps, in itself, speak of our common heritage and our shared instinctual energy? The South could thus be said to represent, in our understanding of the psyche, the flow and force of the Id. Is not the snake also the primal co-tempter in the Garden of Eden? We 'fall' at the very beginning of life if we give way to the enemy of the South – Fear – and constrict the flow of our feelings, refusing to trust life and give of ourselves and respond to the world in our own authentic way, embracing instead the helpless, weak, victim child so supported by the prevailing psychological theories of our day. Is not 'poor (little) me' a favourite life-script? With such a start, we lose our way in life, and are deeply in need of the new beginning that the Southern aspect of self always offers us. We do well to take up the mirror of the Child Substance Shield and see what we have been doing to ourselves, and how we have been dealing with the world from our earliest days.

The season of the South is the Spring: the time of new life and new beginnings, the time of fresh growth and hope. The colour is Red: rich and vibrant and strong – the colour of our life blood coursing through our bodies. The people of the South are the Red Indian peoples, with their deep and immediate connection with nature, their free-flowing feelings and their trust in the Natural Law.

All these attributes of the South combine to capture, and make alive and communicate, a fundamental orientation of our psyche by means of down-to-earth images taken from everyday life. In my attempt to describe what is sometimes called 'The Power of the South' – which has not been easy, because the living quality of a configuration of energy can only really be picked up through the spoken word and other non-verbal means of communication – I hope I have at least managed to convey how inner and outer worlds can form one body of experience.

It is interesting that no reference to any human parent is included in the child energy of the South – no focus on dependency, no mention of cause. There is literally no one to blame. And no involved theories to enmesh or divert us. There is little to confuse us. We simply visit the South within ourselves and absorb its qualities – remain with it for a time – allowing feelings and sensations, images and insights to emerge. We have entered the sacred circle of the self and thus our focus is on *our responses* to our parents, our very specific responses, rather than on them as external beings causing our problems. Once we have entered the circle, we know we are the cause of ourselves. At the same time, our interdependence, and the connectedness of all livings things, are part of the Natural Law which is the law of the South, and is thus acknowledged as the very foundation of life. Allowing ourselves to experience the sustaining power of Mother Earth (rather than concentrating on what we ought to be getting from our particular mother), we fulfil this Natural Law, becoming both whole in ourselves and a child of the universe.

Chapter Six: The Circle of Self

The freedom from blame, from dependency, and from any interest in explaining ourselves by means of external causes – all these pertinently express the quality of innocence carried by the South. In such a place we can learn to shed blame, we can begin to wash ourselves clean of blame. By contrast, in our blame-ridden culture, we either hold on to the idea of innocence in children as a cover for infant manipulation, or we actually equate it with 'being the victim' – the innocent one, the victim of a crime. It has come to mean being blameless in relation to someone else who is to blame. It has become a notion that feeds the dualistic, moralistic, either/or division into 'good' or 'bad', 'innocent' or 'guilty'.

On one level, of course, a child is open to being a victim because there is a real sense in which it is dependent, and alarming abuses take place within the power structures of both the family and society. (Do not most power structures spawn abuse, especially if the power relationship is 'permanent' in nature?) However, we remain interminably and exclusively the victim child if we give dependence a fundamental place in the psyche; and the South 'knows' this.

The Healing Wheel of Life does not lend a false status to the victim position, although it does dedicate an entire direction to the open and vulnerable child self and our personal life history. Identification with the victim position only arises if we remain stuck in the South and fall prey to its enemy, Fear, at the most primary level. We are then taken over by the dark mirror and hug it tightly to ourselves, rather than taking time to look into it. If we refuse to move on and complete the circle of self-healing, avoiding meeting and drawing on and balancing our full range of energies, then we shall naturally be held in the grip of fear, and remain ever incomplete – and thus open to victimhood and ready to blame.

Let us now move to the North. When we actually enter into the experience of moving through The Medicine Wheel, and take our leave of one direction, we may, in a simple ritual of silence, choose to note what we have learned; and even as we mark our appreciation, we can sometimes also feel the need for a balancing energy of a complementary nature.

The Direction of the North

In the North we connect with the element Air, and the aspect of our human-beingness that we address is the Mind. The mirror that it holds up to us is called the 'Adult Substance Shield'. Here, we engage with our adult self, the full woman or full man. (Even a child who 'does' the Medicine Wheel has an adult aspect of her- or himself with which to connect.) We look at our personal activities as an adult, for this is the area of our psyche which deals with the practicalities of our world. The law of the North is the social law, the law which is evolved by the society in which we live for purposes of enabling the smooth, efficient and just ordering of our social affairs. (Of course, if many in the society remain stuck only in the dark aspect of the South, in infant victimhood, then the dynamic of impotence and omnipotence will underlie such social arrangements.)

The time orientation of the North is the Future. The adult in us needs to use her or his ability to think ahead, work out consequences, and make plans. Unless we have dealt with our past in the South, we shall be hampered in our ability to make clear and helpful predictions about the future. In this Northern direction we claim the operations of our mind. We focus on our thought processes, and hold the mirror before us to reflect the outdated beliefs, attitudes and confused ideas that obstruct the activity of thinking freshly. We note how they provoke old feeling states and grievances, and thus rule our behaviour accordingly.

This mirror can all too easily become misted over, or even completely surrounded by the 'fog' that our mind so easily produces. We may intend to look attentively and allow reflection, but we rapidly get caught in our attachment to certain thought patterns and obstinate repetitive images. And so the activity of the element Air is invoked to keep clearing the mind. The quality of wind is called upon, not only to awaken the mind to arise and be alert but also to keep it moving – to help sweep it free of the endless clutter that gathers around 'what might have been', or 'how it should have been'. Air reminds us to stay free. Just as clouds appear in wondrous variety of form, sometimes clear and sometimes diffuse but always changing, so, too, we need to let the images of our mind take shape, evolve, and then pass on. We need to let them be and then let them go. Thus the mind breathes.

It is important to note that a low-energy vagueness of thought does not have the same quality as non-attachment, and is more likely to indicate a lack of commitment to know – to see – to find out – to experiment and explore. It is to be distinguished from the vibrant emptiness of 'not knowing'. We need to look keenly at the contents of our mind without getting fixed on any specific aspect that it presents. Fixation does not bring that security for which we long; mental rigidity must ultimately breed confusion in an ever-changing inner and outer world. We can hardly call on 'air' and 'wind' too often, for our mind continually needs freeing and emptying if we are to attain wisdom.

Wisdom is the special quality designated to the North. But it is understood as an innate animal wisdom that balances the rational energy of this adult aspect of the self. Indeed, this is also the direction of the Animal Realm. Animals are seen not only as teachers – our psychology displayed in the external world – but as the 'Receivers of Energy'. We receive with our minds in the North, whereas we give with our feelings in the South. We give from a trusting and open heart, and receive wisdom with a free and open mind. As Krishnamurti states, 'as long as your mind is considering, judging, forming opinions, concluding, it is neither aware nor sensitive'.

The concentrated activity of the mind is reserved for practical problem solving, but true wisdom is attained through continually clearing and emptying the mind and receiving the new; or receiving what is old freshly, as if it were new, or seeing it in a more living form. Thus, the Enemy of wisdom, the Enemy of the North, is Clarity. This comes as a shock to us in our culture. Does not the intellect prize clarity above all else? Isn't it the very purpose of rationality?

Clearness of thought is important in the American Indian teachings (and, indeed, clear communication is represented by the transparent quality of air), but fixed thought is seen as a great danger, and clarity tends to be identified with a sense of arrival at an end-state that must be maintained as such. The quality of wind must be evoked, if thought is to keep moving through continuous and varied moments of precision, pouring forth ever-evolving configurations of form. Once something has been clarified, it can not only become set but can also be mistaken for reality itself. In this way, we misuse the ability of the rational mind to define and make distinctions by allowing whatever we make precise to harden into fixed definitions and categories which we then impose on reality. This common (and usually unconscious) activity has the effect of perpetuating divisions, of creating divisiveness. The enemies of the wise and receptive mind are set conceptual frameworks, and a belief that we know it all, that we have got it exactly right. With short-sighted conviction of this kind, our modes of thinking solidify into rigid dogmas and we become ruled by thought that served another time and place. We are out of step with our true needs, and our awareness of the present is clouded. We can no longer receive new knowledge, nor allow our ideas to grow and develop. We are then bound to be involved in merely defending the status quo. Hubris is closely associated with the kind of obstinately held clarity that is the enemy of the North, as also is attachment.

In the terms of our culture, this direction holds the energy of our Ego Consciousness – and, of course, ego consciousness in both its light and dark aspects. As I said earlier, Northern energy is the energy of practical, rational planning; it is outer directed and achievement orientated. It is a most necessary energy. It is expressed by the animal of the North – the Buffalo. Although the element of the North is air, the animal is not, as some might expect, a bird. The choice of the buffalo to express the nature of the North, large and solid and connected to the earth as it gallops over the wide open plains, stresses the importance of 'grounding' the fast-moving energy of the human mind.

The buffalo gave the American Indian peoples food, clothing, shelter, implements and tools. The buffalo helped humankind in its everyday existence in a very immediate and practical manner. And the horns of the buffalo stand for the wisdom that flows from the union of both the absolute and the relative. Neither aspect of reality is put above the other, and no false imposition is made of an either/or choice between them. Both are accepted as equal partners in the workings of our human mind. The horns are distinct but not in opposition. There they both stand, the twinned wisdom of empty receptivity and practical rational intelligence. The Right and the Left brain modes of knowing. Inarticulate, sure animal wisdom and the learning promoted by language. Open sensitivity and awareness of the whole context of being, and active organization of focused thought.

The season of the North is the Autumn, with its keen, fresh, invigorating air and strong winds – winds which clear the mind of all that we no longer need to hold on to. It is the season of adulthood, of maturity, of visible fruitfulness, of achievement on the material plane of being. Growth comes to fruition in the autumn. In the North, men find their true manhood and women their full womanhood. And this is personal, fitting to each person, although discovered within the context of the society in which we live. Adulthood is not attained simply by copying stereotypes or set models. The North is the place of personal thought and personal meaning. Here, we find and respect and develop our own ideas, just as in the South we trust our own feelings and follow our personal preferences.

In this model of the psyche, ego consciousness cannot be isolated or separated from other forms of consciousness and thus made into some sort of entity in its own right. It is appreciated as one aspect of consciousness only, and is experienced in relation to those other aspects. As pointed out earlier, it is not possible to give any meaning to one direction without referring to the others – *the context of meaning is always the whole circle.* The ego, therefore, is safeguarded from dominating the psyche. We can immediately see, and experience, how the self is violated if, indeed, the North does try and claim some superior position. Also, even within the Northern direction, ego consciousness is balanced by the quality of the receptive mind: open to acknowledging the realm of the Absolute while getting on with dealing with relative knowledge for everyday purposes.

The colour of the North is White – the colour of emptiness, which offers us space for the play of ideas and images, non-resistant, allowing of movement and calling forth the possibility of expansion. And the people of the North are the 'White' peoples who have all too often mistaken the expansion of the mind with territorial expansion and colonialism, with economic expansion and forced growth. We white peoples have also developed practical, rational skills *at the expense of* our innate animal wisdom and attentive receptivity. We have let left-brain activity dominate over that of our right brain. We need to let go our focus on controlling others, and remind ourselves of the truth expressed in the twin horns of the buffalo.

The Direction of the West

We move next, as we venture through the Healing Wheel of the Self, to the West. This is our Adult Spirit Shield, for the energy of the West teaches us the nature of the mature spirit within each of us. (Again, a child undertaking the Medicine Wheel can connect with her or his adult spirit no less than grown women or men. It is a given aspect of the psyche.) *It is in this place of spirit, secure in our knowledge of spirit, that we fully know of our human physicality.*

The aspect of human-beingness that we address here is the body, and the element of the West is the Earth. We learn here all that the earth teaches us of process, continuity and change; the movement of the seasons, the moon and the stars, the cycles of birth, death and rebirth. As we witness the continual succession of generations, we ground ourselves in the repetitious rhythmic stability of nature amid the multitude of fluctuations and surprises that she also unceasingly offers us. Here, we learn to move *with* life, we learn to welcome change, to die to our old selves and be reborn. And yet all this change is also held, or contained, by the more slowly changing body. The West is associated with the Mineral Realm, and minerals are understood to be the 'Holders of Energy'. And so we hold with our bodies, while we give with our feelings and receive with our minds.

It is clear how important it is not to confuse the directions. If we hold with our feelings we distort ourselves and defend against life; and if we give with our bodies we can lose ourselves and our natural boundaries. If we hold with our minds, then we are fixated in our thinking and the prey to old programming and social conditioning. And so it is vital to take note of what each mirror distinctly reflects to us. We hold our being with our bodies; we are gently cradled in its shape and form and functioning, and do well to respect its ways and needs. We also touch and hold others with our bodies. It is a most profound and immediate communication of love and care for another. We celebrate, greet, reassure, comfort and affirm each other

Chapter Six: The Circle of Self

through physical contact. If we are each at home in our own body, then we have a sense of the subtle boundaries between people – we do not intrude on the space of another, nor do we try to possess another's body. We can enjoy the closest of bodily contact, and great intimacy or highly charged excitement poses no threat, once we honour our distinction. We have no fear of losing ourselves in another.

The Adult Spirit in us knows, too, that we can never really escape from ourselves by merging with another. We can delight in that special sensation of fusion in love-making just because we know it as ephemeral and transitory. We do not, from our Western self, set up a life style based on fusion; nor do we pretend that a focus on fusion is an attempt to let go of our ego in order to 'find ourselves'. We recognize that we are more likely to be fleeing into an extension of ego, or else a denial of ego. We are almost certainly regressing, and accessing neither our adult nor our spirit nature. The fully embodied Adult Spirit finds joy in full sexual expression and intense intimacy, but is not driven by the desperate thirst for physical fusion with another. It is isolated ego-selves that incessantly hunger for the only union they ever taste.

Ego consciousness belongs to the rationality and the practical outer-directed intelligence of the North. It is not associated with the West. It is vital that the ego does not attach itself to the body and live out its idea that it is a separate unit. This is the direction, rather, where we connect with the Collective Unconscious or Deep Consciousness. Grounded in an earthly body, and knowing ourselves as an integral part of nature, we open ourselves to the rich storehouse of psychic energy available to us all. This realm of interior emergent knowledge can then be translated into physical terms; and indeed, we only fully know what we have received when we have made it incarnate. We are each heir to a vast underworld of shared consciousness, just as we share common bodily needs on an everyday level.

The animal of the West is the Bear, which the American Indian Peoples regard as the 'Holder of Dreams'. The bear is a large and powerful animal – heavy, furry, earthy – and it hibernates in winter. It follows the rhythm of the seasons, and enters a state of profound sleep until it dreams itself awake to a new beginning. It is able to maintain an inner heat while all around is cold; it is associated with comfort (our teddy bears), hugging, holding, warmth and motherliness. However, we also talk of the 'bear-hug' and 'being squeezed to death by love'; and the lumbering bear can connote heaviness and depression. We can live out a distortion of the West if we become too introverted, in love with darkness and reluctant to stir into movement, even when the spring calls.

Through dreams, through image-making and the non-linear creations of our fertile deep consciousness (whether awake or asleep), we touch our collective source of being. Through contacting the special energy of the West, we draw on the richness of all lived experience from the beginning of time. We embody deep mysteries; we are never mere external bodies. In the West, we honour the hidden depths, all that is held in the darkness and lies dormant until the time is right for its expression. And so the season of the West is Winter – the natural time not of action, but of dream regeneration, contemplation and simple being; the time when life is held in unfixed stillness.

The special quality designated to the West is Intuition. With a subtle holding of our attention, we can pick up knowledge from the universe within. It is a process both immediate and swift, yet arising from a state of unhurried stillness. It is from this point of stillness that we open to hear our inner voice. Through intuition, we mediate between the unconscious, 'below surface', non-linear depths, and the ordinary physical manifest reality in which we live and move and act. It is intuition that enables us to know of the inner being and non-explicit aspects of other people, which adds an extraordinary richness to relationships. And it gives us the power to access our own inner mystery and translate it into worldly terms. When we 'go with' our intuition, we reflect the movement from darkness to light that occurs from the time of the winter solstice.

As the quality of darkness is appreciated by this aspect of the self, it is not surprising that the colour of this direction is Black – the colour of rich containment. Black holds more than can be seen. It is not empty. We go to the North for the emptiness and expansion of the colour white; in the West we contact the fullness of our collective heritage – we tap the 'dreams' of all living beings.

The people of the West are the 'Black' peoples of the world, in touch with their physicality and expressing spirit through dance and song. The time orientation is the Present. We can only intuit in the present. Intuition has the quality of immediacy – direct knowledge and knowing. We can only touch and sense in the present, only witness the ever-changing beauty of the earth in the present. And when our dreams give us new forms and extraordinary combinations of images, we need to take note of these immediately, or they quickly slip back into the night world of our dreaming body.

The law of the West is the Magical Law which again operates in the power of the living moment. We 'magically' change or shift, we know not how, in the 'now' of our experience. The crystal is the mineral which speaks to us of this magical law. We become alchemists of life when we are true to our Western energy and respect the many different dimensions of our being. If we move our focus from our ego consciousness (while allowing it to operate satisfactorily in the Northern aspect of ourselves) and let rationality be, opening ourselves to our unconscious or Deep Consciousness, then it seems that different 'laws' come into being which we cannot explain in the terms of our Northern selves. Neither kind of law cancels the other. They both co-exist, just as all the directions co-exist. If we are true to the powers of each in their fitting context, we shall then live out our full humanity.

It is in the West that men find their 'woman self', and women their 'man self'. It is an integration of a far more immediate and energizing nature than the claiming of some abstract anima or animus. It is not a mere balancing of qualities; we each have a complete Adult Spirit Man in us if we are born a woman, and a complete Adult Spirit Woman in us if we are a man. We are equally both man and woman, although one aspect is expressed in substance, in manifest material form, and the other in spirit, in a more subtle unseen energy. It is in the West that the man sees reflected his ability to be earthed in his body, and dares let go into living process and change. He claims his intuition and opens himself with appreciation, not fear, to the dark rich treasure house of his Deep Consciousness: he embraces his non-rational nature. He learns of birth and death and rebirth. We can see how so many in our culture have been stuck in the North, with our Adult Substance only, which actually indicates that we are even more deeply fixated in the South – blocking our feelings in fear and reluctant to trust, too wary to respond to life and the lessons it ceaselessly affords. It all starts in the South. That is why we begin with the child in us. We have to clear our past before we can deal productively with our future and live fully in the present.

And so, too, women see the reflection of their man self. They find this not in the North but in the West, where they have to resist being lost in their femininity, seduced by the non-rational and mysterious, or tempted to remain sleeping in rich dormancy. (No 'Sleeping Beauties' waiting for their prince.) Here, in the West, grounded in their rich feminine qualities, they are required to stand on their own feet. Here, they claim their own authority, trusting their intuition and affirming their knowledge. In their 'man self', they take responsibility for bringing forth their talents from the darkness into light, and are not content simply to contemplate what they *could* be or do. In the West, we dream in order to bring ourselves into ever-greater wakefulness and awareness and creativity – like the bear who stirs to life, refreshed, when the right time is come to meet a new spring. We let go of last year, of old outdated modes, and move into the living present as a fully embodied Adult Spirit.

It is important to note that the practical rationality of the North is not considered especially male; it is simply a necessary part of being an adult who has to deal with the substance of life. Neither is the 'empty' wisdom and receptive mind considered an intrinsically female attribute. It is the necessary mode of attaining the kind of wisdom needed for satisfactory relationships and the building of just societies. Men and women equally need to use their minds fittingly and honour the two horns of the buffalo. Indeed, these horns only present a dilemma if we split ourselves and attempt to lay claim only to those qualities which we deem as masculine, or only those we regard as feminine. We need, each one of us, to partake of all human qualities while appreciating their complementary nature. The Adult Substance woman is no less a 'buffalo' than the Adult Substance man. True adulthood involves the decision to use our own minds, forging our own meanings while developing satisfying ways of living in community together. Maturity is not attained by copying models of maleness and femaleness.

I have not yet mentioned the Enemy of the West. It is perhaps the most profound of all enemies – the Fear of Death. Not death itself, which is part of the process of life, but *fear* of death. It is the fear of partial deaths within our life journey, fear of going through experiences that feel like a death, as well as fear of our actual physical death. If we do not acknowledge this fear as an enemy, then we waste our life, continually seeking ways of avoiding death and resisting change. It is appropriate that we face this challenge in the West with the energy of our Adult Spirit self; we then face it while clearly honouring our body, but with the energy of our mature spirit who knows the depths of our subtle layers of being, and intuits beyond the surfaces of the material world.

Adult Spirit, in constant touch with the collective unconscious which it can bring into consciousness through an ever-unfolding process of present awareness, can also experience its essential grounding in the eternal source of All-That-Is. Adult Spirit is not tied to linear thinking, which dictates life as having a definite beginning and an end. Partaking of our multi-dimensional nature, it senses the deep underlying reality from which all life forms spring. It knows death is not absolute, that it occurs on one level only, and that it is good that it occurs on that level, for there could be no life without death. The whole natural world rests on death as well as life. Adult Spirit knows these things.

Thus, in the West we can contend with our fear of death. We learn not to contract against life in the fear of our destruction. If we claim our Western self, then we shall no longer be dominated by the fear of our annihilation; we shall no longer continue to distort ourselves in our efforts to freeze the inner movements of our feelings and keep this appalling fear at bay. The more we allow ourselves to be at home in our bodies, the more we appreciate that the human body is perfectly designed to process natural stress and pain, beautifully adapted to live well on this earth who is the Mother of us all. If we draw on the Adult Spirit in us, then the Victim Archetype loses its pull on our psyche and no longer attracts us. It is difficult to remain a victim once we access our Western self.

The Direction of the East

And now we move across to the East. This is the Child Spirit Shield and reflects to us the essential knowledge, as well as all that we dare to discover, of the original unique spirit being that we are. The aspect of human-beingness that is expressed by the energy of the East is Spirit itself – that aspect which has the power to generate self; the power to create and transform. The element of the East is Fire, and its special defining quality is Illumination. The colour is Yellow: alive, shining, brilliant as the sun – which itself represents God-energy and the actualization of our full potentiality. The people are the 'Yellow' peoples, who have long honoured spirit and transpersonal dimensions of reality.

The time orientation of the East is Timelessness, or transcendent time. In spirit, we are free to be in any time and all times – we can move 'through' time and space, and not be limited by its laws. From the point of view of spirit, everything simultaneously 'is', and we simply orientate ourselves to different aspects of what is. We no longer perceive a world of discrete objects, separated by barriers of different kinds, but enter an all-embracing field of subtle communication.

Information does not have to travel – it is there. Thus, it is possible to partake of the powers of telepathy, clairvoyance or clairaudience, prophesy and prediction. We can know of other incarnations and cultures, and experience other dimensions of being. Here, language, of course, can no longer serve us in the same way – we overstep its limits if we speak of these things. We cannot help but use unsuitable and contradictory terms when we attempt to describe trans-temporal awareness, but we can have a common understanding that this is so, and thus minimize distortion while still indicating to each other the immense freedom of spirit. It seems that we human beings have a profound urge, which will not be daunted, to share the heights and depths of our experience.

The aspect of consciousness that we access in the East is 'All-inclusive' or Cosmic Consciousness. This must not be confused in any way with the superego: a construction put forward by the white peoples of the North to acknowledge a sense of our 'higher self' *from the viewpoint of ego consciousness*. From ego's perspective, wary of anything outside itself or 'above' itself, such a construct is bound to degenerate into a loveless admonisher. The concept, superego, cannot sustain itself as a generator of inspiration; it lacks the Fire of the East. It is hardly fitting to approach Cosmic Consciousness from the place of ego consciousness. It can only be known in itself, from our Eastern self, through the spirit in us. If we tamper with it from any other 'place' or direction, we create nonsenses and end up constricting ourselves instead of freeing ourselves, hiding from ourselves rather than illuminating our reality.

The East is the direction of our creativity and unfettered imagination. There is no place here for superego and its restrictive conformity. The East generates the energy of burning and revealing light, not shameful repression. It offers us the power of transformative Fire, not the endless uphill struggle and repetitive failure to be 'good' by rejecting the 'bad', and keeping our dark forces hidden and secret. In the East we express the radical aliveness which naturally emerges from true change. The energy of Fire does not allow for mere rearrangements of old patterns or reshuffles within the same old conceptual frameworks. It can destroy as well as give life. There is no disguise or cover possible in this place of the sun. The season of the East is Summer with its flowering; its fullness of actualization. And yet at the same time, because the sun represents the Infinite, there is always more to be revealed; there is always more to be known. We never cease to evolve and create, drawing continually from that Infinite Source, and manifesting the new in finite form. The law of the East is the Cosmic Law which we can never fully comprehend with our minds, but partake of naturally in our spirit selves.

In this Child Spirit Shield, women find their 'little boy' self, filled with the spirit of adventure and always wanting to press onwards and climb the next tree or mountain. This little-boy energy lives in each of us. It is the excitement of exploring all that is novel; the daring to enter utterly new territory and risk the unknown; the courage to tolerate uncertainty and not-knowing. It is the curiosity to cross boundaries never before contemplated, and the delight in being continually stretched and challenged; the longing to know whatever there is to be known. It is an inexhaustible energy because it draws from the Infinite. It is a free, open and willing energy – as also is the energy of the 'little girl' self that each man discovers within himself, as he enters into the Child Spirit reflections of the East. This little-girl self in each of us is highly sensitive and in tune with the cosmos, receptive to the infinite. She is ever-ready to allow the power of her imagination to bring her into the yet-to-be-known. She is not constricted by the 'normal' and is willing to undergo illumination, to see the subtle levels of being and allow her visions to transform her.

It is with our Eastern self that we humans create our visions, and in this we have to be alert to the Enemy of the East – Pride, and the Love of Power. It is all too easy to become 'high' on the potent, stretching energy of the East, and that is why it is important first to free ourselves of the manipulative child in the South, to be deeply grounded in the West, and to attain a balanced wisdom in the North. There is a danger we could become intoxicated by our own visions and imagination, and take on to ourselves the task of forcing change on the world. We need always to start by transforming ourselves.

The animal of the East is the Eagle who spreads its strong wings and soars towards the sun, but never forgets to keep an eye fixed on the earth from which it gets its sustenance. The eagle has especially keen sight so that it can fly far and free, and yet still see its prey – its daily food – the source of its nourishment while in material form. So also, human spirit, however great its powers, must not disconnect itself or disassociate itself from matter and the earth. However high we fly, our vision must be turned towards the earth; our imaginations must serve life on this planet. Only then do we actualize our dreams and, drawing on the infinite store of timeless possibilities, we bring new forms into being in the living present.

While the South is associated with the Plant Realm and the giving of energy, the North with the Animal Realm and the receiving of energy, the West with the Mineral Realm and the holding of energy, the East stands for the Human Realm. As such, we are seen as the determiners of energy: and the aspect of self that determines our lives is our spirit. It is this ability that makes us free; capable of making meaningful choices and bringing our deep intentions into being. It is from our Eastern self that our creativity springs, rendering us capable of inner transformation and thus of altering and shaping our experience and our reality. It is an awesome capacity.

Chapter Six: The Circle of Self

It is important that we acknowledge that this power of determination stems from spirit, the originating aspect of self. It must not be taken over by the mind (how often do we all, in our own way, attempt to determine our lives, and thus the lives of others, with our rational ego energy in the North), or by our feelings (as when we are ruled by our emotions and manipulate others through our emotionality), or by our bodies (as when we allow ourselves to be overwhelmed by our immediate bodily needs to the exclusion of our other needs). All aspects co-operate in our determining ability, and play their part in living out this human power; but it is spirit which enables us to be the agents of our lives and take real responsibility for ourselves. If we allow ego to claim the power of agency in the North, then our creativity soon degenerates into control.

Sun energy expresses both our full potentiality and our power to actualize what we determine to be. An untold array of possibilities is available to us if we live with and through our whole self. Our Child Spirit dares to acknowledge and explore these possibilities. It connects with all that resonates with its deep intention in coming into this world in this distinctly human form. It actualizes its very self. And so the Child Spirit of the East completes our circle of Self, and once completed, we know it also as our beginning. Thus we live the full mystery of the circle.

We can see why it is so vital that one direction does not merge with another. It is essential that in their simultaneous presence, they are also kept distinct, and that the special quality each holds does not contaminate the other directions. To let ego consciousness from the North seep into the place of vision-making would be disastrous, as it would equally be to allow the amazing cosmic power of the East to sweep aside the personal 'substance' realms of the North and South. For this reason it is fitting, when moving through the Healing Wheel of self-reflection, to come last to the East, even though its energy is, in a vital sense, prior to all other human energies. As mentioned earlier, we should be hard-pressed to handle both its powers and its enemy if we had not first grounded ourselves well in the West – in Adult Spirit, in our earthed body, in the deep roots of our collective source of being and our intuitive sense of our interconnectedness with all life. This provides both the ground for our vision-making and the steadying of our imaginative zeal.

The directions within us must always be balanced. The actualizing energy of the East betrays itself once we get lost in pure fantasy, or overtaken by entirely abstract ideas of how to reshape the world, ignoring the laws and ways of the other aspects of our being. We need to re-enter and complete the Medicine Wheel many times, re-enter and complete the circle of self, ever-deepening the sense of our wholeness. While open to utterly new ways of being in the East we must not violate what 'is'. The actions of Stalin could be seen as an example of grandiose abstract planning, with no care for the personal or the practical realities. In him we see how the Southern aspect of his personal childhood was so dominated by its enemy, fear, that all trust and responsiveness were undermined until eventually, as an adult, only omnipotent desire to control his motherland remained. Given such acute imbalance in the North, ego expanded into the East where it got firmly entrenched, perverting the creativity and transformative power of that direction, and rendering it ever-vulnerable to its own enemy, Pride. Essential grounding in the West, with the awareness of living process, was lost. He thought up 'improved housing' and ordered millions of people to be moved, for their own good, into homes not yet built. It might well have looked like a wonderful idea on the drawing board.

The Space of Pure Consciousness at the Core of Each Self

Having completed the circle, we also open up the possibility of experiencing its centre – the place of what the Buddhists call 'No Mind', and Christians call 'Beingness'. This is the place of pure consciousness when the observer and the observed are experienced as one – there is no one looking on and no thing to reflect. 'No Mind' is not the same as the integrated mind, that integrated consciousness which is reached through the unity of the four directions of the self – although that integration provides a natural access to the state of 'No Mind', which in turn is open to Universal Mind. The centre of the circle represents the unnameable: the empty space at the core of each self and at the core of the universe. This is the living space that can never be destroyed, never disturbed – not even by a nuclear holocaust. This is the empty plenum, rippling with energy, referred to by the physicist David Bohm; it is that which the American Indian Peoples call Great-Great-Great-Grandmother Space – she who unceasingly gives birth to everything that is.

Chapter Seven
How Responsible Are We?

With a linear causal model deeply entrenched in our thought structure, so deeply part of the way we think that we are unconscious of its imposition, we then try and handle the challenge of free will. No wonder we always seem to flounder. We may then resort to the declaration that it is all a paradox and quite beyond us, as opposed to embracing paradox to reveal the subtle workings of a truth.

Determinism Sits Uneasily with Our Lived Experience

It seems that we cannot escape the challenge of free will; we cannot rest content in the safe confines of determinism, even though it fits so snugly with our familiar causal frame of reference. Not only does morality demand choice on at least some level (and we are deeply moral as well as moralistic beings), but in addition, we personally experience making choices even as we blame the world and other people for our predicaments, and feel that 'we cannot help it' if this or that occurs. The aggrieved cry, 'But what else could I have done?' is interwoven with the daily activity of choice and decision-making of one kind or another. It is hard to believe that we were 'determined' to have a bath at a certain moment, or that we could do no other but eat a peach rather than a pear, given that we enjoy both fruits.

In fact, much time is given over to the choosing process, much energy is involved in our making of decisions as well as in trying to 'make up our minds'. It is thus as incongruous to our lived experience to say that we are caused to do such things through a chain of mechanical external causes, as is the theory it is based on. Only a certain part of our intellect, divided from other aspects of our thinking as well as from our feelings, senses and intuitions, can espouse the abstract idea that if we knew the velocity and position and mass of every particle in the universe, then we could, in principle, predict everything that occurs – including the movements of our psyches because they are 'nothing but' the firing of neurons in the brain. Of course this Newtonian theory is now outdated, but its neat order still pulls at the intellect of many of those whom we entrust to do the 'hard thinking' for us all in our essentially 'Victim' culture. Both our impotence and our omnipotence are perfectly expressed and accounted for by the deterministic model; we cannot help how we are, but we can control the external world if only we get to know enough about it.

Control without responsibility is what has characterized our relationship to the earth and all that lives upon the earth. It leads to ever-more appalling demands on the planet, our collective Mother, however destructive these may be to her. As life is one vast circling network of interaction, we are preparing the way for the destruction of ourselves. Action that springs from the victim mode of being is bound to be destructive; the victim cannot truly care either for the 'other', whom he blames or craves, or for himself, whom he has betrayed. No movement or political party devoted to ecology can be effective as long as we remain loyal to the Victim Archetype. However much energy is poured into tackling the ecological crises that we have inevitably, as victims, brought on ourselves, it does not begin to balance the continuing increase and proliferation in our collective desire and demand to consume. The omnipotent child in us simply will not face the fact that 'Mother' has her limitations. We believe that she should provide all we want and that we ought to have all that we can get. And societies which have developed the most sophisticated means of doing this are thought to be 'ahead' of other nations; they proudly export their consumer notions and habits in the name of 'progress'. The victim will always see problems of supply as Mother's problem. And when, at last, we are forced to wake up and make some connections and take some action, we still remain attached to the idea of 'conquering' the awkward difficulties that keep emerging, and desperately seek short-sighted methods of control – hoping, perhaps, to ward off that all-too-familiar sense of overwhelming external power. The victim knows only of impotence and omnipotence, and very little about co-operation. And we shall continue to feel and act this

The Unnecessary Choice between Free Will and Determinism

We do, indeed, directly experience the power to choose even if only in fairly trivial ways. It says a lot about our split psyche that we do not trust this experience, that we keep it in a separate compartment, and opt to give more weight to the clever constructs of abstract rationalism. I do not believe that it would be possible to maintain this unnatural emphasis unless it was underpinned by the energy of our collective victimhood. How ironic that science was born from empiricism and yet has given birth (among other things) to a style of thinking which spurns the direct experience of the senses. 'That may be how it seems in ordinary experience but *really* it is so and so...', rather than respecting the various different ways of seeing, and giving each validity in its own terms (just as we know the sun as rising and setting and yet also know that the earth is moving around the sun as a constant point of reference).

The two horns of the buffalo free us from the limitations of either/or thinking. And so, if we understand the mind through the innate wisdom of the Northern direction, then we shall cease to impose unnecessary dilemmas upon ourselves and force an unnatural choice between *either* being determined or having free will; between being held responsible for everything or nothing. We shall, if we are wise, *draw on the evidence of the whole self in all its aspects*. We shall listen to what the South tells us, as well as the North, the West and the East. If we are ever to understand the nature of choice and responsibility, then we must let go of linear causal models. They are far too simplistic, serving only a mechanistic mode of thinking and leaving our lived experience of free will dangling as some sort of disembodied epiphenomenon or inexplicable habitual fantasy. On the other hand, once we enter into the fullness of a circular and multi-dimensional model that is more expressive of our lived reality, choice and responsibility are rendered richly meaningful.

In addition, linear models demand and depend upon having a clear beginning and an end. (Unless we are dealing with mathematical infinity, which we are certainly not doing when looking at the

Chapter Seven: How Responsible Are We?

phenomenon of personal choice. If we resort to such an abstraction in the exploration of choice, then I think it likely that we are merely seeking a rationalized excuse for no choice.) Yet with linear causal models we make arbitrary starting points, incessantly, and cannot help but do so if we are not to be caught in an infinite regress; at the same time we require these starting points not to be arbitrary, or the whole system falls. Unless we can pin down the 'true' beginning, then the cause, or designated event, cannot be the cause but only part of a chain. The causal model requires that the emphasis is unequal; some events, some actions, must necessarily be assigned more power than those others which are named mere effects. Starting points need to be 'real' starting points. We have to know the beginning of the sequence.

In a circular system we can begin at any point, and all is well because no special weighting is required – all that matters is that we start. To use the simplest of examples: if each person in a circle is asked to speak in turn, then we can start with anyone and all will have their say. Once we enter a circular system, all is potentially available to us. What matters is that we pick up the thread somewhere, and it will then lead us into the dynamic interwoven pattern of the whole. And so, if we are unable to free ourselves of linear causal thinking but are going to have to make an arbitrary beginning anyway, then we are best served by choosing the self as its own starting point. The very starting point arbitrarily chosen – the self – can release us from the linear mode; for once we give attention and respect to the contents of our direct experience in its many different modes, then we can be led to acknowledge our highly complex nature, and come to know ourselves as more than rational egos in material bodies – we can come to perceive ourselves as multi-dimensional beings.

Just as reality is not a linear chain of events, so also the stream of human consciousness is not a linear strand of images. There are many strands, happenings, images, on many levels – all co-present – and we light on one level and then on another, pick up this thread of thought and then flit to a completely different one. And all these rapid, multi-directional, minute movements connect on the surface of our consciousness – meet in our awareness – and so can give the impression of a flowing linear stream.

I should like to share an experience that I had early this

morning. I caught the mini-movements between levels and sensed, for a micro-second, the other strands that my awareness *could* have followed and knew the enormous richness of hidden activity from which that surface stream draws. Each 'dot' in the stream of consciousness connects with an intricate web of other strands, continually interacting and creating a vast and deep cavern of potential experience. I was spellbound by the beauty and power and complexity of the psyche. It was as if I had caught it at work. I had slowed down the process in some way, like a slow-speed film, so that I could detect the ceaseless multi-directional movements behind each instant of conscious experience. I had a vivid sense of the mirroring of the structure of consciousness and the structure of reality – of knowing inner and outer as one.

Once we know ourselves as multi-dimensional beings, we are freed to examine the living paradox of human freedom.

Paradox as the Vehicle for Elucidating Free Will

It is widely agreed that our concept of free will is a paradox. What is more, our actual experience of free will presents us with many more paradoxes. And paradoxes rest on a multi-level context. Otherwise they are mere contradictions, dead-ends, nonsenses. Here again, if we remain in the linear mode, then we shall land ourselves in mind-splitting conundrums. For instance:

1. Bertrand Russell's famous 'unsolvable' paradox – 'The statement on the other side of this piece of paper is true' while on the other side is written 'The statement on the other side of this piece of paper is false'.

2. To give another example: Both of these statements are true: 'She couldn't help breaking her leg – it was a most unfortunate accident and not at all what she had wanted to happen', and 'She chose to break her leg – it solved many of her immediate problems because she was then looked after and cared for'. Taken within the same frame of reference, this makes as much nonsense as Russell's linguistic paradox. But if we assign the first statement to one level of experience, which has its own reality and is valid on that level, and assign the second statement to a subtler level of reality, the level at which we attract

happenings and live out instructions from our deep consciousness, then we enter into a position of understanding.

Paradox offers us the creative opportunity of focusing on a dual meaning: it speaks to us of the essential connections between meanings that would indeed be contradictory if held on the same level, but enrich and extend our understanding as we come to realize that one meaning in the paradoxical structure expresses something on one level of reality (or a given context), and the other meaning expresses something on another level of that reality or context.

To take another example: 'You must lose your life to save it'. We let go of and lose one aspect of our life (something on the ego level, perhaps) in order to enrich the quality of our life on a more significant level. Both meanings refer to the same 'event' or happening in the universe, but to different ways of viewing that reality. They must also each be held apart, in spite of their shared denotation, and not collapsed into one another and their meanings merged – although each have a valid weighting or we should not be attracted into the paradox. This distinction provides the dynamic tension in the paradox, a tension which stretches the mind to entertain a richer meaning. The koans of the Eastern traditions are designed to promote just such a transcendence of the linear mode of thought, and invite us into an experience of a multi-dimensional nature. 'The sound of one hand clapping' does indeed remain incomprehensible if bound to its linear linguistic level. Consciousness is thus urged towards contact with reality from a subtler and more all-embracing perspective. It is this perspective which renders choice and personal responsibility intelligible.

Personal Responsibility Rests on Knowing Ourselves as Both Defined Entities and Ceaselessly Interconnecting Energies

There is something important that the causal model, and our linguistic structure, do offer us. Both deal with entities. They imply that people are entities, distinct objects with boundaries. However, it is essential that we do not rest on this understanding alone, but acknowledge that the discreteness is only true on one level – the level of ego perception. The two horns of the buffalo again: all is one on the most ultimate level, allowing consciousness to participate ceaselessly in shared connections; and at the same time, boundaries are indeed a feature of the manifested physical reality in which we human beings also operate.

A sense of responsibility draws on, and draws together, both these levels. (To put it another way, it rests on an appreciation of both the 'particle' and the 'wave' model of reality.) First, we need to feel defined as separate entities so that we know what small chunk of the universe we are directly and especially responsible for. To achieve this, we need to let our bodies 'hold' our psyches (as the Adult Spirit in us knows in the West), and we need to experience directly our own inner events – the movements of our own feelings and thoughts. This entails re-owning our projections: those parts of ourselves that we reject and place outwards, on to others and the world. It involves recognizing, with the help of ego consciousness in the North, what is 'ours', and being able to distinguish between our own psychic material and someone else's, taking notice of what we ourselves generate. (Only a secure ego, supported by other aspects of self, can utilize its skill to perform this task.)

Secondly, we need to know ourselves as spiritual beings who create our own experience – who attract certain happenings through resonances on the subtle levels of being; through activity in the unseen realm of our most profound interconnectedness. We are bundles of interlocking energy; and dwelling in the immense energy field of life, we cannot help but make energy connections of an untold variety. It is this that makes it possible for us to be the agents of our lives: we bring our intentions into being through these connections. As sources of energy, we also contribute to the vast store of vibrating potential manifestation out of which we fashion our ideas and evolve new forms. This we know of in our Eastern self as Child Spirit. Of course this knowledge does not really come second: it is prior to all else, but owing to our regressed position, most of us need to gather ourselves up as Adult Spirit first. We need to experience that we are held as a responsible entity by our spirited bodies.

(In this way we avoid the pitfall of *identifying* with ego consciousness, while still drawing on the power of the ego to make conscious distinctions. The body gives us a fundamental and primal experience of definition in a simple, direct and immediate manner. Knowing our self as a singular entity is of more 'matter' than an intellectual exercise, although the intellect elaborates and refines the continual processes involved in keeping our boundaries during the complex interactions of the psyche with the world.)

So to understand ourselves as responsible beings, we have to know both that we are, each and every one of us, an enspirited material entity as well as knowing that, in common with all earth dwellers, we are constructed of pure energy, and cannot help but be in ceaseless contact with All-That-Is. The universe in which we creatively participate is like one vast mind firing continuously, making connections and disconnections, forging pathways which eventually perhaps even reveal themselves as recognizable causal sequences on more manifest levels.

The Necessary Distinction between Creating Our Reality and Controlling Others

It seems important to emphasize again that being responsible for our lives and being free to create our own reality are not a matter of manipulating other people on the level at which we are boundaried and discrete entities. It is not achieved through attempting to control each other and force our will on others. If we confuse choice with control, and try to exercise will in the place of making connections, then we shall all-too-likely imagine that we are causing others to do things (the great generator of guilt), or feel that we are a mere effect in *their* 'game of billiards'. If we understand ourselves *only* as separate entities, then we can indeed experience ourselves as shoved around like billiard balls. We sentence ourselves to an illusory mechanistic world, and pretend to be puppets and puppet masters. It is one of our most habitual 'entertainments' and diversions in life. But it is only an agreed system of interaction. In fact, we can only effectively impose our will on others if those others are colluding with our will *on a deeper level* – if they are themselves selecting, at the very different level of their own deep psychology and for their own particular and profound reasons, that which we are busy imposing on them at the manifest level. On the surface they make real and heartfelt protestation, and display earnest resistance, and of course such experience must be recognized and respected; but it does not, and cannot, contain the whole expression of that being.

We do not cause each other, and unless we know this we shall be permanently plagued by guilt. It is a travesty, yet is also deeply significant, that we have come to equate guilt with responsibility. We hold ourselves responsible for all sorts of things that we could never 'make' anyone do. We feel guilty for someone else's act of suicide, for instance, taking on to ourselves an enormous and erroneous power of determination. Or we 'take responsibility' for another's happiness – feeling guilty and resentful if they do not comply by being happy. We have confused our boundaries; we have stepped over our given arena of power. Or else we assign guilt to others and declare that they are 'responsible' for what other people do or feel – or, indeed, for what we do or feel. ('You made me do it' and 'You make me feel guilty' are great favourites.)

As soon as some disaster befalls a community or a nation, energy is immediately directed towards the task (presumed essential) of placing guilt and responsibility on to specific people. On one level – the practical level of social organization – this procedure has a limited but important application; and on this level responsibility must indeed be taken by those who have sought, and been given, certain powers; for lessons need to be learned in order to organize more efficiently in the future. This is an activity of the Northern aspect of self; but it is usually heavily contaminated by a merging of all four 'directions' and is thus prone to be overwhelmed by the enemies of each.

We do not cause each other. We connect with each other on the subtle level of our being – resonate with like energies and pull away from energies which we find repellent, tune in with complementary vibrations and experiment with dissonant ones. We achieve a living and meaningful sense of responsibility when we appreciate this level of interconnections – having also acknowledged our separateness so that we know clearly which self we are responsible for and do not confuse our boundaries – and then consciously delineate, attend to and attract what we want. This, of course, entails knowing or discovering what we really do want. It is a process of continual experiment: we find out what we do and don't want through our lived experience, through daring to explore diverse ways and means. We can then constantly change whatever is unfitting, or no longer fitting, in the actualization of those wants. Thus we can increasingly 'be' what we intend.

Like other organisms, we are self-regulating beings. We hypothesize and test out and change our hypotheses if they cease to serve us or fail to connect us with reality (or the reality that we require). If we are aware of this process then we feel the joy and exhilaration of a creative endeavour; we are being true to our creative nature. We experience ourselves as self-generating beings.

The Different Levels Involved in the Process of Choice

It makes no sense to declare that we choose our lives unless we expand our understanding of choice and become conscious of the different levels at which it operates. We need to explore below the trivial level, the one on which we usually acknowledge our faculty of choice, and view our more significant interactions. Here it is most likely that we shall be confronted with our victim experience. We are bound to come up against our set patterns of behaviour, our habitual ways of dealing with situations which generate the same familiar old feelings. They are strangely comforting, however distressing the circumstances. At least we are on known territory. Any suggestion of changing our modes of response or action usually stimulates obstinate justification of the status quo, irritation at not being 'understood', or expressions of hopeless resignation. We insist: 'But I can't help it', or 'It's not *my* fault', or 'I've tried and tried and I can't seem to stop doing it'. Or perhaps we declare, 'Yes, but I always feel this way', as if that settled the matter.

Unless we find some means of accessing a still-more fundamental level, meaningful choice will remain unreal for us. Unless we extend the arena of choice from the surface level of our activity to a more potentially 'causal' or 'source' level, a sense of true responsibility will elude us. I maintain that only if we recognize that just such a level is actually the subtle level of our interconnectedness, does the concept of choosing our lives make sense. Only with a living acknowledgement of this intricately potent level of connectedness, with its laws of attraction and repulsion, can we entertain the possibility of self-generation within a network of fellow self-generating beings of all kinds. If we want or intend something on this subtle level, then we key into and resonate with a fitting situation or person or event *at the same level of their subtlety*. Equally, if we actively do not want or intend this happening, then we refrain from engaging with such a situation, person or event; we do not tune in with the equivalent level in them and so we pass each other by. There is no spark of connection. We have all heard of those extraordinary cases when someone, for no apparent reason, suddenly decides to take a different route to the one consciously planned and, in so doing, avoids an unforeseeable accident.

Just as earlier I suggested that we needed to extend our concept of self in order to embrace a self that *could* be creative and responsible, so now I suggest that *we need to extend and develop our comprehension of choice*. This involves unpacking the various aspects of its operation on different levels of our being. We need to do this, also, in order to make sense of the all-too-common experience of non-choice. Any theory of free will must address the reality that many people experience having little or no choice, just as any theory of determinism needs to account for the lived experience of choice-making. It is highly unsatisfactory to simply dismiss such troublesome challenges as illusion.

And so I draw on the Medicine Wheel of the American Indian peoples once more. I have devised a wheel of my own and mapped it on to the four directions – I call it 'The Wheel of Responsibility'. I maintain that we, in our culture, are utterly confused about choice. We both claim it and deny it; crave it and evade it. With a limited view of the self we can only note choice as it is manifested on the superficial level; we cannot see how it serves and expresses our fundamental being through the subtler aspects of consciousness. We are thus ever liable to fall into contradiction, vulnerable to psychological paralysis and prone to take up a position of victimhood. But if we spread the process of choice on to the Wheel of the Whole Self, and keep moving through its directions while respecting the quality of each, then we are released into a dynamic multi-dimensional model of choice which naturally emerges from, and thus more elegantly mirrors, the structure of both consciousness and reality.

Chapter Seven: How Responsible Are We?

The Wheel of Responsibility:
A Multi-dimensional Model of Choice

I wish to emphasize once again at this point that I am exploring, and offering for your consideration, my own choice of belief system and my own conception and development of the Medicine Wheel. It has proved richly meaningful for me, and of practical value; and others with whom I have shared these ideas have also found this to be so for them. But it is only one way of seeing, one model for dealing with the complexities of human life, and you may well order your experience more effectively by evolving your own vision and methods. As we are creative beings, there are endless possibilities of shaping our reality in personally significant ways.

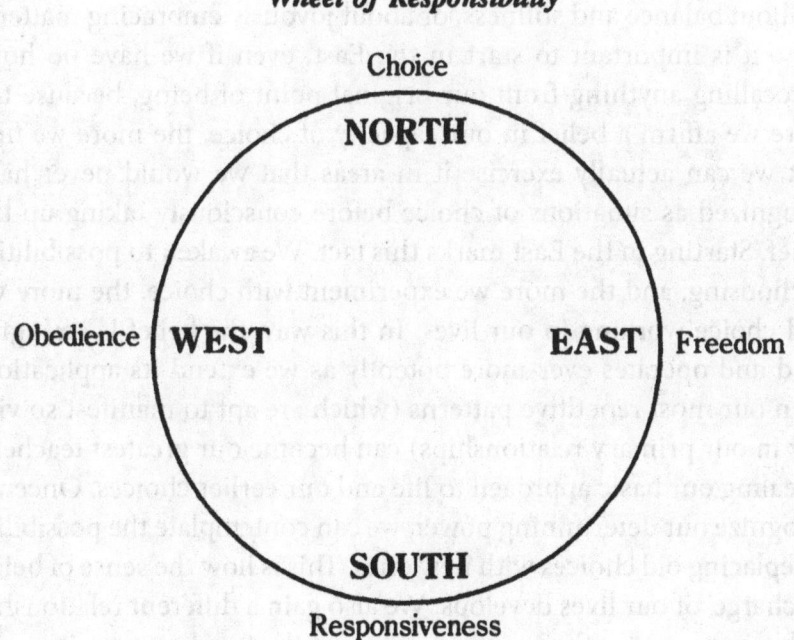

The East: the Source of Choice – Our Original Intention

The Wheel of Responsibility starts with the Child Spirit in the East, for it is only at the level of spirit that we can truly take responsibility for ourselves. The unfolding process of choice starts with our deep intention at incarnation; that unique aspect of All-That-Is which we were drawn to express with the help of material form, that 'lesson' we felt the compelling need to explore. Here, in the East, we learn, we remember or remind ourselves, of the underlying theme of our embodied lives. However, as this may be inaccessible to our consciousness when we embark on the Wheel, we may only be able to give *acknowledgement* to the source of our power of choice, and entertain the *possibility* of our capacity to create our own experience of life. Or we may, perhaps, sense some quality of energy for which we have no words – some sense that our life is about challenging the extremes, or about balance and stillness, or about joyously embracing matter.

It is important to start in the East, even if we have no hope of recalling anything from our original point of being, because the more we affirm a belief in our capacity of choice, the more we find that we can actually exercise it in areas that we would never have recognized as situations of choice before consciously taking up the belief. Starting in the East marks this fact. We awaken to possibilities of choosing, and the more we experiment with choice, the more we find choice working in our lives. In this way, the belief is strengthened and operates ever-more potently as we extend its application. Even our most repetitive patterns (which are apt to manifest so vividly in our primary relationships) can become our greatest teachers, revealing our basic approach to life and our earlier choices. Once we recognize our determining power, we can contemplate the possibility of replacing old choices with new ones. This is how the sense of being 'in charge' of our lives develops. We also gain a different relationship with our context – the beyond – learning the freedom of going *with* the flow of larger movements and forces rather than feeling at the mercy of them.

It is in the East, then, that we can claim our *intrinsic capacity* to create our experience, and this forms the deep foundation of all other levels of choice. It becomes evident that the 'health' or liveliness of our day-to day-choices is underpinned by the prevailing security that an awareness of spirit affords. It is in the East, too, where we contact the energy of illumination, and find that choice widens and increases its range and power with the opening up to our more inclusive consciousness. The more conscious we are, the more 'sun' we allow into our lives, and the more we can actively use our faculty to choose. The ability only becomes fully operational with such an extension of consciousness, informing our understanding of *how* we are responsible, and nourishing the desire to live out that responsibility. On the other hand, if we are not wanting to be responsible, then we do not directly contact, or become aware of, our faculty of active choice, and it lies virtually dormant within us. We still create our lives, but we do so blindly, bereft of that most human experience – the joy of meaningfulness.

But do we choose this not-wanting? Is it, in fact, a *refusal* to be responsible? Many of us have actually voiced this reluctance and powerfully experienced our resistance to choose. We may even, at times, be aware of a conscious and obstinate determination not to accept responsibility for ourselves. With our Eastern aspect of self we can begin to face and explore both the source of our choice and, thus, the source of our refusal. If we do not intend to be responsible, then we would be unlikely to evoke or enlist our ability to choose.

Could it be that most of us living in this era did indeed incarnate precisely to explore this issue? It is the most relevant of all issues, as the human species struggles to move into the next stage of evolution and leave its outdated infant mode of victimhood behind. Our very humanity depends on how we deal with this profound refusal of responsibility.

The Holocaust stands at the centre of the twentieth century as the most appalling challenge to non-victimhood. Here, we have almost enshrined and made holy the victim position, and dare not suggest responsibility in those who suffered. We place it all on those 'inhuman' persecutors (who are so unlike we could ever be) and identify with the helpless. Such victims seem to have lived out some awful need for us all – we treat them almost with reverence, like sacrificial lambs at the altar of external control. The Holocaust has become the Archetype of Impotence and Omnipotence: manipulation of human beings as mere objects to be removed systematically and mechanically from the scene. But in it do we not recognize extreme non-choice as something utterly abhorrent and not to be countenanced? And is not the balancing energy of ruthless and relentless imposition on the liberty of others seen clearly to be a crime against humanity? Did we need to act out these extremes on a big scale, centre stage, in order to know how untenable they are?

The war against Hitler is thought to stand for all time as a just war. (We are not so quick to recognize the same ingredients of extreme non-choice and ruthless imposition in a possible nuclear holocaust.) It is sad that, when faced with the challenge of deeply shocking events, we resort to thinking in terms of absolute guilt and complete innocence, rather than enlightening ourselves with such a tellingly clear example of the *abdication* of our humanity. We react with despair or virulent blaming when we could, instead, journey to the depths of our own souls to find the source of our collective aberration. This is the hero's true journey. But not the slaying hero of ego-dominated myths of the past. We need, rather, to call on our Eastern self and access that child spirit energy which is prepared to venture into the most painful and difficult of inner territory, combining courage and curiosity with psychic sensitivity. It is an inner journey into the fullness of All-inclusive Consciousness.

We intend to be responsible or refuse to be responsible from a deep place in ourselves. This intention informs our whole way of being in the world. It has nothing to do with education or privilege; the source of responsibility does not lie in the Northern direction with our adult substance self. Many people try and place it here where it can never find its proper rooting. It is not an ego decision. It is not culturally given or a matter of social custom. It cannot be dictated by law, nor do we acquire it simply by reaching adult status. Knowledge of our freedom – of our ability to create our lives – depends on our recollection of spirit, and thus springs from engagement with the Eastern aspect of self. Any person, however simple or sophisticated, can intend towards being responsible for themselves, or intend towards escaping responsibility.

However, if it is true that we are passing through the victim archetypal mode at this stage of evolution, then those who have elected

Chapter Seven: How Responsible Are We?

to clear themselves of victimhood will have the experience of *attaining* choice. It can thus look to us like a privileged or elitist acquisition (only possible for saints or materially satisfied, consumer-weary navel-gazers). But I believe that anything as extraordinary, defining and *fundamentally* transforming as the ability to choose must be there within us, available to be activated, or we could not attain it. If we believe this to be the case with regard to the human ability to acquire language, then how much more compelling to afford choice the status of an innate capacity. It is hardly a gift from the external world. But we have to intend to use our choice; and it is in the East that we honour this intention. We remind ourselves of its possibility each time we visit the Eastern aspect of self.

If we intend to be responsible for our lives, if we deeply wish to live our unique self as fully as possible, if we long to grow and go 'with' life and be creative, then we discover choice within us. We uncover, bring to light, that faculty of choice which is there in each of us. In the East we come to terms with our most fundamental orientation in life; are we going to see ourselves as choosing beings or determined beings, creative entities or mechanical objects, artists of life or victims of circumstances? It is the Child Spirit in us that 'intends' how we shall be in the world. According to our primary intention, our ability to choose develops and widens and grows in power, or it remains dormant, blocked and constricted.

For the American Indian peoples, the Human Realm, which is placed in the East, is characterized by *our determining energy, and our conscious power to use this energy and determine ourselves is the defining quality of our species*. Self without such a power would simply be incomplete, and the 'victim self' is thus always an incomplete self. Are we then free to choose which model of the psyche we like? Having made my choice, I can now conceive that we are likely to choose whichever model accords with our deep intention.

Often, we can do no more than acknowledge our origins in the East, and much work has to be done in the other directions before we feel direct contact with our Eastern energy. It is not the place for dwelling on mere abstract ideas. If we engage with the East with our intellect only, then we shall be overcome by its enemy – idealistic fantasy and pseudo-power. We are then likely to fall flat on our faces and feel let down and cynical, or else we may displace the notion of freedom outside us – on to nation states, perhaps. Are we not only-too-ready to wage wars in the name of national sovereignty, rather than claim our power to determine our own lives? We can get involved with notions of liberation on a grandiose scale – proclaiming that we belong to the 'Free World' – while feeling utterly dependent on, and defined by, the approval of others in our everyday affairs. It is the fire of direct experience that characterizes the East. Unless its 'sun' energy enlivens our being, we need to move to the South and get in touch with how we are feeling.

The South: The Responsive Self

Having acknowledged our spirit self and the possibility of freedom, we then move to the South to our Child Substance self. Whereas in the East we were calling on our imaginations to envision and experience the self we *could* be, here in the South, we attend to our actual personal feelings as they arise in the course of our daily lives.

As we are focusing on choice and decision-making in this Wheel of Responsibility (and usually turn to 'medicine' when all is not well with us), we are very likely to be feeling anxious, or, to put it more accurately, we are likely to be caught in a state of anxiety. The whole point about anxiety is that no feeling can flow through to completion and clear itself. We are in a general state of contraction while at the same time stimulated emotionally. We can neither act nor let go and relax. Instead of working in a complementary manner, both the sympathetic and parasympathetic nervous systems are simultaneously aroused, and we are overwhelmed by a cascade of hormones. At such a time, we experience having no choice. At the crude level it is fair to say that we cannot exercise choice. At a subtler level, we are simply living out an old choice. It is in the South that we address our past. Unless we claim our past, our ability to choose will, in all likelihood, remain submerged. When we experience no choice, it doesn't mean that we don't possess the faculty of choice but that we are dominated by a deeper level of choice, by an older decision that we have held in our being – in our body – on the cellular level. We are still attempting, on an unconscious level, to live out our primal choices that were evolved by us when in a state of acute fear, insecurity and dependence.

We can see here the danger of confusing the four cardinal directions of the self. Let us untangle the confusion. In The Wheel of Responsibility the essence of the South is *responsiveness*. The Child Substance self, expressing the quality of the element Water, is naturally responsive. The important point to note is that we respond to situations in our own special and specific way. Right from the beginning we have our own particular response to our mother, for instance. In the South we need to claim this primal responsive self, for here the nature of our responsibility lies in our ability to respond as a unique being. However, because at our present stage of evolution we so soon come to resist the natural passage of our life energy, we tend to hold these early responses of ours so that they become set positions. We negate the flowing water energy of the South from the beginning and, by freezing certain key responses, we form primal emotional templates which then order our feelings and behaviour into repetitive patterns. It is essential to stay psychologically fluid during the period of rapid biological growth that our Child Substance self undergoes. But instead, we crystallize our initial infant responses (as well as later childhood ones) into hard-core decisions that thereafter pervade our entire being. (An example of this phenomenon is explored in the following chapter.) Do we not all-too-frequently continue to act, albeit in disguised forms, as if we were as dependent as a babe in arms?

Decision-making belongs to our practical Northern self, as does conscious commitment to certain choices, and projection into the future in order to make provision for likely eventualities to come. These are all activities of the rational mind and the province of adult wisdom. Our responsiveness in the South must stay ever-mobile. It has nothing to do with the future. We must not mould responses to deal with what could possibly be, or we are no longer responsive. When we respond, we fit the living situation, we flow with life in our own unique way. This is the aspect of human responsibility that we learn of in the South.

Again, we can see mirrored here how we confuse not only South and North, but South and West. We utilize the 'mineral' aspect of self and hold our energy, rather than let it course through us;

rather than simply giving ourselves to the situation in our own special way. We turn our flowing and necessarily flexible responses into fixed choices. And stuck primal choices are immensely powerful, not only because all other choices are built upon them and influenced by them, but also because they hide so tenaciously below the surface of consciousness. They are fashioned with our cellular consciousness and are held in the cells of our body tissue. These old choices can all-too-easily remain entrenched in our organismic memory, and are seldom brought forward into the arena of conscious decision-making. In fact, they surreptitiously take over that arena and nullify its appropriate use. Thus, as adults we genuinely experience a state of severely restricted choice, or purely trivial choice, or even non-choice, if we flounder in the grip of anxiety and compulsive obsessions.

And so our basic primal organismic ability to respond, which is the first stage in our unfolding ability to be a responsible human being, becomes solidified into set 'decisions' or positions which are held in our bodies in such a way that we become victims of our own biology – or, rather, of our own biological distortions. No wonder that drugs can seem the only effective way of dealing with the psychological states of disturbance that eventually emerge.

If we are true to the Southern aspect of self, then we shall not hold our emotional energy; we shall give of ourselves, and from ourselves, in our own inimitable way. We shall experience our own deeply personal response to a given situation, experience it as *ours*, and be in touch with our feelings and tastes and preferences. We shall instinctively trust our right to be who we are, and we shall therefore also trust each other person's right to be who they are. We shall respect diversity, and be released from the restrictive plague of conformity.

Each time we visit the South, we can come to recognize ever-more clearly some attitude or action as *my* response; this is the course I myself took, as me, given my circumstances, my ground, my context. If we let our preferences and needs show, if we let them be seen and felt, then we not only *give* our energy, our particular qualities, to the world, but we can more easily claim them as ours, and thus get them met in a more direct and responsible manner. We can act more cleanly.

In addition, just to know what we need or want or like, regardless of whether fulfilment is possible, is a very centring activity. We rest in our truth, and feel the special comfort and inner nourishment that is born of being at one with our self. It becomes increasingly apparent that no one *made* us be the exact way that we are: we do not *feel* 'caused' if we dare to allow the inner flow of our energy. Once we know self as a source of energy (from our contact with the East), then in the mirror of the South, we can see that we mobilized our energy in a particular way, allowed it to take certain paths and make specific patterns that later manifested in traits and habits of behaviour that can be characterized as ours. We are clearly being responsible if we can say, 'All courses taken on every level of my being were taken by me – including the hanging on to old positions and confusing the energies of North, West and South'.

The 'child' of the South is often labelled irresponsible because, sadly, responsibility has come to mean taking on the burdens of adulthood, the labour of life and agony of making decisions. But we only experience ourselves in this way if we have never fully lived the Southern aspect of self. We feel burdened if we are not being ourselves, if we are working 'against the grain'. We then enter the North, desperately seeking a socially given self-image and having to sustain a definite position in life. We exhaust ourselves trying to keep pace with fashion, with what others are doing, and we cannot begin to recognize the variety of possibilities that could be available for our particular mode of expression.

If we belittle our responsive nature in the South, we actually negate choice in the North. Not only do our various preferences and tastes provide the basic 'stuff' and 'matter' out of which authentic choice takes shape, but adult choices are rendered vacuous if we are secretly ruled by the fear-ridden frozen responses of our child self. It is no wonder, then, that choice presents itself to our ego consciousness as a problem. Life can only feel exactly 'right' and 'good' for us human beings when we allow our individuated beingness. We are a self from the moment of conception. Our essence is the seed which generates our individuation, and our first mode of being needs to be one of responsiveness to this essence.

It is tragic that the very responsiveness and spontaneity of the child is associated with irresponsibility, and thus envied and curbed, for if only we truly respond to our unique self, then it is the exact reverse – we are, in fact, being utterly responsible: appropriately responsible not only in relation to this stage in life, but also in relation to the Southern aspect of the self which plays its part in the operations of the psyche and our structuring of reality for our entire life span.

Whenever we enter the Southern direction in the Wheel of Responsibility, we have the opportunity to respond now, as ourselves. We also have yet another chance to claim and appreciate our past responses as ours, as well as to recognize those responses which we solidified into set decisions that then ruled and blocked our future responsiveness, and took the place of choice in later adult life. We need to discover those specific personal 'organismic' fixations, those frozen primal positions, that still organize our present choices and decisions (or non-choices and lack of decision), and will continue to manifest in our feelings, thoughts and behaviour throughout our lives if we fail to look into the mirror of our Southern self. The process of unfreezing such responses will be explored more fully in Chapter 10.

The North: the Place of Choice and Decision-making

We then move to the North – the appropriate place for both decision-making and commitment to certain decisions. Decisions are needed for practical and social purposes, but they need to emerge from a continually emptied and uncluttered mind if they are to serve us in our unfolding process of individuation. Commitment is not synonymous with rigidity; it evolves in its form and expression as we develop and grow. New decisions are constantly being called for.

In this Northern direction of personal meaning, we make up our own minds; we strive to be alert to unnecessary conditioning and outdated social norms. We keep tuned to our 'wind' energy, which enables us to sweep over and scan vast landscapes, both within us and without, for the empty mind moves rapidly and freely. Thus, we become aware of the future implications of our decisions and the likely consequences – without getting diverted by our projected fears from the past or through contemplating every little snag that could possibly arise.

Chapter Seven: How Responsible Are We?

As social beings our choices cannot help but involve consideration of others and awareness of their needs. It is enormously important that ego consciousness is placed in its social context; it is never allowed to remain isolated, and the special energy of the Northern direction keeps this connection intact – it is the direction of the Social Law. Our orientation in the North is outgoing, and the quality of 'air' and wisdom indicates clear and unprejudiced perception of others. Our 'practical selves' naturally want good relationships and satisfactory social encounters, and we use our common-sense intelligence to make decisions that will tend to bring this about.

While we are spontaneously responsive to ourselves and to the world in the South, we consciously *take* responsibility for ourselves in the North. This involves a willingness to be aware, to be as transparent to ourselves as air, and to communicate with ourselves and others with as few mental impediments as possible. It involves deliberately deciding to search for those old primal 'choices' which undermine our ability to choose as an adult; consciously deciding to visit the psychic space of the South where these frozen responses, or 'premature decisions', still lie embodied in our being.

Unless we deal with our past in the South, we shall never experience true choice in the North, even though this is the direction in which we come into that very power of making conscious choices. We shall always have a sense of being pushed or pulled by unknown forces. We shall not feel free to choose, except in superficial matters. Or else we may be convinced that we have made a real and new choice, only to find ourselves caught in the same old mistakes, reacting in set ways and compelled to travel well-worn emotional grooves. We shall constantly land up in all-too-familiar situations, feeling the same familiar feelings, however hard we try to alter the course of our behaviour, however ardently we exercise our faculty of choice. No wonder the rational mind is drawn to theories of determinism.

It requires many turns of the wheel, many visits to all four directions, to uncover the basic frozen responses which dominate our choices. We cannot discover them by remaining forever digging in the South, nor can we unveil them solely by means of our ego consciousness in the North, however well intentioned. All aspects of consciousness are needed in order to know ourselves at the level of our organismic being. We shall need to sink into ourselves and tap our unconscious, or Deep Consciousness, through focused relaxation and times of stillness. (In order to do this, we could avail ourselves of psychotherapy, various meditation practices or a visit to a place of retreat.) Drawing on the experience of our Western self, accessible to us through intuition and dreams, we must also allow the light of illumination in the East, perhaps using active visualizations, or the creative arts. We shall need to call on our finest sensitivity and extend our consciousness across our usual inner barriers, daring to know whatever is necessary to be known. All this knowledge lies within us – all our past 'choices', our fixed responses, are there like the rings of a tree – carried at the cellular level.

Thus we lay bare the rich hidden aspects of the self until we get to the nodal points which are ordering our beliefs, attitudes, thoughts, feelings and, therefore, our present stunted choices. With such awareness we can recognize and begin to dissolve those frozen responses of long ago, and release our responsive nature to flow once more. Freed from the clutches of the past, we are then in a position to claim that capacity to choose which is always within us but is so often rendered unavailable for active use. We come into a maturing of these capacities in the North and thus can make conscious choices, choices nourished and enlivened by our personal preferences and particular ways of being. The responsive child in us can then continue to work with our adult self and we can meaningfully take responsibility for our decisions and our actions. We can deliberately choose not to allow ourselves to be diminished when someone tries to 'put us down'; decide to stop harassing ourselves with the attempt to do something 'perfectly'; give ourselves permission to undertake difficult tasks in our own time, or turn to what we enjoy at the moment when we need nourishment.

When South and North work together in this way, we can learn *how* to take responsibility for our feelings – not only by acknowledging them as ours (as we do as the responsive child) but by alerting our consciousness and developing our awareness to a point when we can catch our emotional energy just as it is about to slip down the same old groove and produce the same old feeling and, instead, allow it a fresh pathway. We can choose not to 'get into' hurt when someone misunderstands us, or to feel abandoned if a loved one has something else that they need to go and do; we can see the situation simply as an expression of how they are. Or we can choose not to feel rejected if our sexual partner is impotent. Although we may feel disappointed (free response), we can choose not to treat the episode as a comment on ourselves and thereby avoid the 'done to' or 'not wanted' position (frozen response).

Our Northern self can help in this transformation by actively choosing to suspend the repetitive 'hard done by' feeling as it begins to gather momentum, and allow this energy a different course; and we thus experience a new feeling. Strangely enough, emotions of rejection can hold a sweet sadness even if they are later followed by dissatisfaction and resentment. We are very attached to what is familiar. But life is far richer once we allow a whole new range of responses to open up in us, and it is worth relinquishing the negative 'pay-offs' that old feelings tirelessly offer us.

Choice of feeling in the North is a developed and sophisticated application of conscious choice, and it is important that we first learn to accept, in the South, all our feelings without judgement, knowing them as neither good nor bad (any more than different colours are good or bad), but simply as inner realities of our human state, and as movements of energy through our bodies. It is essential that we experience the full variety of human emotion before we attempt to make the choice of not repeating those that have long served an old idea or belief. And then it is actually the *belief*, which provokes and shapes the feeling, that we drop. If we judge a feeling in itself as bad, and for that reason wish to exercise our choice to feel another, then we shall more likely suppress it, covering it up with a pseudo or secondary feeling – as when we smile or laugh when we are angry. We are not then at one with ourselves or daring to be who we are. It is actions that are good or bad, not feelings. However, we can get into the habit of allowing certain feelings at the expense of others (always crying when someone is angry with us, for instance), and it can be fruitful to suspend the expression of such feelings and be open to the possibility of our energy moving in a different way.

The key point is that we allow the movement. Choice of feeling must not involve trying to make a feeling 'go away' – clamping down on a certain feeling in order to deny it. If we do this we shall soon have forfeited future choice. Feelings must always move, but the emotional tone and quality can be transformed as we refine our ability to tune into our inner processes – physical and mental – and choose the course of that flow. We can let irritation move into humour, for example, in that moment when we loosen our minds to let go an old perspective or receive a new one.

The West: Obedience to the Voice within

On the Wheel of Responsibility the West is the direction of obedience – but not obedience to external authorities or systems. So often, we place obedience, or compliance, in the South or North, and so live out our wounded infant victim selves to the full. Adult spirit of the West draws from the infinity of inner space, gently held by the vessel of our body. With this aspect of self we can connect with our deep consciousness, and bring its rich wisdom into our daily lives in the present moment. It is the intuition of our mature spirit self that we obey, not the dictates of our ego, nor the commands of others. We stand in our own authority in the West, while sensing our rootedness in the Source of All Things. In this direction we are aware of our collective being, our commonality which body expresses, and thus our true inner voice is always in tune with the ultimate, profound well-being of the whole community of earth-dwellers. It may sometimes look otherwise on the surface, or for a period of time; but our deep inner voice cannot be out of key with that very ground of shared consciousness from which it sprang.

No wonder obedience to it calls forth frequent instances of synchronicity. If we trust and follow our own truth, then we experience that sense of everything falling into place. As we are not obeying our ego, we are not here operating in a competitive system of 'one up, one down'. We are not into control, or social game-playing, or power politics. It is crucial that we do not muddle North with West and obey our intellect or rationally devised 'answers'. We consider these, and try them out, but we do not obey them. We only obey the messages that arise from our mature and authoritative Adult Spirit self; messages which emerge through a completely different process, and which we experience in a very different way.

Intuition is effortless and immediate. A particular intuition, or communication from our Western self, comes with the spirit of its own authority; and if it does not, then it is most likely an interesting idea or thought which invites a different kind of consideration. We do not work for intuitions. They come to us. We only need to clear the way for them, through trust and creating a fitting context in which to receive them. We need pockets of space, both focused in some way or unfocused; times of peace, of doing nothing. Such intuitive inner knowing is compelling in that we feel we 'have to' take a certain path, or perform a certain action, or embrace a certain attitude, and yet there is no sense of compulsion; no sense of being driven. It is one of the purest and simplest of experiences, both mysterious and ordinary. We are not drawn into the activity of deliberation. There are no two ways about it – no cluster of tangled possibilities to sort through. An intuition stands alone, inviting full acceptance. Our response of obedience is not one of pre-choice or a diversion from choice; it is beyond choice.

So part of the process of becoming a fully responsible human being is to trust the intuitive knowledge which points to what we need to do to be true to ourselves; to obey what emerges in clarity from the depths of our being. This experience of inner communication carries conviction because it is accompanied by a sense of connection with both the core of who we are and the foundation we all share. It has a genuine ring, like the sound of a true note when a bell is struck: it resonates with our sense of truth. It also seems to appear vividly out of the depths of consciousness, with the impact of a sudden light falling on to what before was hidden from view. It is a burst of new consciousness, and we violate ourselves when we refuse to act on it. And obedience itself is an action. It has nothing to do with passivity or subjugation. Obedience in the West is far removed from a 'slave mentality'. (That belongs to the dynamic of manipulation on the level of ego in the North, or subservience to an external authority or parent figure, having never sufficiently cleared our past in the South.)

However, the word 'obedience' has unfortunate connotations for many people; we connect it with suppression of our own desires in favour of someone else's – whether parents, God or the dictates of some system. Because it is meant to be for our own good, or the communal or national good, we are not supposed to complain. And so we rebel against the very concept – it presses a button in us. For that reason it can be helpful to envisage the act of obedience as a *coming into alignment* with that which we recognize as necessary or meaningful or 'right' for us. If we have a sense of our whole being aligning itself with the particular insight or intention, then we simply live out our truth, and the notion of obedience is irrelevant.

Yet we seldom stay in this state, and I believe that it is unrealistic to expect to do so. The need for obedience is likely to occur – along with the inner rebellion (or resignation) so often associated with it – as soon as we move on from that moment of alignment. Resistance can creep up on us even when we know that we are only obeying our deeper selves. When we move out of the orbit of the intuition and lose touch with the quality of its energy, we slip into ego consciousness and everything takes on a different perspective. What emerged with the compelling ring of truth can then be treated as just an idea – and it is usually a troublesome idea that disturbs the psyche's status quo. It is then that we need deliberately to remain committed to the intuition that was so clear to us when we received it, and we experience this as an act of obedience.

As we are so prone to slip into ego consciousness, I feel that it is valuable to retain the concept of obedience, and to embrace its power in a new way. I remember once marking for myself – on receiving an intuition which had an awkward consequence for the easy running of my life – that I was pretty well bound to see it differently when I moved out from that still place of sure conviction; and I pledged myself to hold to the knowledge, whatever clever counter-ideas I would later entertain. The subtle holding of the West is indeed a grace. It has held secure some vital and vulnerable turning points in my own life.

The act of obedience could not be further from victimhood. We consciously undertake, with our whole being, to actualize the inner communication. It has been given many names: 'The still small voice within', 'The will of God', 'The movement of the Holy Spirit' (for the Adult Spirit that can never be a purely external 'Father' God, nor the isolated voice of the ego). And the fitting response is the act of obedience. There is no sense of choice but, equally, no sense of constriction or constraint. We apprehend the experience of freedom that it will open up for us just because it so exactly fits our most profound needs. We are the complete reverse of the blaming, complaining victim who also declares, 'But I have to do it'. In fact, we recognize that, through this willingness to obey, we are but fulfilling our own nature, and expressing in a specific way who we need to be at this particular point in our unfolding amidst the larger movement of life.

There is nothing to react against if we are exactly who we need to be. Such fittingness gives us a glimpse of both perfect freedom and clear responsibility.

The East: The Freedom to Actualize Our Self

If we have really entered into the energy of the West, then we are taken naturally towards the East, the direction of actualization. Here, we come into our true power as determining beings and experience freedom – freedom to be who we are and to act as we are. We can only be fully responsible human beings if we complete the wheel and return to our entrance point, claiming our whole self with our distinct aspects of consciousness, along with the concomitant perspectives that make up the process of choice. We have come full circle, and each time we complete the circle we attain a further degree of individuation.

As multi-dimensional beings operating in space and time, it is hardly surprising that choice is a multi-dimensional process that takes place through time (although the culmination of the process can 'gel' in an instant; we suddenly find that we can make a decision we know will hold). We have been beleaguered with confusion and contradictions in this area because we have been too mono-dimensional in our approach and thinking about this most vital and fundamental human activity.

We can only bring the capacity of choice and responsibility into full functioning by recognizing and utilizing far more of our psychic apparatus than the modern discipline of Psychology is, for the most part, willing to acknowledge. It is not surprising that theories of a deterministic and behaviourist mode have dominated the academic and clinical scene. When choice is identified with ego (always a delicate aspect of consciousness if isolated from its grounding in the rest of consciousness), with only a critical guilt-provoking superego to aid and guide it as they together attempt to control the enormous irrational force of the Id, true choice is a slim possibility indeed.

Moreover, many other models of the psyche are so simplistic and crude that they couldn't possibly provide a working theory of choice. Indeed, highly influential psychologists such as B.F. Skinner do not even admit to a model of the psyche at all. Obviously such 'reduced' human beings could not be expected to have much to do with choice. For choice can only make sense if we make use of a multi-dimensional model of consciousness, and it can only operate in a multi-dimensional reality. Otherwise, we cannot hope to escape the contradictions into which the subject of free will always plunges us. It can only be understood by letting go of causal theories of the psyche and glimpsing the possibilities opened up by theories of connection.

And so obedience to our inner self in the West, that call from the depths of our being and our collective consciousness, takes us forward into actively living our human freedom of self-generation. The East emanates the energy of actualization and fulfilment. We begin and end in the East. We open our imaginations to new possibilities, and contact the transformative elemental energy of Fire. Here, we extend our conception of who we are, we envision our future 'possible selves', and know these as living realities that can lend us energy right now, enlighten us now, because in the East we draw on our trans-temporal consciousness.

We are not projecting into the future with our rational minds, as in the North, and looking at the consequences of present decisions in a linear fashion. We are creatively extending ourselves – extending our consciousness – and directly entertaining new ways of being and new ways of relating. We feel them as realities. They are not vague shadowy images or abstract ideals, but vibrant possibilities energized with the light of immanent actualization. In the East, the future is now; all time is one. It is our apprehension of this that renders human beings free. And it is thus that we are able to actualize our visions – even though it may 'take time' to give them form, depending on the nature of the vision.

Chapter Seven: How Responsible Are We?

The trans-temporal aspect of self gives us a tremendous sense of freedom. Creative freedom. Freedom to create. It is more than just not being bounded by the past. Perhaps this is beginning to sound like pure, ungrounded fantasy – the very enemy of the East. I should like to share a somewhat ordinary example from my own experience. I vividly imagined a possible version of myself in ten years time; in every detail and in very specific situations. She was an older 'me' who simply was not jealous. This person felt alive and real to me. I knew I could be her. She took form as one of the many possibilities, already existing in some sense, for me to embody. I had but to choose to be 'her', rather than one of those other possible selves that I could equally choose to be. I then had an experience of all my possible selves – past, future and present – existing simultaneously, and I knew that I could avail myself of any of them, if I so determined. All that information was there, in me. I experienced the sphere of my whole self. Since then, that 'future' self has become part of the present me. Eastern energy transforms. (I wish to emphasize that this experience could never have borne such fruit if I had not already accepted, in the South, my feeling of jealousy – and accepted it with compassion. I was not rejecting the feeling, nor repressing it; I was moving to a position within myself from whence I no longer needed to generate it afresh.)

I am reminded at this point of quantum physics and Professor David Bohm's theory of 'fields of information'. As I understand it, each particle has its own information field, and is contained within a series of ever-more extensive information fields. It 'knows' all its possible movements; and if split in two, it carries the information of its partner and thus knows how to complement its behaviour, even if it be the other side of the universe. Given this internal information connection, it does not need to signal messages more quickly than the speed of light. Do we, too, move in and out of different fields of information? When sharing such a field, coincidences, which are inexplicable on the manifest or 'billiard-ball' level of reality, could not help but occur. And can we perhaps, at the subtler levels of our being, draw from the information field of our whole life? Or the even larger field of many lives? And is it thus that we dance our microscopic way through the universe, twinning and untwinning with other sources of information, being attracted to some fields and not others, ever moving in joint creation of our own personal and shared realities?

We can know the vast spectrum of our possible ways of being through the Eastern aspect of our consciousness, for here they all co-exist. The sun represents the energy of our full potentiality. Not only do we have access to our possible future selves, but also to our possible past selves – all the unlived aspects of our childhood and young adulthood, all those untrodden paths. Their *energy* is still available to us. The energy of success in a particular area, which we never let ourselves achieve, can be ours now; as also can be the qualities that we denied ourselves. I have a sense that we can even learn from the mistakes that we never gave ourselves a chance to make!

The power and the freedom of energized human imagination are enormous. We make real that which we can clearly conceive, given always that, like the eagle, we keep an eye on our earthly reality. Our free flights into the realm of imagination must finally end at home on earth; must be translated from trans-temporal reality into the present space/time mode. In some extraordinary sense, perhaps all pathways are open to us – as they are to the sub-atomic particle. Certainly, our range of choice is vast, if we but dare to use our full and all-inclusive consciousness.

In the experiments of quantum physics, the actual pathway a particular particle 'decides' to take can only be known retrospectively. It could be anything until it has arrived at its destination, and its process of 'choice' remains utterly inexplicable to the rational mind. Quantum mechanics cannot be understood, only applied. It is not an explanatory theory, but the fruits of its application are astounding. (So, too, do not we also, in the shaping of our lives, make use of beliefs and visions that we cannot always explain, although we clearly experience their efficacy?) All that can be predicted is that the particle in these experiments will indeed arrive at its destination (the screen) and make its mark, its contribution, in forming a clear and ordered pattern composed of billions of similar particles that have each taken their own unchartable path. And so with us. Only at our death do our choices become sealed, only on completion of our life do they fall into place.

And so we complete the Wheel of Responsibility where we

began it, by positing our freedom to create who and how we are. Here, we can envision not only future possible selves but future possible societies. Again, not just with the one-sided abstract mind and regressed infant energy of victim impotence and omnipotence, or we become Hitlers and Stalins. We must use our full human imaginations, ever-grounded in our common humanity in the West, and honouring unique personal feelings and meaning in the South and North. The Child Spirit in us is fearless of change, exhilarated by innovation, ready to let go of whatever obstructs our vitality and joy. If we dare to be fully responsible, fully *human* beings, the next stage in the evolution of our species will have taken place. We shall be freed of the Victim Archetype.

Chapter Eight
The Wheel of Victimhood

The Distortions Brought about by Our Engagement with the Victim Archetype: The Wounded Child

It is very revealing that in Britain, the Southern direction of the Medicine Wheel, after only a few years of its teaching, is becoming known as the place of the 'Wounded Child'. This assumes an *intrinsically* given 'Victim' childhood (the South is the place of the Natural Law, not the Social Law), and negates even the possibility of the trusting, spontaneous, responsive energy that marks the child of the South – an actual, living, substantive child with personal feelings, talents, tastes and preferences which express that unique being. This distortion cuts out the lifeblood that nourishes true choice in the adult Northern aspect of the self.

The Wheel of Responsibility is hampered from the start. It can never really get moving if we assume that we are a poor wounded child and a victim of our parents, set to become a victim of society in adult life. The assumption that the natural child is a wounded child shows how deeply we are involved in the Victim Archetype. Indeed, it does seem to us that our wounds started from conception, or soon afterwards, and thus our whole personal history is contaminated and organized by the energy of victimhood. Unless we claim our origins in Child Spirit, and know that aspect of self as prior to Child Substance, we shall take up the belief that we are automatically wounded and flawed.

Acknowledging our Eastern self – our trans-temporal self – is a way of dealing with our forgetfulness of spirit, which seems to be part of the process of incarnation at this stage of our evolution. It is a way

Chapter Eight: The Wheel of Victimhood

of reducing the length and strength of that initial one-way shutter (see Chapter 4) which blocks out everything other than awareness of our biological reality in order to establish our direction forwards into time and space, enabling us to gain a rooting in matter before we open up to our All Inclusive Consciousness, and naturally experience our being in spirit once more.

If this process of forgetfulness of spirit is truly at the core of our human predicament, then we are bound to find it hard to believe in our power to determine our lives; we shall therefore start the Wheel of Responsibility from our wounded victim self. Nevertheless, we do sense our incompleteness; and the important point is that we feel the need for healing – the need for medicine of some kind for our psyche. We know that we are not as we are meant to be, what we could be. Whether we view ourselves through a religious doctrine or simply open ourselves to our own personal experience, we sense something is awry. Our prevalent self-confusion arises from the fact that we are not dealing with our wounded child while in the South; instead we place our regressed infant self in the North, disguised outwardly as an adult because biologically mature. The denied child in us is then given the task of making choices, of actively and consciously 'taking responsibility', when that is the very thing that most terrifies that child.

On some secret level, therefore, we feel psychologically oppressed by adulthood rather than extended by it. We either put on an act of bravado and pretend to take things in our stride; or we procrastinate and manipulate, and slip out of being responsible for our lives in all sorts of different ways. Taking responsibility is inevitably experienced as too much of a burden – an impossibility – for the hidden and distorted child. And, indeed, that is just what it is.

What a paralysing 'double bind' to be attempting to exercise choice from our infant victim self who is continually disclaiming choice, and saying 'I can't help it'. Situations of choice are then bound to evoke anxiety, or else dissociation from our feelings, or perhaps a flat denial of the options involved. If we are still dominated by our past wounds, then our actual experience of choice will be seriously undermined, which in turn reinforces our victim 'reality' and the no-choice position.

It is essential that we recognize the wounds of childhood while in the direction of the South as belonging to the past, and not elevate them into viable adult viewpoints and modes of relating. Not only do we negate adult choices by displacing our infant self to the North, but in addition, by straining to make conscious choices and decisions with our infant victim self, we have no chance to be that ageless 'responsive child' of our Southern self. We give ourselves little opportunity to express our natural responsiveness to life: we eclipse that wholesome child energy which is such a vital aspect of our psyche. We lose our ebullience and trust and carefree joy when we catapult our hidden infant self into the social arena of the North, which requires adult choices and decisions, and the deliberations of ego consciousness. This is false responsibility that undercuts true and appropriate responsibility. We become responsive to others rather than to ourselves. Note that this misplaced responsiveness is quite different from an aware consideration of others, just as the natural organismic responsiveness to self in the South is completely different from an isolating absorption in ego.

Once our immediate responsiveness is focused on others rather than starting with our own truth, then we lose our unique path. We are liable to sop up social conditioning and fixed ideologies, to respond automatically to authority figures, and thus become caught in an unending need to please and a dependency on gaining approval from outside ourselves. We have completely distorted both our responsive child nature and our choosing adult self.

Of course a responsive child will naturally be responsive to others as well as to its self because other people are an inevitable part of its world; but responding from a base of trusting our selves and our own feelings is quite different from responding out of fear – fear to be our self, which then generates all kinds of fear of others. In fact, once we stop responding to self, we stop allowing our own feelings to flow: we become a fundamentally defended personality, and response of any kind is rare. We are thus caught in the grip of reaction, and our behaviour is all-too-often ruled by reactive patterns. The spontaneous, trusting child lies submerged in us.

If, as a child, we are first and foremost responsive to others rather than to our inner selves, then we shall naturally fall into blaming.

We cannot even start the process of self-responsibility. Whatever befalls us we shall feel bad, because we have denied who we are and betrayed ourselves, and so we shall blame those to whom we are busy responding, and say that they must have got it all wrong. Or else we shall heap blame on ourselves for somehow never managing to get it right – because nothing will *feel* right. Beating up on ourselves is a very common preoccupation, deciding that *we* are bad rather than *her* or *him*, because it keeps intact at least one 'good' parent. In the utter dependency we experience, once we lose our natural gift of self-regulation, we desperately need the security of a benign authority figure.

Once self as an original source of energy is ignored, responsiveness degenerates into its shadow – reaction. Once a sense of self is abdicated, then *you* make *me* the way I am. We claim that 'I have to act this way because of how *you* are', rather than moving from the core of self outwards into the world and responding and interacting from that live centre of our being. Self-entrapment and self-limitation result, rather than self-expression. Fixation rather than spontaneity, distrust rather than trust, suspicion rather than innocence. We are fear-ridden rather than filled with energy and life. Thus do we distort ourselves.

If we can remain responsive to self, then we know that we are only really dependent in certain practical ways. We have a direct sense of well-being, of being well in ourselves, that no one can destroy; a sense of self that cannot be taken away, even though others may evoke painful, distressing and frightening feelings in us. The more we respond to ourselves, the stronger our sense of self becomes; and as more of who we are is expressed in the world, so are we more able to see ourselves and be seen by others, who then reflect back what they see. It is much harder to violate or harm a person who is being utterly themselves, although of course that person can feel deeply hurt. It is much easier to abuse those who keep themselves locked away in unknowable secrecy, available only for projections. Self-revelation and expression constitute a far more resilient protection than hiding from others – and from ourselves.

If we have never been responsive to our child self in the South, then we have much more difficulty, when in the West, to be obedient to our intuitions. It is difficult even to recognize and hear such internal communications, let alone obey them, if we have been geared only to pick up messages from outside ourselves in order to adapt to others or manipulate them. If we have never trusted our immediate feelings, how are we to trust the more subtle movements of Adult Spirit? Also, if absorbed in a battle with ineffective choice in the North, then we can resolve never to obey anything – unaware of being slaves already to the frozen responses of our childhood. And it is unlikely that we shall be able to connect with the free spirit of adventure in the East, eager to explore the unknown and daring to create new visions for ourselves. It is fundamental to our well-being that we find the quality of trust where it belongs – in the South; that we start by trusting ourselves. And yet this is the direction dominated by the victim in us. We do well not to trust that victim self, for it draws us into the vicious circle of reaction.

THE CIRCLE OF REACTION

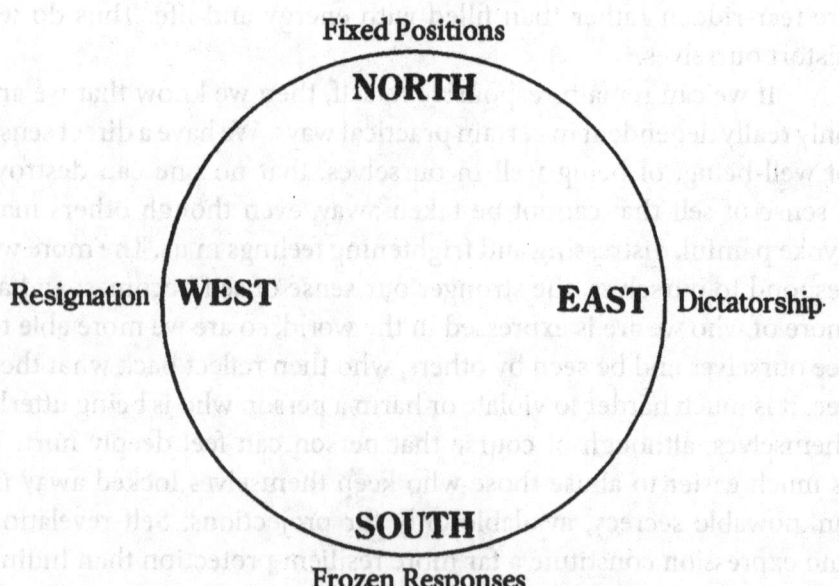

The Frozen Responses of the South

To deepen our understanding of the Wheel of Responsibility, it would perhaps be helpful to trace the distorted victim version which I have called the Circle of Reaction. We undertake the Wheel of Responsibility by starting in the East, but if we deny our origin in spirit then, instead, we begin in the South as the wounded child (without a grounding in spirit, we are bound to experience ourselves as wounded), and thus come to act out the Circle of Reaction. We do indeed appear to be born into victimhood and, in this way, support is given to the notion of 'original sin'. We never do, nor dare, then claim our responsive child, we never do truly respond to ourselves; for we have contracted our whole being in order to block our fear of annihilation, and are suspicious and mistrusting of our feelings from that time on. Thus, we cannot claim the quality of the South, which is trust; and not trusting ourselves, we can hardly trust others. We cannot flow *with* our energy for we are preoccupied with adapting and manipulating; we lose all sense of our natural 'water' mode of being and our life energy is continually obstructed. We gradually take up a defensive position which is materialized in our physical posture. We become limited and constricted and on guard against life. We are dependent in *every* way on parents and family, and allow ourselves to be completely defined by them. They tell us who we are rather than us 'giving them' who we are – as plants do.

Threatening situations are bound to occur, and some of them will be singled out by us for special attention. Our own highly individual responses to such key situations are then frozen and held in place by our now established habit of muscular and mental contraction. Eventually they become set positions which are automatically stimulated in circumstances that resonate in any way with the original ones. It is hardly surprising that these fixed positions then organize our experiences and behaviour in a repetitive manner. The new circumstances that trigger these set reactions may be very different in all sorts of ways and quite unrecognizable on the surface, but as long as the resonance of the same emotional dynamic is present, the old frozen response will be called forth to meet it and all other evidence is ignored, is simply not seen or heeded, or given any value.

These frozen responses could be called 'primal choices' in that all our future choices are based on them. However, as choice is associated with ego consciousness and rationality, it can be a misleading term to use when referring to the non-rational Id energy of our organismic expression. I prefer to use the word 'response' when describing the Southern aspect of self. Furthermore, we freeze our responses at the cellular level – it is a very physical and unconscious act. Holding our old patterns of response in place, we automatically serve and fulfil our outdated and set beliefs. In the Wheel of Responsibility, we express in the South our unique primal responses; in the Circle of Reaction, we freeze selected responses in an equally individual way.

The Re-enactment of Old Fixed Positions in the North

Choice belongs to our adult self in the North; but if underpinned by the frozen responses of our past rather than supported by a flexible responsiveness to life, if undermined by fixated energy rather than nourished by the flow of personal expression, then it is hardly surprising that we seldom experience full choice. It remains elusive and problematic (and the rational mind gets busy with its theories of determinism).

It could be put in the following way. Because we 'choose' from our victim self in the South by committing ourselves to certain organismic positions or 'decisions', we in fact cannot freely choose as our adult self in the North – the direction from which it is appropriate to exercise this faculty. So instead of choosing, we react. (Put crudely, we have placed 'choice' in the South and 'responsiveness' in the North, and both are thereby distorted. How many adults have we heard protest, when they have acted without social awareness or got themselves in a mess, 'But I was only following my feelings'.) Once our child energy solidifies into set positions, then only trivial choices remain open to the adult in us: choice at the 'soap powder' level. Even choosing a friend may be beyond us. As soon as personally significant situations arise, we are arrested by resonances from the fixated responses of our childhood, and we find that we then manifest repetitive patterns of feeling and behaviour. What is more, our autonomic nervous system is stimulated, quite outside the range of conscious ego control, and we feel either that we are driven or that we are paralysed; we seem to be at the mercy of incomprehensible forces, and feel that we cannot help ourselves. Even the law (the social law of the North) pronounces that we are sometimes not responsible for our actions. We simply react, re-en-act our hidden, unconscious commitment to our earliest modes of defence. We are fixed in our past and become beings of diminished responsibility.

The perennial power of fixated responses to hook or divert future flows of energy is revealed, on the more overt level, as anxiety, depression or manic enthusiasm; and choice is effectively annulled. If we hold on to our feelings, imprisoning our responses at the cellular level and betraying our 'water' self that allows free movement of inner energies, then we cannot empty our minds of fixed ideas and beliefs or repetitive thoughts and fears. We are subject to prejudice as adults, and our minds lose their receptivity to new and more fitting ideas. We can neither think nor feel freshly (thought and feeling are merely different aspects of an energetic process and so are continually influencing each other). We cannot come into our adult wisdom; and thus, not only is our very faculty of choice severely curtailed, but our tools of choice are distorted, and the material out of which we form our decisions is all too likely to be unsound. Neurosis is commitment to the outdated.

And so in the North, just when we need to take conscious responsibility for our actions as adult social beings, instead we are all too likely to react. Anti-social acts abound. In the North the victim in us seeks an adult dress, and is liable to manifest as persecutor or rescuer. Both are usually compulsive modes of being. We seldom consciously decide to persecute another (unless given over to a system that has legitimized or proscribed persecutory methods of control, and then we have fallen into inappropriate obedience rather than having exercised conscious choice). We 'find' ourselves persecuting, we are drawn into the persecutor/victim dynamic, and then hastily justify our actions retrospectively, cut off all feelings, or switch to hating and beating up on ourselves.

Rescuers, equally, are not usually in charge of their compassionate or protective acts – they cannot bear another's pain or discomfort, and find they have to act. Many mothers and 'helpers' are caught in this behaviour, and have little choice in the matter. They seldom realize or face how intrusive, how diminishing, or how seductive their 'help' can be. The choices of the adult on the Reactive Wheel are not only very limited but are also liable to be based on self-hate; either valuing others as always more important than self, or punishing others – which also springs from hate of self. And this hate is hardly experienced as choice. Such is the legacy we unknowingly receive when we stifle the responsive child in us.

Choice is so intrinsically part of our nature that we can never entirely negate it. Even when we let ourselves be held in our own past fixations and premature decisions, and have little leeway in the type of relationships we choose, we still plan and deliberate, and decide to act at a particular moment rather than at another. How is it that incest has remained so long in the dark? (As usual much blame is laid on mother for not being more aware and protecting everyone, and little attention is given to the depth of her betrayal, anguish, displacement: the utter upheaval of her whole world that she is expected to deal with the moment she does 'let herself know' the truth. It is a terrible knowing that promises to tear her apart. She is not only a mother.)

Does not father actively employ his ego consciousness to pick his time and place, even while driven by a compulsive urge to act out his desires? Although he may well be out of touch with the level at which he could exercise full choice, he uses great ingenuity to keep the secret. He (or she) was not *just* carried away, even if freedom of choice has been eroded and consciousness clouded and options of expression limited by some devastating frozen response at the primal level. And even then, that frozen response is still a highly personal manifestation, a specific activity of that particular human being. It was he who experienced that response all those years ago, and no one froze it but himself. We do not cease to be responsible beings even if we do appear to ride only on the Wheel of Reactivity.

The Passive Resignation and Refusal of Consciousness of the West

We move now to the Western aspect of self to discover in what way we are likely to bypass responsibility in that direction when once we

Chapter Eight: The Wheel of Victimhood

are caught in the throes of our reactive patterns. Here we can get into full-blown victim mode once more, undisguised by persecutory activity. We can easily slip into resignation and confuse it with dormancy. Dispirited by problems of choice and the anxiety involved in decision-making, we can become entirely passive and allow things simply to happen to us. We can remain in daydreams, in perpetual 'hibernation', having no intention of bringing anything to fruition in the world. We wish to hide in darkness and be absorbed into nothingness. We long to merge with the cosmos and be a universal spiritual being untroubled by mundane problems. This kind of passivity is vastly different from consciously going with the processes of life, allowing and experiencing death and rebirth. It is opting *out* of life, not letting go *into* life. It is a kind of stagnation. Everyone else must do it all, and then we can never get it wrong.

Our unconscious is no longer a rich storehouse of possibilities waiting to be experienced; it becomes, instead, a refusal of consciousness. The light of awareness is neither beamed into its depths nor ready to receive what it spontaneously brings forth, and we are ruled by what we claim we cannot know. We miss our intuitions, and so cannot even attempt to obey them. We do not recognize them. We pronounce ourselves a mystery, not in order to honour our infinite nature but in order that we may remain in ignorance. We do not revel in the dark inner domain of our being which nourishes us and connects us with the source of all things. We feel excused by our complexity rather than challenged by it. Once we refuse consciousness of energies moving forward into the light we can be beset by paranoia, by demons of all kinds, by unbidden images – projection on a grandiose scale takes place. Nothing seems to belong to the entirely passive being because everything is experienced as being done *to* her or him. We are called mentally ill and 'looked after' – perhaps in an institution of some kind where we have even less sense of responsibility. The perfect patient. If we refrain from listening to ourselves and acting on our own behalf, if we refuse obedience to our deep inner self and sink instead into a reluctance to do anything, then we are in great danger of losing our way completely.

The Fanciful Dictator of the East

From this collapse in the West we are unlikely to take the initiative to contact the energy of our Eastern self in a constructive manner. We are sometimes transported there through our dreaming or the dynamic updrift of repressed energy seeking release from its imprisonment; it is not easy to stagnate and stay dormant for ever. (Catatonia is a rare achievement and not often sustained, while spells of depression frequently alternate with manic phases.) Intoxicated by a sudden rush of power, we pick up our energy and our imagination runs wild. Fantasies abound, and we may be fired to transform the world and enter into frenzied adventures. Creativity run amok. Such are the Hitlers and Stalins of this world. They certainly dared; they certainly used their imaginations. They displayed, in their different ways, the shadow of the transformative energy of fire – the frantic desire to actualize their own flights of fantasy in a relentlessly expansive mode.

If we are driven by compulsions arising out of the frozen responses of our childhood, then we are all too likely to distort our determining power into generating destruction – even if only our own. What a sad betrayal of our human freedom occurs when we try to transform the world (or ourselves) out of hate and distaste for 'what is' and a denial of present realities, rather than being willing to enter into the transformative process out of love of life and awareness of its further possible fulfilment – the creative challenge of what 'could be'. Pride, the enemy of the East, must eventually bring about a fall – just as the eagle will fall if he flies too high and ceases to gain nourishment from the earth. Egoistical pride in our determining power is the enemy of freedom, not its friend.

Of course most of us on the Wheel of Reactivity will not venture to such heights in our flip to the East. (Once caught in the reactive path we cannot simply *visit* the East.) Mostly, we attempt to regain our abdicated infant power by actualizing the persecutor or the rescuer in us in some more imaginative or creative form than we were able to give these modes of behaviour in the North. Or we simply escape off the round of life altogether and flee into death.

The Circle of Reactivity only occurs if we opt out of acknowledging our Child Spirit self in the beginning. As soon as we do that, we are prone to annihilation terror and vulnerable to the Victim Archetype. We start our journey from a defensive position and are bound to end up as a wounded child. But we can heal. Once we claim our spirit self we can learn not to be a victim, which, in itself, shows that victimhood does not lie at the centre of our humanity – it is not an essential aspect of being human.

The Distinction between the Circle of Reaction and the Dark Mirrors of the Wheel of Responsibility

Although clearly related, it is important not to equate the victim vicious circle of reaction with the dark mirror of the Wheel of Responsibility. Each direction always offers us a dark and a light mirror – both have a special quality and particular energy, and they are held up together as our teachers. The enemy of responsiveness in the South is the fear which makes us solely responsive to others. The enemy of our choice and decision-making in the North is guilt, vindication and punishment. In fact, the superego could be seen as the dark mirror of the North.

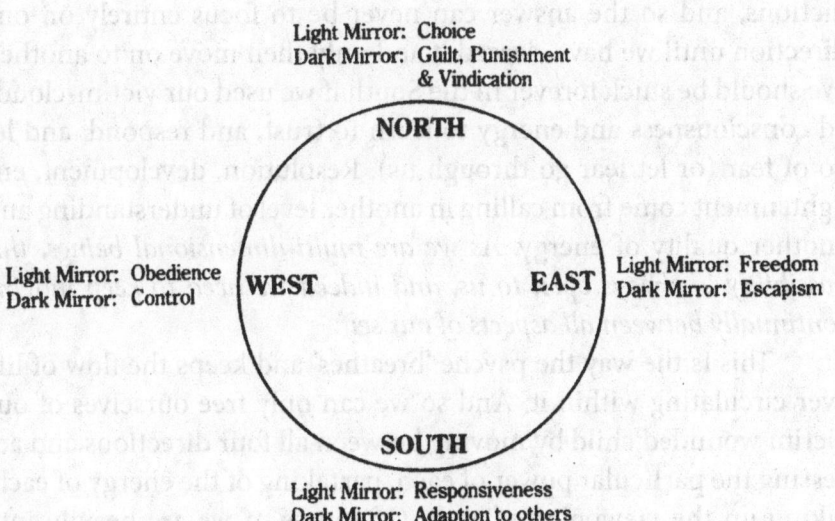

The enemy of obedience in the West is control. If we are busy controlling ourselves then we cannot listen, we cannot hear that which it is fitting to obey. Instead of going with our deep intuitions and obeying our inner voice by calmly stating, 'I will this to be', we are driven to improve ourselves and declare, 'I must do this' or 'This *has* to be done'. The enemy of freedom and creativity in the East is escapism – a refusal to engage appropriately in our earthly reality; the enemy of actualization is avoidance of the ordinary, and attempting to remain 'above it all'. These modes of behaviour may be carried out in a relatively benign or well-intentioned manner, but they take us off centre, expressing a lack of balance, and pulling us away from self-fulfilment.

I will trace the dark mirrors of the Wheel of Responsibility as well as the compulsions of the Circle of Reaction in an example later in this chapter. We can then see how starting with our victim child rather than the spirit child of the East leads to the domination of the Dark Mirrors, and the eventual circling impotence of pure reaction.

Perhaps it is quite evident now that we need all the directions. We can only heal, and be whole, if we view self with and from all aspects of self. Conflicts and contradictions cannot be resolved if we remain in the domain that produces those conflicts or contradictions, and so the answer can never be to focus entirely on one direction until we have cleared it and only then move on to another. We should be stuck forever in the South if we used our victim-clouded consciousness and energy to learn to trust, and respond, and let go of fear (or let fear go through us). Resolution, development, enlightenment come from calling in another level of understanding and another quality of energy. *As we are multi-dimensional beings, this possibility is always open to us, and indeed we need to keep moving continually between all aspects of our self.*

This is the way the psyche 'breathes' and keeps the flow of life ever circulating within it. And so we can only free ourselves of our victim wounded child by moving between all four directions and accessing the particular power of each, partaking of the energy of each, taking up the viewpoint of each. Of course, if we are heavily into victim material, then we can only do this in a diminished manner, but with every visit we touch and are touched by the power of each direction, and more and more of our many layered consciousness is gradually made available to us.

Clearly, we need to deal with what holds us in the past in order to move into the future with the ability to make real choices; but if we still approach our future from the perspective of the past, then we limit the range and quality of those choices. Although they may no longer be set by old frozen responses, they remain within a certain context. We can, perhaps, act more productively, but only within the contained framework of a known understanding of the self and the world. To use the analogy that I mentioned in Chapter 1, we remain 'Newtons' of the psyche and can never discover our 'Einstein' selves.

We can remedy this situation by opening to our West/East axis of spirit *at the same time* as living our South/North axis of substance. The West/East axis recognizes our rooting in the collective source of being, and avails us of the freedom of trans-temporal experience expressed in the present. It gives us a completely different ordering of reality in the light of which we can transform our way of seeing ourselves and our interactions.

The Medicine Wheel thus spells out for us with a simple elegance how, by acknowledging our human beingness 'in the round', by engaging in a continual process of completion, we can escape from the treadmill of the victim/persecutor/rescuer dynamic. Only by extending our context of self-knowledge can we even see what systems of belief and models of reality we are serving and how we could be other than the way we are. Only when sustained by more than the Id, Ego and Super-ego of the South/North axis can we experience enough security and sense of living power and well-being to dare to let go of our ways of grasping at power. Coming from the East/West axis, we can recognize the personal 'story' we have constructed for ourselves and the 'history' that we have collectively woven. We can then evolve utterly new *kinds* of stories and models rather than repeating endless variations of old themes – or, as it seems from my present perspective, one dominant theme. We can at last become 'Einsteins' of our own inner space, and move beyond the power struggles of inequality which characterize the old 'Newtonian' psychological framework. Once we claim our West/East axis, ego domination *cannot* continue, and we are no longer limited to linear causal thinking, though we are still able to utilize it when it is fitting to do so.

The beauty of the human being is that we hold, within ourselves, the necessary meta-position – necessary for extricating ourselves from our conundrums, double-binds and dilemmas. In the East we know of our infinite nature. If we keep re-attending to the realities of our Eastern self, then this knowledge gives us the necessary context within which it is possible to let go of, and move away from, our victim viewpoint. Once we know the self as an original source of energy, then we can experience ourselves in the South as a 'giver of energy' rather than as a wounded child. We discover that we are imbued with an enormous resilience and strength through this very process of giving to and from our true selves. We are strong enough to be vulnerable.

An Analysis of a Classical Victim Situation: Rape

At this point I wish to take up the challenge of the classical victim situation of rape. First I offer a few comments about rape in general, and then I should like to look at the labyrinth of choice and non-choice, and the see-saw of the victim/persecutor dynamic, in a particular example.

Obviously the victim of rape is not responsible on the surface level at which the action occurs. A confusion and distortion of levels takes place when the rapist pleads that his victim really wanted it or asked for it. She (or he) did not want it, nor did she ask for it on the level of the action itself, even if her deep dislike of herself drew towards her a person needing to humiliate a woman, his own energy of humiliation long trapped within his body since some early frozen response, and connecting with hers as he tried, vainly, to regain a sense of his power. Perhaps she was party to attracting and creating a situation in which she could experience the familiar feeling of self-disgust, but she may be utterly horrified and shocked by the mode of action that brought this feeling into play.

It is quite inappropriate to say that she is responsible for the act of rape that she suffered. It is, however, important that she herself look for any connections between her particular way of being and the quality of the event; not in order to blame herself but in order to be in charge of herself, not to judge herself but to see herself. Just because the rapist feels guilty or frightened, in that he knows he took the action, he may be eager to displace this unwanted feeling on to his victim *on the level of the action itself*, and so he claims that she specifically wanted to be raped, at that moment, and by him. Or he could conceivably be boasting.

Another way of fleeing from responsibility for the action he took is to protest that he felt compelled in some way and didn't know what he was doing, blaming his past for messing him up as a person rather than seeking to learn from his past. It is connections that he, also, needs to be looking for, not someone or something to blame.

Of course, if we take action from our wounded infant self parading as an adult, then these actions will inevitably not *feel* like choices, for the persecutor no less than for the victim. The motivation for such actions is not operating at the ego level. The ability to exercise meaningful choice has already been eroded by unconscious allegiance to old fixated responses from the past; and because the experience of choosing lies within the domain of ego – the level at which we concentrate on the notion of causal chains and objectivity – we look outwards, rather than turn our attention inwards to learn of the forces which block or move our being at a deeper level. Genuinely feeling that we were compelled, that we couldn't help ourselves, we look outside ourselves to see who or what could have caused the reprehensible action. As I can't be responsible, he or she or they must be.

The victim in us is always insecure, frightened and dependent, so there is bound to be that attachment to externals and 'flight from self – as well as a hidden 'fight with self' as we block and deny our consciousness. The profound guilt that every abdicated self carries buried within finds expression in an urgent need to 'justify' ourselves; and the more appalling the action, the more elaborate and distanced from reality this process can become. But underneath this facade, the crude dynamic of the Victim Archetype is at work. 'I'm not choosing – I'm an effect', says victim/persecutor. 'But I can't bear being an effect – I deeply know that it is not fitting and that I should be powerful – so I'll get you back.' And so we enter the hate position and punish others, or the resignation position and collapse into being an 'inadequate' human being and wait to be helped or abused.

The overt consequences of the interconnections made on the subtler levels of our being can still be appalling to experience and intensely unwelcome, even if the event was in some sense intended. Here we have a paradox rather than a contradiction, because the whole point is that our deep intention in life is directed towards exploring the meaning of something far more comprehensive than the specific external event in itself. We are unlikely to incarnate intending to rape, or be raped, or go to prison. We incarnate intending, perhaps, to live out victimhood in such a way that we discover that we are more than just an effect after all, or we may intend to reveal the misguided abuse of power. In finding ways of living out these intentions, given our opaque contact with our knowledge of spirit at this stage of evolution, we may get tangled in a web of complex connections, and experience highly unwelcome situations. And so, for instance, our fear of exploitation (which could be an aspect of the challenging task we have set ourselves) may simply resonate with another's fear of exploitation, and each may be drawn to complementary modes of reaction to that fear.

It is an abuse of our humanity to dismiss any level; to say that it doesn't ultimately matter because it is only the explicit end of a more complex happening and deeper things are at work. All levels of our human-beingness have their own validity and must be respected, must be kept distinguishable and not collapsed into each other and thus discounted. They must be held distinct in a living tension that does justice to the extraordinary multi-quality of our being. No level is simply cancelled out just because a subtler level exists, although our experience of it can be altered by consciousness of that subtler level, and full awareness can annul the power to harm that a destructive event carries when our consciousness remains only with the level of that event.

Exposing the Levels of Choice and Non-choice in an Episode of Rape

I should now like to trace the possible choice process of two people involved in an episode of rape – in this instance, between a brother (aged 19 and whom I shall call James) and his younger sister (aged

15 and whom I shall call Susan). All through his adolescence James was taunted by Susan, who was far more intelligent than he was. He felt humiliated to have a younger sister so much brighter than himself, especially when she 'showed him up' in front of his peers. There would be a lot of laughter at his expense, and he felt he had to join in and pretend it was 'just fun'. Although on other occasions he would make the odd nasty comment to Susan, he never expressed his anger and he felt paralysed in his humiliation. He had many fantasies about paying her back. Even if she was brighter and more talented than him, at least he was stronger. He imagined pinning her down and scaring her. He warded off awareness of the sexual overtones in his fantasies, and only admitted to the surge of excitement he felt at the thought of being able to humiliate her. The stored energy of his repressed anger was being offered a channel of release, and the more he fantasized, the more this frustrated energy was mobilized.

The internal pressure became increasingly uncomfortable. He couldn't work out what was happening to him: something was the matter, but he didn't know what. Susan, meanwhile, was perfecting her little barbs. She was enormously vulnerable about her sexuality and feared that she was not attractive. Her father had completely ignored her ever since she had reached puberty, and she felt something must be wrong with her. She had not yet had a boyfriend. She feared that she was 'just' clever.

One night James came home in a very agitated state – he had been out for a night of drinking with his friends and they had taken up Susan's jibes. And then there she was sitting on the sofa, looking prim and scornful. He was suddenly aware that no one else was in the house. Hardly knowing what he was doing he grabbed and shook her. She fought him first with her usual verbal weapons calling him a 'thick thug'. His rage burst in a flood. The more she struggled the more determined he became to overpower her and 'get his own back'. He couldn't understand his own excitement and unexpected energy – anything, *any*thing to humiliate her. In the midst of his frenzy she became strangely passive, frozen. He felt driven to complete the act. He raped her.

Who could say that Susan chose to be raped? Both of them had long been following the shadow Wheel of Responsibility, without looking at its dark mirrors, and so finally got caught in the Circle of Reactivity. From very early in life, Susan responded to others rather than to herself, and found it harder and harder even to recognize her own needs and wants. She was fearful of not being liked and craved approval, although she was also determined to show that 'she couldn't care less'.

It seemed to her that her parents favoured her big brother because he was a boy. He went off and did special things with her dad while she did her homework alone in her room. She could never catch him up, never be in his position. And anyway, the more she grew up, the less her dad had to do with her. She felt helpless – a victim. And then she found that she could get attention through her cleverness and her wit. She now called upon her adult Northern self and chose to use this capacity. Soon, her crafty victim child discovered that she could gain the power of the persecutor if she used this wit to undermine her big brother. The victim in him rose marvellously and unfailingly to the bait. What is more, even his friends began to notice her. However she never found satisfactory release (i.e. true self-expression) because she was using this skill as a weapon, hitting at James when she was really desperately wanting something from her dad and was angry with *him*. Her success was always marred by a vague sense of guilt and a growing dislike of herself. As time went on, she felt *compelled* to jibe at James; she couldn't stop herself. And she disliked herself more and more. She was driven to try and control James and yet felt out of control herself.

By this time, Susan was in a poor position to avail herself of the light mirror of the West and listen to her own inner voice. She ignored her own deep needs and was stuck with her outdated choice of using her quick wit in a negative way in order to make her mark. No longer even attempting to know her true needs, she was caught up in trying to control others. Once in this situation, she could only engage with her Eastern self through escapist fantasy. She spent hours imagining herself to be a totally different person who didn't have any 'horrible traits'. She envisioned a situation in which she didn't have to deal with difficult relationships because she was studying in a special kind of monastery where she was given great love and respect by all the monks. This scene was clearly impossible to actualize – not a creative extension into new possibilities. It was a final abdication of the responsibility to be herself and make choices *as* herself. (Even at this stage, if she had accepted her fantasy as a mirror from which she could learn, then her interaction with her brother could have been a different one. Facing dark mirrors takes us into the light of awareness; allows us to step out of the Circle of Reaction.)

Then one night, James inexplicably attacked her and raped her. She was stunned and shocked, and felt deeply damaged. She had only made the usual kind of remark, so how could this appalling event have befallen her? The familiar guilt and self-disgust were heightened – were somehow fully actualized. Her mother was flooded by her own distraught pain and horror, and Susan felt the centre of a general atmosphere of disgrace. She got attention, even from her dad, as never before. And somehow it was a ghastly kind of *relief* to be a recognized victim – a proper victim. It touched something deep in her, some primal place. How can anyone who is raped be expected to be alright? She could go with that old, familiar, helpless feeling and blame him, blame them all, for what had happened to her. She alternated between waves of terror that shook her entire body and then sudden stunned, blank, stillness. This, too, felt familiar in some vaguely perceived way. She wouldn't have to be responsible for her life any more. Anyone would understand if she was horrible now – especially to James. Life was awful, but at least it sort of 'fitted together' and wasn't her fault.

So of course, Susan did not exercise choice when she was raped. Even her conscious choice to taunt James with her wit had slipped into an automatic reaction and a compulsive need to control. And the freedom of even that choice had always been 'undermined' in the sense that it served a need to put him down that grew out of her lack of responsiveness to herself in her own right. Having lost that, she could then only value herself in relation to others and by comparison with others – a very fragile, elusive means of gaining self-esteem, and likely to generate poor choices. Her persecutory need clearly came from her victim self – from the insecure inner child who, never having claimed a profound-enough vision of her spirit self in the East, had lost the natural responsiveness to her own being. She felt dependent on recognition from her parents, on being the 'special one', and yet also felt helpless and hopeless about attaining this position.

Some would have gone into resignation and become the quiet 'good girl', but with her spirited energy Susan turned to the activity and creativity of cruel wit. As a victim she gained a welcome sense of power through manipulating someone else into that role by engaging as their persecutor. But even with this decision she soon experienced herself once more as a victim: she felt compelled by a dynamic stronger than herself, thus precluding choice.

It was only when her brother suddenly and dramatically switched to persecutor himself, catching her off her guard, that she eventually gave in to resignation and passivity – possibly complying not only because locked in frozen terror but also because the act resonated so strongly with her self-hate. This passivity, however, does not cancel out the act of rape or mean that it was not rape; it does not mean she wanted that specific action imposed on her, nor that she wished it on herself. She did not seek or ask for rape as such: she was genuinely violated by the act, but she was deeply *connected* with it as a happening in her life. It would be utterly misleading to say she caused her rape, but equally misleading to say that she had nothing to do with it.

Note that the example of rape offered here is not intended to be an exemplar case study of rape per se, as a phenomenon. There was certainly no 'grooming' involved. As will be clear from the details above, it was a power struggle between two neglected and insecure teenagers suffering from minimal parenting, and often left alone together in the evening. What the example does do is to illuminate some of the dynamics of victimhood in so far as they play out in an incident of rape.

We can see how a crude causal theory would cut across the living process of a dynamic, multi-layered reality by demanding judgement and, thus, a concrete division into fixed victim and persecutor positions. Either innocent or guilty; a pure nonsense when attempting to honour the fullness of our human functioning. Such decisions, such judgements, can only be applied meaningfully to the surface level of manifest action, which is the appropriate level for the operations of the law and social control. The making of judgements therefore needs to be ritualized, marking it as a social event and displaying the specific and limited nature of the activity. Unless we are a dedicated behaviourist, we cannot be referring to the whole person when we make such judgements, although it is also clear to whom we are referring. We human beings are infinitely more than our actions on the explicit level. These form the tip of the iceberg, and they matter enormously; but we cannot judge what we cannot see. Socially agreed action of some kind may need to be taken in relation to those actions which are offensive in some way, but to be orientated against another person in their whole being is to set ourselves against our own form of being – our own humanity.

In this exploration of the different levels of choice and responsibility, I have not yet referred to the source of Susan's particular expression of victimhood; those formative frozen responses of her infant Southern self. We can only access those through the process of a deep inner excursion of some kind because they are buried in our cellular consciousness and not immediately available to ordinary ego consciousness. (This process will be dealt with more fully in Chapter 10.) Clusters of beliefs and thoughts and feelings, themselves held by an interlocking resonance of energies, keep our primal organismic responses in a state of fixation – reminding the body to hold firm in a certain position and continue a specific mode of breathing. These clusters of old beliefs and feelings are also concealed below the functioning of our everyday awareness. As they have become automatic generators or programmers of our further thoughts and feelings, they are the last thing we think to look at – it is rather like trying to look behind our own eyes. We have to let go of ego consciousness and allow other aspects of our consciousness to emerge, if we would know of our organismic 'decisions'.

What about James? He clearly felt himself to be the victim of his sister's persecutory behaviour. But in order to be so vulnerable to her, he must have long been tailoring his responses to others, rather than being responsive to his own unique being. He had learnt years ago to block his feelings – especially hurt and anger – and pretend to feel what he was not really feeling. He had become highly adaptive, and didn't trust himself, gauging his self-worth only by how others saw him. Coming into adulthood with much fear, hurt and anger locked within him, he felt lost and uncertain about the process of making choices and decisions.

He was anxious to be seen in a favourable light. He was always nice (except for the occasional remark in private to his sister, whom he had grown to hate) and tried to be good fun. He was aware that his parents liked him, but after all, they were his parents and so they didn't really count. Anyway, it was only because he was cheerful and polite. He consciously chose to act this way in an effort to make up for his lacks; he sensed their disappointment in his poor academic achievement. Nothing much was said, but plenty was implied – the general atmosphere was often heavy with their anxiety about his future. So he tried to laugh when he was hurt, smile when he was angry, fool around when he was frightened. These modes of behaviour all too soon became automatic reactions, out of his control. He *had* to be the 'pleasant chap' – his sister was the shrew. He became passive and resigned, and began to put on weight. He couldn't help not being clever – he couldn't help anything.

James had no sense of obeying his deeper needs or intuitions. He was so busy keeping his act together that he dare not explore below the surface. Only in his fantasy world did he fully come alive; only then was he fired with energy. Here, he would dare to be active and aggressive. Little did he know how close to his everyday reality his fantasies were, how all too easily they could be actualized. The 'nice guy' suddenly exploded into action, overwhelmed by the pressure of his unlived feelings. He had been humiliated just once too often. However, in the midst of his excitation and agitation he was also fully aware that his parents were out. His adult Northern self registered, in a practical fashion, that it was a 'good' moment to do something. And so he gave in to the process of release, he allowed his long-refused feelings and the dark unacknowledged energies of his unconscious Western self to merge with the actualizing energy of his realistic fantasies. His whole history lay behind his act. It was not a 'free' choice.

James had no conscious control of his actions because he had long ago suspended his spontaneous responsive mode of being, become locked in programmed reactions, and thereafter allowed the larger part of his inner life to remain unknown and unexplored. He had attempted, as do so many of us, to live life from 'the tip of the iceberg' of the self; and if we do that, if we attempt to give all our power and all our consciousness only to that visible tip, then we render that very tip impotent. The ego cannot be called upon for the exercising of fitting conscious choice or control of our actions once it has been split off from the massive 'bulk' of motivating creative energy within the self, and denied familiarity with the more profound aspects that underlie it. A split self cannot help but be lost; cannot help but be overwhelmed, eventually, by the forces that are imagined not to exist – or else dimly sensed but kept tightly tethered. *We can never be a free self, making meaningful choices and able to regulate our actions, unless we have a concept of self that extends beyond the 'tip' – beyond rational ego consciousness.* Of course, a purely ego-based self is determined by external events – whether external by way of arising from deep inner terrain excluded from any direct connection with the ego, or external in the usually understood sense of the physical world in which the individual resides. The behaviourists and cognitive psychologists are correct within their own frame of reference.

And yet it was *his* act; James, himself, had acted thus. It was an act which involved both choices and reactions that were his alone. Who else could be responsible for the action but himself? We can see here how if only he had accepted his initial feelings of anger and hurt without judging them as bad or silly, if only he had expressed them as they arose in the appropriate circumstances and at a manageable 'voltage', then this destructive act would never have taken place. Destructive of self and other; they always go hand in hand. If we continue to reject the feelings which we regard as bad, refusing to give acceptance to the life energy within us, then we end up performing acts which are judged as evil.

Even at a later stage, if James had faced that he wanted to humiliate his sister in the most powerful way open to him, if he could have let himself know that a part of him even wanted to rape her, then he could have chosen not to do so. The less he condemned himself for having such a disturbing desire, the more he could have looked into that dark mirror and seen what he needed to see; the less he judged himself, the sharper his capacity for discernment and the more in charge of his actions he would have been.

Acceptance of self, compassion for self, is our greatest protection and our greatest liberator. Our fear of being 'bad' brings about the very thing we dread. We do indeed create our reality – even when we are not consciously choosing such a reality in the conventionally understood sense. (Note that we cannot in fact create our reality from our ego consciousness alone, and neither can ego take full responsibility for it. An imagined ego-self will always be a victim self.) Self-acceptance, made possible by an acceptance of the full nature of the self, is ultimately the only safe path; love of self the only fitting foundation for human(e) interaction and relationship.

So, we *can* be victims on a surface level, just as we can be persecutors. There is clearly a sense in which we can hold the rapist more responsible than the raped for the action of rape, or the torturer for the action of torture upon the tortured. But if we could extend our consciousness and encompass the whole of their being, we would then see the two participants connecting in different configurations of energy. And if we are still determined to organize and punctuate our understanding of interactions around the terms 'victim' and 'persecutor', we shall find that someone who is a victim on one level will be a persecutor on another, and a victim again on yet a further level. Was not Hitler one of the greatest victims of all time, as well as the greatest persecutor? He was completely at the mercy of his own fearful prejudices and obsessions and thus set for self-destruction. And did not James and Susan take it in turns to be victim and persecutor, performing a 'dance' of mutually exchangeable positions *on different levels*? The victim James became persecutor, and returned to victim again when he had to suffer punishment for his crime.

As noted earlier, the case described in the section above relates to a particular incident, showing the way in which the dynamics of victimhood can illuminate the relational dynamics at play. It is important to emphasize that in no way is it intended to be an exemplar case applying to all instances of rape. There are circumstances where, for instance, grooming is involved, and especially where it involves child abuse we can indeed find true victims. The latter requires and involves different considerations.

Chapter Eight: The Wheel of Victimhood

Sexual Abuse, Grooming, and the Real Victims

Bullying and sexual abuse in public school boarding houses has been known to occur, but an area where silence has often reigned is on the shocking prevalence of sexual abuse within families. In earlier times this was never acknowledged or discussed in even the most holistic therapies.

The despicable thing is the clever manipulative 'grooming' that goes on in order that their victim comes to believe that they are co-creators in this horrible thing that is happening to them. Treats, sweets, taking young children shopping for pretty dresses or a football or for 'nice' drives in the countryside. All this done so as to transfer the abuser's heartless shame on to the terrified and confused and lonely recipient. Of course they are then highly unlikely to tell anyone, as the abuser well knows. No wonder they very often manage to repress it completely and forget that it ever happened, forever scarred and left battling with its consequences.

Such people are real victims. Profound harm has been willingly done to them, and they have absorbed his share as if it were their own and it is they who had somehow caused it all to happen. How could they deal with such skilful manipulation? And the worse the abuse, the less they can dare to tell anyone.

As time goes on, some abusers even use occasions such as extended family holiday get-togethers – the participants knowing nothing, and being utterly ignorant of the enforced secret between the abuser and their prey, and very likely enjoying his charm and humour. Laughing at his jokes while he slips in a sly wink at her. A horrible kind of bond.

The holiday becomes a ghastly ordeal rather than a welcome break, as far as their unfortunate victim is concerned. Plus the dread of how to cope with all the holidays to come. Some abusers get almost intoxicated by their success, and become ever-more confident that they can get away with whatever they want. And their subtle reminders that it all did indeed happen can continue for a long stretch of time. It lurks within them unexplored.

Once locked in by this awful grooming process, the level of his sexual acts will escalate, becoming ever-more overtly sexual during their secret meetings. And the worse the abuse, the less the victim dares tell anyone. And it is all being inflicted by her or his own father, grandfather or uncle. Who can she possibly turn to for help? Certainly not her mother. That most fundamental relationship will be deeply affected, and will never feel quite the same again. In fact, it is a primal wound – the Wound of Abandonment. (It is helpful if, when an adult, Primal Therapy is undertaken.)

Unfortunately, the methods used to repress such suffering, or divert its effects, result in other problems for the victim in their efforts to create benign contact with others who have nothing to do with the abuse. However, I know people who have triumphed in spite of all these woundings, but only if, at some point in their adult life, they seek to find a therapist who knows that whatever they might have intuited, they must develop a good and trusting relationship while they deal with their client's current concerns.

Much of their further work will be about how to deal with the fact that they are very likely to be burdened with Obsessive Compulsive Disorder (OCD) and Post Traumatic Stress Disorder (PTSD) which will be affecting so many of their interactions and decisions – ceaselessly having to monitor these symptoms and work out how to temper them. This is especially the case when they arise during family interactions with their partner and their children and others who are really important to them, such as close friends or their boss at work; people who are significant in their lives who they do not wish to alienate.

Paradoxically, the result can be that they become extra skilled at relating because so much thought and consideration is given to how not to impose themselves on other people in a burdensome way – when it is best to stand back as well as when to seek connection.

But most important of all is their choice of a partner: if possible, someone sound and reliable and really committed to them and the well-being of their children, but who has also coped well with their struggles, with their particular wounds, now nourished by the love between them. And then there are always the mundane things like handling their daily chores.

The seed of love, that I believe lies within us all but certainly does need watering, can truly flower. Victims can overcome their victimhood.

The Importance of Understanding Guilt in Its Social Context

Moving on now to the important issue of guilt, certain acts sometimes require to be publicly named by society as bad, but it serves no one to declare, at the same time, that whole person to be bad. If defined in this way, then he or she is all the more likely to perform more bad actions. Furthermore, the judgement of 'guilty' needs to be seen as a social event, a technical legal label, not as a pronouncement of full and sole responsibility for an event. It refers to a specific act performed by a specific person, and that act is judged to be unacceptable. But if that person enters into a state of guilt that contaminates all levels of their being and brings about a fixed position of self-hate, if the 'guilty' person indulges in endless beating up on themselves and decides that they are thoroughly reprehensible in every way, then they will never be able to act well. They will never experience that sense of well-being from which creative actions flow. Perhaps, also, they may sense that something does not ring true, and they will be filled with forbidden resentment. This self-flagellation is no road to virtue or redemption – it is a diversion and a *cul-de-sac*.

Once we are busy demonstrating that we know that we are bad, then we are unlikely to see clearly exactly what it is that we have done, and who we really are. Paradoxically, such guilt renders us unable to take fitting responsibility for the very act which we are making such a fuss about. The energy of total condemnation brings about a reactive denial in us – a preoccupation with vindication, even while heaping blame on ourselves. We are absorbed in self-conflict, quite unable to be still and allow ourselves to see our actions for what they truly are. Self-awareness is unlikely if we know that we will not accept the contents of that awareness. Committed honesty requires an ambience of deep compassion towards oneself; it is this combination of honesty and compassion that forms the most favourable ground for discovering and facing exactly what we are responsible for – and what we are not responsible for. We cannot take responsibility for, or from, some vague guilty sense of wrong-doing; we require to know as precisely as possible what it is that we are claiming as ours. We need to discern, as well, where the boundary of our responsibility lies, so that we don't inflate with self-hate and take over the domain of other peoples' feelings and actions.

I have found in my own experience, as well as in my experience of others, that we can only fully recognize the unacceptability of some action that we have performed if we, at the same time, know ourselves to be an intrinsically acceptable being. Does not every incarnated being have a right to be in the world? Ruthless honesty is only possible from a place of love. Guilt and overall self-condemnation are our greatest and most common enemies, as we endeavour to contend with the complex process of learning to be responsible. For we do, at this stage of our development, have to *learn* it. As long as we are dominated by the energy of the Victim Archetype, taking full responsibility for our lives is bound to be a struggle and a relatively rare achievement. Only when freed of its grip will the Wheel of Responsibility, still carrying both light and dark mirrors, turn easily for us as a species.

Labelling people as victims or persecutors releases no one. Rescuing victims and condemning persecutors likewise releases no one, although such activities may provide temporary relief and necessary protection on a practical level. Such an approach, being based on reactive behaviour, cannot lead to freedom or fulfilment. We must dare to find another way of viewing ourselves and others.

****

It may well be thought that I have side-stepped the real challenge that incest poses to the question of choice by picking an episode of sibling incest rather than one between parent and child. Of course the greater the imbalance of power (and the reality of material dependence), the more profound the consequences are likely to be if that power is abused. The difficulty is that the issue of 'child abuse' is so disturbing – so highly charged – that it is almost impossible to write about it without either causing offence or generating misunderstanding. I wish, however, to share an observation. I have noticed that those who have suffered abuse as a child seem to achieve real healing when they manage to contact the true energy of the experience *from their own point of view*. This may be pure terror and disgust – especially if violence and threats are involved – but it may possibly include pleasure.

The fact that this is likely to greatly increase the confusion and distress of the child does not cancel out that pleasure. The child can feel not only impotent but powerful (the special one) and, if the sexual contact is gentle and sensitive, may even be angry and hurt when the interaction suddenly stops. An aspect of the silent and unspeakable agony can be that a loved one inexplicably cuts off all intimacy, and retreats.

Recognizing the occurrence of these emotions in no way validates the irresponsible acts of the parent or adult; but if we are wishing to be of help to the abused child, then it is far more important to respect and affirm the actual reality of her or his experience, *whatever* that might be, than it is to pour the focus of our attention on the inappropriate or appalling behaviour of the other person in the interaction. In our desire that the child should not carry the guilt of the parent, we can collude with the negation of their own living energy: only with acknowledgement of that energy – by going *with* it – can the child free her- or himself from the tangle of confusion and pain centred around the forbidden happening.

The starting point of release, of healing, is our *own* reality, not that of another. It is our own energy that can move us on, aided by an overview and understanding of the whole context of the interaction, which can be gained at any time after the event. In our concern for the pain of the child, we can get lost in condemnation of the parent and thus leave the child isolated yet again. All that has then altered is that which is considered unspeakable.

Chapter Nine

The Dynamics of Power

I see the distinctive power of the human being in terms of a readiness to access and consciously employ our life energy – to both trust and allow its unfolding, as well as to take actions which enhance our fulfilment as a whole and undivided (individual) self. This naturally *entails* an open and sensitive awareness of both other selves and the shared context in which we live. Thus, our willingness to embrace our personal power contributes to the evolution of the whole species in conscious relationship with all life forms. Only when we are willing to choose what leads to our personal and collective development and completion can we be said to be partaking of our full human power. Power without intelligence is not human, not humane.

And so our power rests on our ability to trust – to know when to allow and when to 'do' – and thus *we become powerful through a commitment to increasing awareness* and the capacity to know what gives us true security. In fact, power could be seen as the ability to feel secure – at ease as a being in the universe. We come into this power through acknowledging spirit as the source of our being; and gaining increasing freedom from fear and release from blaming, it becomes possible to discover the reality of choice and to know ourselves as the creators of our experience. The distortion of power – power 'over' others – stems from insecurity, and generates insecurity. Those who engage in power games have lost their power – the power to generate a state of well-being – and are trying to regain it. They display the tactics of the impotent who play at being omnipotent.

The Initial Collusion of Infant and Mother: Impotence and Protectionism

If, as a species, we are to handle our power appropriately, then we must find the seed of our insecurity. We must look to our starting point as a human being; the relationship of Infant and Mother at the archetypal level.

Arising out of our incomplete state of evolution, the story of human development has been profoundly complicated by a debilitating collusion at this very level. Both Infant and Mother have been pouring their energy into a self-perpetuating illusion: they have been lending their power to a suffocating alliance of impotence and protectionism. In earlier chapters I explored the notion that the infant who forgets its own wholeness in spirit, becoming focused purely on its biological reality, cannot help but feel utterly dependent on mother and at the mercy of her process – whatever that may happen to be. The 'all-powerful' mother, for her part, is also rendered powerless, powerless to be who she needs to be. She must serve her child. He gives his power to her, and she gives her power to him. A tangled mess of impotence. Just as the infant's life depends on the mother's response, so the mother's life depends on the infant's response – on how well he feeds off her. Rejection of mother eventually becomes essential. Defiance is the only path to self-definition. And we accept this as normal.

A 'blameless' mother is no more the causal agent of her child's psyche than an inadequate or reluctant mother. When we encounter an even reasonably individuated person, we experience how inappropriate it would be to attribute their way of being to their mother. Indeed, it is very hard to tell what their mother must have been like. Ponder on the Archetypal Individual – Christ. The qualities of Mary have been guessed at and lauded for centuries, but never has it been suggested that they included the power to cause her son to be the way he was. He unfolds, rather, from his knowledge of his inner divinity. Even a perfectly loving and willing mother *cannot* take responsibility for the *essential* well-being of her child. It is an abuse of that unique, living being, that unique channel of spirit, even to attempt to do so, and a denial of the principle of distinction which is the essence of material form.

It is desirable that the infant get physical protection, but not psychic protectionism. Psychic protectionism is not only unnecessary for essentially whole spiritual beings, but also death to their freedom. So even as we demand this protection in our fear, so we rail at her in fury for moulding us. As soon as we imagine that someone outside ourselves is wholly responsible for us, we lose our unique path. No wonder we are so full of rage: we have betrayed our very selves. We exchange our birthright of creative freedom for a state of passivity. We set up the life-script of 'being looked after' – looked after on all levels – creating, in turn, misguided 'looking after', including flight into neglect, from one generation to another. We need to end this confusion and collusion.

Infanthood is a collective responsibility. We are all infants, and our collective experience goes to inform and form future infants. If we would alter the length and strength of our initial period of forgetfulness of spirit and start physical life knowing that we are a whole entity in our own right, then we must begin to feed new and different ideas into our Collective Conscious and Unconscious.

If mothers knew themselves as whole beings – and acknowledged that they always had been – then they would regard their infant children as such, and the collusion between them would dissolve. We must water the seed of a new archetype – the Archetype of Self-generation; and in the mean time, we need to bring into consciousness, without self castigation, our present involvement with the Victim Archetype. If we recognize its workings within us, on both profound and trivial levels, then we shall begin to loosen its hold over us. Every time we state 'I couldn't help it', we are partaking of its energy. Compassionate awareness, on a day-to-day basis, of its power to organize our thinking and feeling (and therefore our decisions and actions) will, in itself, lessen its power. Perhaps there will then come a time when our Collective Infant Consciousness can say, 'Yes, mother, look after my baby bodily needs and, if you cannot, then let another do so, or I must let go and take new form. But I will not trap you in the task of *making everything right for me* as, indeed, I must do if I know myself as only body. If I trap you, then I trap myself.' The trapped infant enters the agony of resentful dependence and inevitable betrayal, while life slips, only partly known, through its grasping fingers, as it evades connection with the true source of its being.

Powerlessness and Violence

The resultant experience of powerlessness calls forth violence: violent actions uncoil, often when least expected, from the depths of this hidden infant impotence. *What is violence but fear combined with frustrated life and freedom?* And then, as a society, we attempt to counter violence by means which actually raise that fear level and that frustration of creative expression.

It is important not to be unnerved by the fact of violence in the world, responding with despair by 'giving up' on the human race and cutting ourselves off from its socio/political arrangements. Perhaps we need to remind ourselves that there are billions more people walking, digging, pottering, sleeping, chatting at any given moment than there are people actively engaged in violent acts. Violence is a minority happening. There is always far more peace in the world than war. It is just that hearing of people sweeping the floor or watching someone sitting sewing does not count as news.

I have deliberately not tried to balance shocking events with those of heroism or altruism. When we come to think about it, is not ordinary 'getting on with life' the norm in both rich and poor countries alike? Although violence may stem from the most primary of all life positions – the abdication of the Self and the fearful dependence that results from that abdication – it is not, in itself, a primary emotion. It arises from a combination of other emotions. It is not an intrinsic part of human nature. It is, rather, a habitual response to the *denial* of our human nature. Were we no longer to perform acts of violence against our fellow creatures, we should not, therefore, be less human.

During this time of evolutionary transition, as we live through the period of informing our collective infanthood with a new consciousness and until we create a more fulfilled and complete Infant Archetype, we cannot avoid some of the troublesome consequences of our confused state. We have to live with them and learn to handle them as best we can, knowing that more fulfilling modes of interaction are unquestionably possible.

If a sense of powerlessness, and thus fear, lies at the source of our acts of violence, then our focus needs to be on providing conditions of safety; safety for *all* participants in a given interchange. A common 'safety net' is what is needed, which takes account of the fear present in us all at this stage of our evolution; which enables us to recognize and accept this fear, rather than scorn it and be ashamed of it, and cloak it with bravado. We must learn not simply to *react* to the *aggression* displayed in much defensive behaviour, however provocatively it is portrayed, remembering always the fear from which it springs; acknowledging our shared fear and our shared need for safety. It helps no one, ultimately, if one person or group attempts to feel safe at the expense of the other's sense of security – or dignity.

Equally, the frustrated life energy held in those who feel powerless, which then escapes in a violent form, needs to be recognized and supported, and not condemned along with the violent act: legitimate and appropriate means of expression must be sought. In any situation of violent confrontation, what is called for is a sharpening of awareness, not a closing against others; an appreciation of the *whole system* of the interaction, rather than an escalation of the divisions and oppositions. Our usual reactions actually increase, not decrease, the level of fear, insecurity and humiliation in those already plagued by their experience of powerlessness. Only with a more comprehensive awareness can we utilize our creativity to find ways, fitting to the living situation, of engendering a greater level of safety and respect for *all* concerned: the conditions that make it possible to truly see and hear each other.

Avoidance of humiliation was not sought, for example, in the case of Germany after the First World War, leaving that defeated nation ready ground for the boosting, purposeful nationalism of Adolf Hitler. 'Face-saving' is an art we would do well to develop if we wish to ease international conflict. The more aggressive the trouble-maker, the more dangerous it is to humiliate that person (or group or nation), and yet the more determined we usually become to do just that. If only we would find the grace to evolve rituals that allow for honourable withdrawal from an interaction, following our innate animal wisdom rather than the logic of the ego that seeks to bully bullies. As long as we view power and security in terms of promoting fear and diminishing our opponents' sense of worth, we are unlikely to live in safety.

A commitment to reduce fear and a willingness to devise fitting ways of preserving dignity could do much to improve international relations, whereas political rebellion within any one nation may more often require an understanding of the 'rebel' need for recognition and opportunities for personal expression. When those holding a monopoly of power judge disadvantaged members of their society who take up arms as intrinsically violent, reacting to them on the basis of that judgement rather than hearing their cry for life and freedom, then violent actions are perpetuated all around. But most important of all, the more we experience that we are whole in ourselves, the less shall we seek to fuse into tight groupings and nations. And the less we identify with, and seek to defend, fixed groupings, the more we are liberated to see the obvious: that we are each part of a whole world system.

The Difference between Taking Responsibility and Taking the Blame

An incomplete self will always be driven by a need for power; not knowing it in itself, it is bound to imagine that it is to be found in others. With no living sense of self-potency, we can only experience power through the victim/persecutor/rescuer mode: either others have power over us, or we have power over them. If, either on the personal level or the political and international level, we continue to think it sensible to gain security by making others insecure, by attempting to render them powerless and experience themselves as powerless, then we merely encourage despair and fury. And so we engender yet more dependence, more resentment, more blaming. Blaming goes on all down the line. Children blame parents and parents children; husbands blame wives and wives, husbands; one nation blames other nations; one religious sect blames another religious sect – on, and on, and on the blaming goes, so often supported by 'good' reasons. And so we play out our long and painful history of victimhood.

Blame-obsessed human beings can also turn from blaming to 'taking the blame'. But 'taking the blame' is not the same thing as taking responsibility. In fact, it merely encourages others not to take *their* responsibility. Absorbing blame, we become like a 'black hole' in which anyone can dump their rubbish, instead of dealing with it themselves and learning what they need to learn from their actions. We cancel out the beingness of others when we take the blame, as well as drawing unwanted debris on to ourselves, to the confusion of all participants in an interaction. It is a travesty to confuse love and compassion with taking the blame ourselves.

Taking responsibility means no more passing the buck – or accepting the buck. It means seeing how we fit into the pattern of the whole Gestalt, seeing the connections between different aspects of our experience, and how we plait them into a strand of being and action – and, in so doing, generate ourselves. This appreciating of connections is a creative activity; participating in such consciousness we create a sense of who we are. If we trace and follow connections rather than pounce on causes, then we begin to really know of our self-generating nature: we gradually and increasingly lose our feeling of powerlessness, and erode our old belief and investment in our victimhood.

If we have been assaulted many times, for instance, we no longer get absorbed in accusing or excusing our assaulters, nor do we draw on ourselves the responsibility for the joint event as if the other person did not exist as a being in their own right. Having acknowledged our feelings of fear, pain and anger, and having given expression of some kind to these inner energies, we then look to see if we could have steered our life otherwise, or how we could have behaved more fittingly. We note what familiar emotions are being evoked and what resonances from the past – what old patterns and themes – pull us into dangerous situations; what signs we ignored in our fear or need. We open ourselves to see what could render us more able to deal with such interactions in future. We determine not to be assaulted again.

At the most fundamental level, taking responsibility means unlocking from our initial collusion with mother. As a species we need to come of age, and leave our infant state of psychological development behind. We do this not by trying to be grown-up, not by attempting to curtail our infanthood, but by knowing that we are full beings from the start; by knowing our infant self as spirit carrier and determiner of its own experience; by knowing the infant-in-us-all is prior to mother, as spirit is prior to matter. In that knowing, we know that the era of victimhood, as a basic mode of human relating, is unnecessary and need be no more. It also implies letting go of a purely sequential developmental model of the psyche – a model bestowed on us by ego consciousness and deeply imprinted on our thinking from concentrated observance of our purely biological growth.

The Archetype of Self-generation is an archetype that makes no divide between our infant self and our mature being: from its perspective, age is irrelevant; childhood is not some separate state; and children are not creatures of another kind requiring specialized treatment. Such an archetype would be a guiding structure within the psyche for the entire span of the embodied self, uniting the phenomenon of the unfolding multi-dimensional human being in one continuous process of individuation.

Psychology as Prior to Sociology and Politics

If infant is prior to mother, so also is psychology prior to sociology and to political thinking. Victims can all too convincingly appear to exist on the secondary level, the socio-political level. That is exactly why it is imperative that we explore the primary level: so that we can free ourselves from generating a victim mentality and thus a victim 'reality' – and, indeed, a victim morality. The more we see ourselves as an 'effect', the more we are, in fact, effected. We need to be aware of the processes that underlie our sense of helplessness and fuel our tireless search to pin down something or someone to hold responsible. We have to get deeper than the socio-political level while, at the same time, serving that level as best we can; neither ignoring it nor imagining that we are somehow 'above' it. Spiritual snobbery contributes nothing to human development. It is precisely because the political level matters so much that we must also go deeper than the political level. We have to get to the non-victim self in each of us.

We can be very complacent about our 'Western Democracy' and imagine that we have reached political maturity. But democracy is obstructed as long as voters are victims – as long as we blame the 'other lot' and think only in the short term; both marks of immaturity. Our infant psyches, dominated by ego, want our private needs fulfilled *now* – we cannot tolerate the frustration of postponement. Anything immediately irksome, however necessary for our long-term welfare, removes a government from office. It is therefore considered unrealistic! Politicians, feeling at the mercy of their electorate while at the same time being dedicated to remaining 'in power', can hardly be expected to present the truth. Voters no longer know what they are voting for. Eventually, few, in a victim culture, experience meaningful choice, however enlightened the form of the constitution. Resorting to old party allegiances and set ways of voting, set ways of using the hard-won opportunities of freedom, we are hardly free. Are we wise enough to vote in our own true interests? Only when we have let go of our addiction to victimhood. The non-victim self would never vote for an exploiter or persecutor (nor, indeed, for a saviour). The non-victim self would never grab power by force or pour energy into devising ways of manipulating others, because it would be secure in its own power. Healthy political activity, humane societies, depend on freeing ourselves from the unconscious grip of the Victim Archetype.

But most serious of all, if we continue to experience ourselves as a victim of mother, then we shall retaliate by victimizing 'Mother Earth'. We shall savage the world outside us as long as we believe that the world outside us *should* be fulfilling our every whim and giving us exactly what we want, whenever we want it, as our natural right. A primal state of blaming passivity leads to exploitation when, eventually, we stir to action. Caught in the energy of revenge, we not only destroy our means of sustenance, but fail to perceive the nourishment that all the time is there for us to draw upon, if we would but live in responsive and responsible mutual respect.

The more we alter our assumptions and re-base our understanding at a fundamental level, the more we are able to approach the obvious problems of our human existence in a new way. We are not then paralysed by hopeless resignation. Nor are we caught up in a false belief that the solutions lie in merely stepping up, or seeking to develop, our present modes of operation: something that we all too often witness and support on the political level of human engagement. With a fresh perspective we are energized. We are freed from the automatic and fruitless extension of both our internal and external defence systems, as well as from our attempts to validate our entrenched defensive stance. Only a more complete way of seeing ourselves, of experiencing our self, can begin to relax our absorption with the refinement and maintenance of inner and outer modes of control and relieve us of our insistent vindication of this focus. Only then can the gaining and giving away of power ease from its central role in personal and social interaction, allowing space for the transformative dynamic of an alternative force, that we also know something of but dare not trust: love.

Willing consciousness is what is needed, and contemplation on the possible source of our beginnings, rather than slipping into mere regression and infant impotence. We need to shift our viewpoint so that we can approach our human predicament in a new way. We can reframe our reality by seeing *ourselves* differently at a primary and fundamental level. To this purpose I invite you to play with, to entertain and consider, the theory that I outlined in Chapter 4. We creatures, with our highly developed brains, need to be able to account for our incredibly unintelligent, shortsighted and wayward behaviour without losing faith in ourselves; without sinking into cynicism, escapism or despair. Perhaps, in our age, we require a 'rational' myth – a myth which is firmly grounded in our biology while still drawing on the infinite and mysterious.

Primal Self-betrayal and the War within

To recap: the elongation of our necessary biological bias at conception, the forgetting and disclaiming of our natural potency and wholeness, lead to our complete rather than partial dependence on mother; an all-embracing dependence on mother as if she were responsible for our entire mode of being. As we are not, and cannot be, the sole focus of *her* being, she is bound to 'fail' us in some way or other. We are not the centre of her universe, however doting she is – nor her immediate access to life. She has her own unique journey to make, which includes her relationship with her child but which cannot be the same as that of her child. (Indeed when a mother tries to make her child her life, she confuses the relationship yet further.) Any 'failure' of hers then places us in the 'done to' or victim position, and our energy is diverted into blame and manipulation. This stunts our growing at a most vital period of our development when growth is most fresh and rapid. A small diversion at this period of infancy shows forth an enormous distortion in the adult. It is then all too easy to condemn human nature itself, and fall prey to a sense of meaninglessness.

Is this not how dictators like Adolf Hitler develop? Wasn't Hitler eaten up by a need for power over others and a suitable cause to blame? Overactive egos are a desperate cover for a deep fear of impotence and dislike of our own self-mutilation; an abortive grasping at the freedom we have mislaid. He was an exaggerated case of an everyday phenomenon: the fury of the unaccepted self. He displayed, in extreme form, the projected suspicion and distrust of the 'other' that arises from primal self-betrayal. We never really can forgive ourselves for this. Self-hate lies at the root of our hate of others, and underneath all inflated egos, an energetic rejection of self attempts to stay in hiding.

The human race pays dearly for the prolonged eclipse of the knowledge of our eternal spiritual potency. Our primal reaction to the subsequent fear of annihilation sets up a pattern of resistance to other powerful inner movements and, eventually, to change itself. We become fixated on the goal of 'no change'. Are we not in love with sameness, with fusion? Is not our libido orientated towards the womb? We are ever susceptible to the pull of the familiar, and become creatures of habit. Having frozen our system in an attempt to block our fear, we distrust the movements of our own life energy and pour our creativity into devising modes of defence. As soon as suitable modes are achieved, we have little inclination to let go of them, and only update them when pressed.

From very early in our personal histories, we are in a state of siege; we are 'naturally' neurotic. Once feelings themselves become regarded as potential enemies that need vigilant censoring, we take up a defensive stance, also, towards the world that evokes such feelings. Our bodies and psyches, geared to tamper with the passage of troublesome feelings, come to lose that most necessary flexibility of response to the ever-changing movement of life both within and outside us. Encapsulating our fear, we use much of our remaining energy in elaborating ways and means of manipulating temporary, ephemeral security – initially from an ever-failing mother and later from a larger and equally failing environment. This inevitable failure fuels further blaming. We resent the very person we most need to love. In more recent times we have come to expect this critical resentment, and regard it as perfectly natural when it becomes crudely explicit in adolescence; when mother is hated for still mattering so much, even as we now openly declare, in new-found adult words, how useless she is. Because in our society we have decided that we 'understand' this phenomenon, we ride it fairly easily. When it reappears in marriage or in partnerships, however, it is a different story – we feel devastated. The more we blame, the more we spoil our relationships, the more we taint our interactions, and thus we diminish the quality of the very environment that we require for our nourishment. The more we blame, the more we hate ourselves and expect to be hated by others. And so we blame some more. It all feels so unfair. We know something is wrong. It must be *their* fault. Aren't they the powerful ones? No wonder we have a world so easily dominated by the victim/persecutor dynamic when the Victim Archetype reigns supreme in the underworld of our unconscious being.

Exploitation of others springs from our fear of the pseudo-impotence remembered from infancy and the primal hunger that arises from our initial abdication of self. Such hunger is insatiable. What is outside us will always fail as a replacement for our essence. No socio-political system can work, humanely, if we do not lay claim to our full human-ness at source.

Insecurity and Consumerism

Meanwhile, we each play our part in the present mode of conducting our social, political and economic transactions. We are all party to manipulation by power-hungry infants (perhaps just a little hungrier and more energetic than we happen to be) who are in flight from the victim impotence which ever lurks in the unexamined psyche. Do not the rich nations bully and persecute the poor nations, controlling the prices of the cash crops they wish to import and demanding a return on their ill-conceived investments? They are determined that their freely chosen financial 'risk-taking' should solidify into another's debt; even if it can never be paid off, it keeps the power position clear. So much of our living becomes diverted into control and subjugation, attack and defence – such modes of interaction are the natural outcome of the victim/persecutor unity of opposites. A profound insecurity, and thus competitiveness, forges our socio-political and economic arrangements.

For as long as human consciousness is ego-dominated, we are bound to be out of touch with our true source of security, and to busy ourselves with translating our need for safety into purely physical, and thus materialistic, terms. This unbalanced view of security leads only to further insecurity – on personal, national and international levels. Capitalism (and its attendant remedy, Communism, which is now seeking to remedy itself by a return to capitalism) is the natural and obvious economic system for insecure ego-dominated beings who believe in a world of separate units and who are in competition for the possession of material goods and status based on material wealth. The same erroneous thinking underlies both these offerings of Western civilization. Capitalism exploits the splits and divisions in society; and Communism, equally devoid of a living belief in our underlying interconnectedness, strives to force the split-off pieces into cohesion. Western capitalism dominates the globe just as, at present, ego dominates the psyche. Desire for ownership of material wealth (which is fast losing its connection with matter and becoming ever-more abstract and ephemeral), as a bastion against our insistent feelings of insecurity and our inner emptiness, is born of an over-weighting of ego consciousness and an ignorance of other aspects of self.

Those who have abdicated their awareness of spirit, thus deeply fearing death, grasp at matter for dear life. Material goods become the sought-after breast for 'adults' – the 'grown-up' answer to this somewhat odd business called life. Once we are 'big', we attempt to possess as much as possible; we 'consume' these goodies addictively in our insatiable hunger for the fullness of our spirit self. Or else, in our dispiritedness, we fall into apathy. The perfect victim lets others get on with it all.

Western capitalism misleads the world with the myth of unceasing material growth, which eventually only nurtures growth of greed – all stemming from the deep insecurity which arises from ignorance of our full nature. There is no evidence that material wealth purchases psychological security; those who 'have' seem to need more and more. And when our high standard of living is even partially threatened, do we not act as if our very survival were at stake? The depth of our agitation is quite inappropriate, as if a lower income would bring the starvation that it surely does presage for the very poor. Bankruptcy seems to speak of death to both rich and poor, and clearly this mismatch of realities produces real fear in all alike.

Capitalism relies on our forgetting our true source of wealth. Its proponents, having no confidence in the reality of our interconnected state, also have no wisdom or skill in handling what so obviously needs to be shared. And yet it is only sharing that promotes safety in a shared world. Both capitalism as a method of dealing with our outer resources, and ego-domination as a mode of dealing with the operations of our inner world, depend on our losing sight of the whole. They both focus on the decompartmentalizing aspect of our psyche, whereas security is born of our knowledge of oneness.

The more insecure we become, the more obsessed we are with attaining security, and the more we create the conditions of insecurity. Perhaps we are nearing the peak of ego-dominated capitalism and are poised, in crisis, towards the evolution of new economic and social arrangements based on the emergence of a balanced awareness of spirit and matter. But right now we are in the ridiculous position of placing our security in money (not even in land or produce) and in weapons. Grasping at purely physical security, we have ended up depending on monetary systems, the forces of which we do not begin to understand – so dematerialized and overloaded with unexplored significance that we are caught in puzzling compulsions and impracticable transactions.

Moreover, the nations with most money spend an enormous amount of that money on weapons of destruction – all in the name of security. We have become the mad human race. We who are concerned with biological security, above all else, look to the erratic movement of figures and ever-changing values of small bits of paper, along with concrete instruments of physical devastation, to make us feel secure. We have created the most profound bio-insecurity imaginable: the increasing disturbance of our planet to a point which could render it untenable for human habitation. Under such a threat, we comfort ourselves all the more with consumer goods, or divert our energy with plans to attain them, and devour 'Mother Earth' for all we are worth. The people who consume the most and use the greatest resources think it quite unreasonable to be expected to lower their day-to-day purchasing power in order to pay for the protection of the rain forests we now know are absolutely essential to our well-being on earth. Only the poor are expected to hold back, and, not surprisingly, no one has much confidence that they will. Nothing must disturb our ability to consume. And thus we generate even more insecurity, and feel ever less powerful.

It is no wonder that human anxiety runs high. Unlike all other species, we seem to have a marked tendency towards sickness. Leaving aside all the dreaded serious diseases, do we not expect to put up with ailments of all kinds – endless coughs and colds, backache and indigestion? We seldom gather together in a room full of really well people. We take easily to being patients. It is hardly surprising, then, that our socio-political systems also show forth, in their own terms, this same tendency. No wonder we become obsessed with 'health' and make doctors gods, clinging to the hope of medical miracles, just as we place our faith in science and technology to heal our wounded earth for us, while requiring as little change from us as possible. Here again, we believe that the answer must come from outside ourselves. Has the vast self-regulatory genius of Nature given birth to the mysterious virus that lays us open to AIDS – that intimate invader of the human race, communicated through our most private interactions and yet touching the lives of any and all of us? Has Nature found a way that at last challenges us to dethrone our attachment to external answers and external authorities, calling us to wake up, in time, and grasp our own destiny in our hands? AIDS demands of us that we take personal responsibility for ourselves even as it unequivocally demonstrates our interconnectedness.

Chapter Nine: The Dynamics of Power

Although we are capable of processing a massive amount of information, we are, at a fundamental level, a misinformed species. How can we be otherwise as long as we continue to operate from a basic mistake: our belief in our impotence which leaves us ever vulnerable to attempted omnipotence. Is that perhaps why we are so involved with gaining information? Are we instinctively, but blindly, trying to put things right in our own passive way as we look at our television screens and read our daily newspapers? But, in the end, victims cannot help but turn any striving into yet another game of power and powerlessness. We begin to swallow mass information like addicts who have given up hope of finding a true source of satisfaction. As we sit absorbing television programmes, do we not risk becoming somewhat programmed ourselves? Many of us now bombard ourselves with information and other peoples' opinions from morning to night – information that we cannot possibly act upon. All too ready to trust what comes from outside sources, we imagine that we are receiving hard solid facts about the real world: we give up trying to discover things for ourselves.

So we are in danger of becoming ever-more 'ungrounded', ever-more distanced from our immediate and manageable personal reality. We violate ourselves as organisms by habitually splitting our five senses – seeing and hearing live events in our world while not being able to touch, smell or taste them. We are incessantly being encouraged to feel involved, invaded by situations that cry out for a practical response while appropriate action is quite out of the question. As time goes on, our consciousness is more likely to be dulled by this mode of receiving information rather than broadened and extended. It is only the *information* that goes on increasing, relentlessly, as we devise new defences to keep our split selves functioning reasonably. (Of course this violence to our sentient nature does not occur when the media is used for reflective thought, or for those subjects in which it is fitting that our principle engagement is one of the mind and imagination.)

How different was the role of the media during the Romanian revolution of 1989. In relaying local events in the living moment, information carried the full and immediate energy of communication. Action was possible. People watching television could walk out into the streets, show their outrage and dissent, and visibly lend support to each other. And this action was conveyed via television back to others who could then also decide to act. A creative self-referring loop was formed, and people could respond and participate in making their social reality together. Television became a valuable extension of the power of some senses, while only a very temporary means of splitting them.

If we remain a race of victims, then our species will continue to live out a misguided balance of passivity and control. The energetic ones take control, become the persecutors and rescuers amongst us, and the resigned ones sink into helplessness and blame. In spite of our absorption with issues of power, we actually know very little about empowering ourselves. Many experience less and less hope of fulfilling that deeply intuited sense of our potential humanity.

The Demand for a Perfect Society

We who are entangled in the Victim Archetype are bound to claim that we are helpless; we are bound to imagine that before we can really 'do' anything, society must be cleansed by those powerful and responsible and blameworthy 'others', those 'parents', so as to be a fitting context for the individual – the individual that we, in fact, refuse to be. If we see ourselves as mere pawns in someone else's political game, then naturally we can do nothing until it is put right 'out there'. From the victim's point of view, the structures of society are formed in some mysterious way that has nothing to do with individual people at all. 'Look to the top, not to the ground', the victim declares. Look to the institutions, not to us. Be objective. Look to those inhuman excrescences that have established themselves through no doing of ours but which we are also now terrified to do without. The root of the trouble can't be us – we are too small and powerless to be responsible for anything. We can't possibly be sources of fresh thinking and creative personal action because we are dwarfed by these external giants. National defence systems and international corporations are the latest 'parents' in the blaming game of diminished selfhood.

If we merely translate our demand for perfect mothers into the demand for a perfect society 'before we can be all right', then we are lost indeed. Was not this the experiment of communism? If we wait for any external state of perfection or completion to get it right *for* us, then this transitional state of evolution will be spun out to our further pain and confusion. If complex beings such as us look not to ourselves, and continue to block or divert our life energy, then the result is a proliferation of 'complexes'. However developed and brilliant our brains, it becomes harder and harder to see clearly.

It is not just a matter of arrested development, but of misdirected and distorted development, because the life force itself is not stopped. Evolution begins bending back on itself if it cannot go forward. Cancers of the psyche develop: misguided growth in unfitting areas of our lives, or on unsuitable levels of interaction. Energy has to go somewhere. We multiply our problems when our energy is misplaced at base, at the start of our unfolding process in time and space. For finely tuned creative beings, a small imbalance at source is disastrous, so that what is unfinished appears as bad, as a mess. And in believing and experiencing ourselves as a mess, we are bound to evolve societies that are also a mess, at the same time as feeling helpless in the face of the pressures of that society.

The Level at Which Radical Change Is Possible

However, the sense that somehow society must be cleansed first, so as to be a fitting ground or context for the individual, is perhaps an echo of the truth that it *is* a collective responsibility to shift the power of the Victim Archetype. The general climate of our consciousness must be informed with a fresh understanding of the self – the kind of understanding offered by the Circle of Self with its four directions. Only then can the psyche be released to transfer its allegiance to a new archetype – that of Self-generation, for instance.

It is at the subtle level of our deep consciousness – the source level of creative possibility and fluid potential – that radical change is possible. Here, *in contact with energy prior to manifestation, beliefs have the power to create our reality*. It is contact with this potent, ever-responsive, yet-to-take-form level of our being which enables us to transform our mode of existence. It is this level that we must access if we wish to relate to each other in a radically new way. Trying to alter what has already become manifested or 'formed' – whether a personal habit or a corrupt social system – is starting at the wrong end of our reality. Force is then required, and force is met by resistance; it all feels a long and hopeless struggle – both personally and politically. We get worn down by continual self-sabotage and the intransigence of established institutions. Action and reaction. Reaction and counter-reaction. Formations at this concretized level are entrenched and far less responsive to our conscious attitudes and beliefs – far less influenced by our deliberations and decisions.

It is at the deep subtle level of collective consciousness that we remedy our primal ills, for only at this level, through our rapid remembrance of spirit, can the source of victimhood be erased. Only at this level can freedom and responsibility have any real meaning. If we put all our efforts into reorganizing our world through will power alone, at the level of hard concrete reality (which is the realm of political action), then we find that we keep making the same kind of patterns, structures and systems even though, on the face of it, the rearrangement looked very revolutionary and innovative.

True transformation can only happen at the level of our deepest consciousness and intention. We most fully and effectively serve the collective physical level of our being by focusing on the collective level of our psyche, and we most fully access this collective level of our psyche through our unique being as an individual. The word 'individual' means undivided; and the undivided being, the whole self, easily falls into a mode of co-operation with other whole selves. As a unique self we have true power, for we have direct access to the Source of All Things. Individuals who are true to their full natures are, by simply being themselves, the expression of the Infinite shown forth in diverse forms. We experience and influence and reveal collective truth through our uniqueness.

Any one of us who taps our present potency, by claiming our given initial wholeness, shall be confirmed in the truth of this state by joy in living and a new sense of freedom. Joy speaks of the presence of spirit, as form speaks of physical presence. Our five senses have been evolved to tell us of form, and our inner intuitive sense has been developed to tell us of spirit, in ourselves and in others. And knowledge of spirit brings joy. It could be that our intuitive mind had to be somewhat suspended to allow our analytic faculty, with its ability to differentiate, to come to full power; but we can progress no further until we reclaim our intuitive means of knowing. We need to honour and develop our intuition, trust it, if we wish to go with the flow of evolution and participate in bringing it to fruition.

All this may sound very metaphysical and far removed from stark, everyday existence. From the socio-political perspective, victims *do* seem to exist. It is, unfortunately, meaningful to talk of victims of corrupt economic systems; victims of international, national and factional power struggles; victims of rape, crime and incest. Members of corrupt societies can be rendered virtually powerless economically, socially and politically; can be caught in a poverty trap and affected by inadequate provision of housing and other social amenities, or can be limited and restricted in freedom of speech and movement. But even in these situations, we are never absolutely powerless because we are never spiritually powerless. Our particular experience is not dictated to us, and varies enormously, even in the starkest and most controlled of situations – as Bruno Bettelheim has shown in his descriptions of the concentration-camp experience. The power of spirit cannot be taken from, or denied, anyone. It simply 'is', and is ours for all eternity.

However, in material terms, and in crude and agonizing ways, we can experience ourselves as victims. Given our deep unconscious attitudes, it is hardly surprising that, both individually and collectively, we manifest situations of victimhood with appalling vividness. Indeed, our victim status is bound, eventually, to be brought into being by these attitudes. It is essential, therefore, that even on the political and economic level where victimhood looks and feels so very real, and has solidified into a manifest aspect of reality, we still consider how it is that we become victims, rather than just rail at our institutionalized persecutors. We do well to see how our own victim attitudes increase and reinforce our victim state, and how they help to bring about the persecutory behaviour of the politically powerful leaders of our ailing societies.

Do not entrenched victims need, and therefore unconsciously seek, persecutors? The more that political leaders victimize, the more these victims seem to find plausible reasons for voting for them; or if they have no vote, they tend to accept them as the necessary order of things, and in this assumption they justify their helpless state. They so deeply believe in their impotence and the power of external causes.

Even when crowds of victims join together, and dare to overthrow a dictator, they are soon blaming their new leaders for not making everything better immediately. In so doing they lay themselves open to the emergence of another dictatorship to keep the deluge of diverse complaints and squabbles at bay. A strong hand is called for: some external authority must set the bounds. Also, is it not the blaming infant buried within corrupt leaders, attempting to control and manipulate the 'horrible world' to make sure that at least they and 'theirs' get the best of a poor deal at whatever cost to others, that reinforces the victim position of many members of the society which they head?

Serving the System: The Power Games of the Impotent

The crucial shift that needs to take place in order to free us from the victim/persecutor/rescuer dynamic is the transferring of power from systems to individuals. Only empowered individuals, who have trust in themselves, are not threatened by others; they can, therefore, co-operate for the mutual benefit of all. Only whole selves have no need to play the power games of impotence.

First, we need to look at these systems in operation and realize that we have delegated our power to them. In general we ignore the allegiance we have given them, and are unaware of how we let *them* play *us*. No one is self-empowered, or free to be their full selves, in the victim/persecutor/rescuer dynamic. Paradoxically, the persecutor or rescuer is no more powerful than the victim. Even an attitude or an action which reduces the apparent victim to impotence is itself a reaction, not an action of power. It makes no difference that the one in the 'superior' position believes himself to be the one with power and the one in the 'inferior' position thinks of himself as the one without it. Both are in illusion; both are impotent and serving the system that makes up their particular power game. *Neither are acting in a self-fulfilling way.* The behaviour of all participants in such

Chapter Nine: The Dynamics of Power

a dynamic is merely reactive and no one is a free agent. Indeed, we cannot be free until the belief in our superiority or inferiority changes. We need to see such 'power' interactions differently, see them for what they are – depowering. The power belongs neither to the one nor to the other; it lies only in the shared allegiance to the rules of the game. And illusory power is addictive.

These rules are usually unconscious and unstated in small systems, such as the family (which is occupied with verbalizing more overt rules that, for the most part, cloak the underlying dynamic very successfully), but can be enshrined in laws in the macro-systems of political organization. Once given the tempting stamp of external authority, we can even give our approval to alarmingly oppressive legislation.

It is our desire to be rescued that renders us so extremely vulnerable to leaders like Joseph Stalin. He was no simple tyrant or persecutor. His outstanding skill, which enabled him to get away with so much for so long, was his intuitive knowledge of how to exploit the victim's attraction to being rescued. He brilliantly maintained his image as the great collective Father leading his suffering children towards a better future and a perfect Motherland. He dangled before the people his compelling vision of an all-providing state and ultimate complete security – what other than the mother for whom we have always longed? And he, Stalin, would be her supreme protector.

What could not be sacrificed to this ideal? It became all too easy to forgo, to betray, real and imperfect family members and friends. Combined with Stalin's talent for promising the victim its deepest desires was his willingness to produce a scapegoat whenever necessary. He was never at a loss to provide an outlet for blame as his giant mistakes began to bite, and thus he cunningly channelled the powerful swell of fear, discontent and distrust away from himself.

In common with Hitler, he knew just how to divert negative energy on to his enemies and positive energy on to himself – and the level of both rose, as he relentlessly pursued the absolute power that he craved in the face of the rampant paranoia that he himself had let loose. A mere bully could never have wielded such power. A mere cynic could never have generated such energy – cynicism has low energy value. He knew exactly how to 'play' the victim/persecutor/

rescuer dynamic with the full force of ardent belief. He released people from the burden of individual responsibility while promising to take care of their destiny: the perfect fix for the victim; and exactly what we expect of mother.

Depowering the Game by Accessing Another Level of Being

It is a vicious circle. How to break it? That is the great question. Do we perhaps break the circle by letting go of the search for definite answers; by letting go of the false belief that rational ego consciousness will provide the necessary information; by daring to wait in openness for whatever comes, rather than forever seeking to obtain definitive solutions from some elusive external source – be it parents, society, or God? Once the vicious circle is broken, then the movement of life itself provides the 'answer' – the necessary new perspective; and it brings new questions, and new and transitory 'answers', by completing itself and fulfilling itself.

One thing is clear: it is not persecutors that we must focus on. Our energy is likely to be ineffective if we rage only at effects; if we rage at the opposite pole of the very dynamic that we are busy fixating by our commitment to victimhood. It is the source that we must dare to know – in ourselves. *Everything that we can possibly do to deny the validity of victimhood in our own life is our essential contribution towards fulfilling the evolution of humanity.*

If we know that victimhood is not true of ourselves, then that knowledge will enhance all that we do, infiltrate all that we are, alter all our interactions. We shall no longer reinforce the initial illusion at the start of life: the collective illusion of the powerless infant. We shall not so much 'grow up' as start afresh from a point of true being. Only then are we full human children who can become adult in our own good time; only then is our species freed to come of age.

Without setting out to disturb anyone, we shall begin to interrupt and disrupt, merely by our new way of being, the interlocking web of relationships based on the illusion of victimhood; and we shall bring about the creative dissonance of the unfamiliar. Courage will be called for, courage to be 'different' and out of keeping with the present distorted norm. And we will need to be alert, lest we fall into

Chapter Nine: The Dynamics of Power

experiencing ourselves as 'victims of misunderstanding' when others react to the dismantling of the old games of victimhood. Family systems, especially, are likely to be thrown into disarray. This, of course, is one of the greatest gifts we can give our families, but it is unlikely to be perceived as such.

The essential point to recognize is that these dynamic systems cannot be changed by those involved in them *at the level at which the game is being played*. The participants will always be caught by the rules of the system they have helped to create, however fervently they try to escape, or however inventive their apparent solutions. The game itself must be depowered from a more fundamental level; the level at which we are conscious of our nature as a whole, self-generating being.

We do indeed have true power, but only over ourselves. All other power is illusion. We only have what *appears* to be power over others, and that is gained at the loss of power over self. We may have the *trappings* of power, but all the time we are driven by fear and fleeing from a place of inner emptiness. We place our trust in the collusion of our fellow participants in the game, for they feed us their power while we abdicate our own. We rely on them to fulfil our needs, whether we are playing victim, persecutor or rescuer. We are utterly dependent on others to play their roles in the game to which we have enslaved ourselves. There is a general trading-off of power so that no one possesses any real power at all – that power to actualize our self and find our fullness as a human being. We can only have power over another if they agree and wish to hand over their power to us – so who really has the power? (Note that such agreement of course usually takes place at a deeply unconscious level.) As soon as we need their power, we reveal that we have abdicated our own, because we would not need it if we had claimed our own.

If we are placed in positions of power, whether in a friendship, partnership or an organization, we can be trapped in that power – always seen as powerful whatever we do, or however we may try to divest ourselves of it; the very attempt proves our superiority. We are laden with the projections, with all the unowned power, of those 'under us', or of those who decide that they are inferior to us. And thus, overloaded with power, we are rendered impotent to relate freely. The 'weak' and the 'strong' equally impose on each other, and rob themselves of choice, as soon as they fix themselves in these positions.

As all participants in such systems (those 'in power' and those who are dubbed powerless) are equally lost in the game, the game must be approached from a meta-level of meaning. This is why we must approach the socio-political level from outside that level, or we shall never perceive the true nature of the game and so be able to free ourselves from it. We will simply be drawn into it and end up serving it, whatever we may attempt to do to improve matters. No one really dominates such a system – not even the dictator at its top. It is the position of supreme pseudo-power. Was Hitler in charge of the events that he so energetically and fervently kept in motion, let alone in charge of himself? And yet who could have claimed more power? Or was Stalin? Hitler is said to have become so frenzied as he described his great 'insight' that Jews were not Germans that he vomited on the podium – the great insight that enabled him to project all his unwanted inner material on to them. He was hardly in charge of this disowned material. Such a deeply split self can only destroy itself. He ended up in hiding like a hunted rat. No grand public funeral for this aspiring ruler of a superior race – no funeral at all.

We cannot have power over any system of which we are a part. The system rules us unless we see it as a system, and step outside it. We can have no true power in the political realm if we remain solely in politics. We have to switch levels. Moreover, if any of the participants caught up in the game switches levels, then the game itself is undermined. If participants in any system, whether the family or larger social systems, switch levels to the one at which they themselves are truly empowered, then real social change is not only possible but cannot help but begin to take place. This is the transformation that we seek, but never find, through our political revolutions.

True revolution cannot happen on the political level – the very level that is claimed as fitting because it alone is thought to be powerful, while the individual is dismissed as helpless in the face of these larger forces. Indeed, the actual dynamic of any power struggle is powerful; more powerful than any of those participating in its circular movements, however active they may be. For that very reason, we must acknowledge and experience its power, and be conscious of our part in its workings, *and then access another level of being.*

It is no answer to simply ignore the political level, or try to escape it, as the dynamic of the system will still hold us in its grasp and we shall then serve it blindly. It gets us nowhere to try and seal ourselves off in some idealistic capsule, or float to some imagined higher plane from where we view the antics of our fellow men in superior despair. A living contact with another level of being is required – a claiming of our true power – while still keeping touch with that very world to which we are, from then on, free to relate in a new way. Once we have actively experienced our own power, once we have got a sense of its reality, then we have no need for pseudo-power; we quite naturally disengage from the dynamics of the game. It loses its meaning for us; it loses its hold over us.

So how do we access this other level of being? In the language of the Medicine Wheel, we give special attention to the West/East axis of the self. We give ourselves the opportunity to contact the deep sense of our collective source of being. In the midst of activity we seek stillness, and we learn to remain open to the intuitions which indicate how we are to express our unique contribution to the world. We use our imaginations to extend our vision and free us from set ways of thinking – to enliven us with the knowledge of new possibilities. In this way, we dare to take untried paths and make mistakes; we enjoy our creative natures. And claiming our self-being as we experience our connection with All-That-Is, we are sustained by a far more vital security than that offered by our familiar pains and patterns of behaviour; a more viable security than any afforded by family, organization or national identity. An insecure person, not surprisingly, is focused on attachment, and is unlikely to step outside of any system.

But non-attachment is not a solitary venture. Discovering our individual being has nothing to do with isolation from others. A responsible person knows how to seek, select, receive and give help – taking responsibility does not mean 'doing it all yourself'. Far from keeping ourselves apart, we actively need the experience of being in community with others. The process of 'dropping the system' includes allowing and inviting others to be our mirror. We can never see ourselves fully outside of relationship, and we gain strength and develop through the infinite richness of exchange with others. We especially need the perception of others when we get caught in old patterns – when we get hooked into victim mode. Our obstinacy at such moments is immense; it seems impossible to break the circuit of interaction which we feel compelled to continue, even when we know full well that we are getting nowhere. I have found that it is only when I have opened myself to feedback from a caring 'other' that I am released to access another aspect of myself; it is then that I can claim the metaview necessary for extricating myself from the fixed dynamic in which I had been engaged. It is sad that such learning is often only sought within the formal structure of psychotherapy, rather than being seen as a natural mode of human exchange. It is possible for anyone to trigger the shift of viewpoint, either by speaking from the 'wise person' within themselves, or by shocking us (perhaps by some spontaneous response that is not necessarily enlightened) into turning to the 'wise person' within ourselves.

Personal responsibility, or empowerment, involves two aspects: it requires an awareness of how we experience ourselves at any given moment, and a decision to be true to that experience, as well as an awareness of the context in which we are operating. I call these twin aspects of empowerment 'core-awareness' and 'meta-awareness'. Responsibility and freedom always call on the whole self. We cannot be true to ourselves if we sit only in the South trusting and following our feelings, any more than we reach full authenticity and empowerment by simply following our own ideas – however courageous we may be. Unless we exercise both our ability to assess our context as well as our capacity to tune into our inner being – and *at the same time* – freedom eludes us. Even the most conscientious of us usually opt for either one or the other: we focus on how we truly feel and are in ourselves, as if that defined the limits of our truth and responsibility; or we concentrate on the overview, becoming a detached observer of the episode. The two need always to be held in living connection – only then can we act as a whole unique being within a shared context.

The notion of context must not be confused with taking responsibility for other people's experience: the perception of one's participation in the creation of some event is a very different activity from the merging of boundaries.

The mature being lives its many-layered self and knows the

distinctions within the undivided reality of experience. Learning to hold the different aspects of consciousness is an ever-present challenge; it is not achieved overnight. However, appreciation of context opens us to the rich possibilities afforded by letting others be a mirror for us, and have a creative impact on us, and is an effective way of getting in touch with a fresh view of ourselves and a new angle on our shared reality. It enables us suddenly to see, from outside it, the dynamic in which we are entangled. Having recognized the system that we are serving, we can then choose to disengage from it.

To summarise the ground just covered. Radical political change requires participants in its system to switch levels: to move the focus of their awareness from the operations of that system to the level within the psyche at which self-generation has meaning. The insistence of the political analyst, as well as of the activist, to go to the root of injustice – i.e. the system itself – is apt. However, the system is seen in terms of overt power and institutions rather than the psychological dynamic which underlies their manifestation. It is precisely this dynamic that is left untouched by political reorganization, and so it continues to 'rule' all those participating in its energy (whether new or old players) in another form or guise. The only way to deal with the root of the problem, the rule of the system itself, is to switch to the source point of our very being, which is prior to all systems. Only as whole individuals can we reach this source and claim the vitality, joy and fulfilment that renders power struggles redundant. Grounded in spirit, the root dynamic in which we have engaged withers and dies. No need to be victim, no need to become persecutor or rescuer, in that endless demoralizing circular game of impotence and omnipotence.

And so raging against institutionalized abominations is missing the point. These are merely manifestations of the unconscious grip of the Victim Archetype, and it is this that we need to address. Extension of consciousness in an inner 'vertical' direction (with the help of 'mirrors' from the world around us) is, therefore, even more urgent than further exploration of the outer 'horizontal' level. If we truly wish to evolve new political modes of operation, then we must cease wasting so much of our energy criticising surface expressions of deeper, more fundamental psychic forces. Truly radical change can only occur at the subtle level of our deep consciousness; and once change has occurred on this level, then effective new arrangements on the political level can not only come into being, but can also 'hold' for an appropriate length of time.

Rescuers and Martyrs

We tend to balance the obvious horrors perpetrated by persecutors with admiration for the works of rescuers. They are the 'goodies' of the system. But the rescuer is equally into pseudo-power, although in a more attractive mode. Believing that we can 'put it right' for someone else reinforces their belief that they cannot get it right for themselves: in other words, that they are less than who they are.

Offering help and support with some task that the other wishes to do, or knows that they need to do, is an act of a completely different nature. It is an act of recognition and care for that other: not taking care of them but being alongside them, as equal beings, with ever-changing and interchangeable needs.

Although rescuing others is a benign inflation of one's own power, as opposed to the malign inflation of the persecutor, ultimately it can be just as diminishing to the recipient – who is, of course, equally responsible for the interaction. The same unbalancing misdirection of energy is taking place. The inflation of outer-directed power mirrors the corresponding deflation of inner experienced power, and both rescuer and rescued are less than they could be.

Those who need to rescue others have very likely *rejected* the victim in themselves – a completely different inner state from that of having let go of, and moved on from, the victim position. It seems that they cannot bear to see helplessness in others because they cannot tolerate that experience in themselves. Believing in the reality of profound personal helplessness, they deeply fear it. They therefore keep trying to improve the condition and situation of those who display helplessness. The irony is that they are then often rendered helpless in their ability to help and, given their dread of impotence, rescuers can be driven to use both highly subtle as well as appallingly crude methods of control. Psychic brain surgery is sometimes considered preferable, as a last resort, to the failure to combat depression in another – especially in a woman (or 'mother'). And do we not witness increasing expertise in our society to 'help' the frail and dying not to die.

Another mode of staying within the victim system is to indulge in mistaken claims of guilt. To take on ourselves the burden of responsibility for another's way of being is a very grandiose illusion, however humbling the claim may appear. Mothers are particularly prone to this form of pseudo-power. 'I am the guilty one', they declare, in defence of their child. Each time a mother takes on guilt for 'the way her child has turned out', she encourages that child to be a victim – to feel caused by her. She keeps her grip on him as he also does on her. They engage in the guilt pact – perhaps the stickiest of all arrangements. Each time she assumes guilt she undermines not only herself but also her child's sense of his own power of choice and self-determination. She affirms his evasion of responsibility and beckons on the diversion of his energy into blame. She is not being responsible.

Alternatively, we may keep the system going by taking on the even less-appealing mode of the martyr. When we feed our self-pity by displaying how much we are prepared to suffer for others – attempting to do their suffering for them, and trapping them in guilt instead – are we not wielding a false power yet again? What gives us the right to impose on another the illusion that they are of greater importance than ourselves? Between deluded (and deluding) claims of generosity and guilt, everyone within the system of interaction remains serving the game as both victim and accomplice. False beliefs of guilt are merely false beliefs of power and so keep the system moving, or even escalate its destructive energy.

The Pseudo-security of 'Being in the Right'

All actors caught up in these victim/persecutor/rescuer systems have a shared mania to be 'in the right'. It is a substitute for the security of full selfhood, the security that cannot help but elude ego-dominated psyches. It is this compulsion to gain pseudo-security that keeps us in the game. Of course we can only be 'right' in relation to the others; at the others' expense and abdication of *their* rightness. We may strive to achieve this by calling ourselves a victim and saying that we are the blameless one, or equally by claiming guilt and saying that we caused it all (we are then being 'righteously responsible'). Even the persecutor is in the right – the necessary strong one who takes charge of the situation – while the rescuer aspires to the 'rightness' of the saint. All participants endeavour, after their own style, to be the one who defines the situation, defines the relationships.

This mirrors our longing for the self-defining power that is, indeed, ours, but which we are terrified to claim as ours. And so we attempt to define others instead, or our relationship to them, and find some way of being 'in the right', however bad we feel – to find some way of being powerful. This obsession, which lies at the base of our habitual manner of relating to each other, from the personal to the international level, draws its energy from a profound and unshakeable knowledge that somewhere, deep down, we do have the power to get it right – for ourselves.

The Redundancy of Comparisons and Competition

Enormous creative energy would be released if we experienced ourselves as intrinsically in charge of our lives. Secure in our own power, we would be free to co-operate with each other and so evolve social systems that served us all. With our egos well integrated and functioning properly, rather than expected to take the full weight of self-determination, we would cease endlessly comparing ourselves with, and competing with, others. We would no longer seek to value ourselves by endeavouring to assess how much 'better' we are than anyone else – and then needing to prove it. We would no longer try and elaborate self-confidence through putting others down. Once we know ourselves as unique beings, comparisons simply make no sense. There is no 'better' or 'worse' person, just an infinite variety of different persons. If we deeply assimilated this fact, then it would be harder to underpin the notion of superior classes, religions or groups of persons.

Surely our only fitting standard is our own truth. We can be authentic human beings or human beings who are hiding from ourselves – denying ourselves. If we were to accept such a standard, then our criterion of health or success would be our sense of being at home with ourselves; our experience of personal integration, love, and oneness as a self. And as a whole and undivided self we can, without effort, come to see, and know, and love other selves. Once at home in ourselves, we find a place for ourselves in the world we have chosen to explore.

There is no fundamental opposition between the true individual and society. The fully integrated self will naturally feel integrated with its environment – though of course, integration does not preclude challenge, dissonance and difference: it is essential to our well-being to be continually stretched. What we fail to take into account is that the state of our psyches reflects the world, and the world our psyches. It is only because we are in a transitional state of development as a species, and our different modes of consciousness not yet in balance, that we experience a world in which co-operation seems somewhat exceptional.

We have made such a dichotomy between inner and outer, subject and object, that we cannot believe that there could be a natural fit between our psyche and the world around us. Having devised the split, we then think that there is an inevitable gulf, an inbuilt mismatch, between the interests of the individual and the needs of society as a whole. It is only the isolated ego, dissociated from the rest of the self and therefore from other selves, that poses its very existence in opposition to the whole – in this case, the state or body politic. The integrated self, however, is by its very nature aware of its connections, and knows that it arises within the context of that whole. It calls on ego to define it as separate *on the appropriate level only*; in the appropriate circumstances and at appropriate times. It is only an unsupported ego that experiences the world and other people as alien, and so becomes obsessed with status in its desperate attempt to 'place' itself in the crowd. It is only when we identify with ego, and treat it as the whole self, that we wipe out the knowledge that we are intrinsically interrelated social beings.

An ego which is attempting to function in lieu of the full self naturally translates this interrelatedness on to its own level of operation and converts it into comparison and competition. This approach to others distorts all our relationships and prevents the contact we so deeply need as human beings. It robs us, too, of the security for which we also crave, that which emanates from the knowledge that each being has value by virtue of its very existence.

And so we come back once more to the enormous importance of personal integration. Personal integration implies that there are many different aspects to integrate; it implies the co-ordinated expression of a multi-dimensional self. We are each a micro universe interacting within a shared reality. As such, how can we seriously be threatened by anyone else? Once we have apprehended the infinite aspect of our nature, then the need to compete falls away and we no longer have to struggle with the daunting task of loving our enemies. In other words, we are no longer doomed to moral failure.

If we each had active experience of our intrinsic personal power, then politicians would no longer be so preoccupied with power over others and the dynamics of group pressures. However, in a world of potential victims, politics which is not based on the struggle for power is almost inconceivable. Has not the word almost come to mean the organization of power? Of course, within any social or political system, different people are suited to carry different responsibilities, and some will express their capacity for organization and leadership while others will contribute to society in a range of contrasting ways. The remarkable diversity of human personality provides, quite *naturally*, an immense variety of talents and preferences and needs.

The very intricacy of our psyches supplies the spectrum of qualities that bring forth what is required for the complex patterns of human living, if we really do each *live* ourselves. This does not mean that conflict or competition have no valid place in human interaction and will at some point disappear, but that 'losers' need not be a fundamental aspect of our social arrangements, nor oppressed peoples a necessity. It is the politics of greed, arising from the deep hunger for our abdicated self, that requires 'serfs' and throws up an underclass, and our engagement with the Victim Archetype that underpins such politics.

There is a natural increasing entropy in social systems as long as the Victim prevails: this means that there is a decreasing level of clear information and increasing psychic disorder. We get ever further buried under all the emotional rubbish – both our own and that of others who are engaging in the game. It is especially tragic because, as essentially creative beings, we are empowered to travel in exactly the opposite direction. We are capable of generating an increase of information and of participating in a more profound order; an order based on the deep interconnectedness experienced by individuated beings who are in contact with the source of all life.

An Example of Self-empowerment

I should like to end this chapter with an example of a switch of the psyche to the level of self-empowerment. Someone very well known to me was on a Spiritual Retreat in an isolated area in the South African countryside. One day she went for a long walk, feeling deeply at peace and fulfilled in herself. Suddenly an unexpected car passed and screeched to a halt in front of her. Three youths bounced out of the car, and coming towards her demanded cryptically, 'Where to?'. She looked directly at them, thanked them, and explained that she was enjoying her walk and didn't need a lift. She said there followed a silence in which they simply looked at each other, and then the youths suddenly turned on their heels and drove off. Only hours later did she suddenly see the potential danger that she'd been in, and she was amazed at her lack of fear during the encounter. Although a courageous person, she is normally fairly nervous and prone to panic. However, she had been deeply centred in herself and in tune with her natural surroundings when the incident occurred. Also, being exceptionally free of racial prejudice, she did not automatically assume that black people were 'up to no good' or 'rapists'.

Safely back at the Retreat Centre, she found that her whole body was trembling as she realized intuitively that if she *had* made that assumption, and panicked in terror, then rape was the very event most likely to have taken place. It was an almost standard rape situation: a woman alone with no possible way of attracting help and three young men who had deep historical and political reasons for treating her as an enemy and 'getting their own back' on one of their oppressors. They also had the tempting opportunity to show off to each other and prove their manhood with no fear of any humiliating counter-attack from her. Two of them could have held her down. In retrospect she could see how aggressive they had been, and how utterly non-plussed they had been by her response.

She had simply been herself, clear and direct and confident, and had met them as fellow human beings; met them from the fullness of whom she experienced herself to be at that time. She projected no hate on to them, nor fear. They had nothing to hook into or defend against, nothing to conquer. The only appropriate action, in the face of such a complete human being, was to let her be. And that is what they did. Her energy had not *connected* with the energy of rape in them. Her ability to remain true to herself was her greatest protection. She transformed a threatening encounter into a meeting – a connection of a completely different order.

Thus can we be alchemists of life. If we refuse to be a victim, then the potential persecutor is thrown off balance, is left energetically disconnected and stranded, and in that hiatus of unknowingness has the opportunity to act in a new way.

Chapter Ten

Freedom and Destiny

Creating Our Own Lives

At the deepest, most subtle level of our being, we are creators of our lives – we 'cause' our lives to happen the way they do through the connections we make on this subtle level. Our responses are uniquely our own. Our attitudes and beliefs, which bring themselves to fruition on the manifest level of external reality, are taken up by us, chosen by us, generated by us, and kept in place or altered by us – by the self in its full nature. We will never understand this notion of creating our own experience as long as we limit ourselves to an ego-based concept of self.

When viewing this claim from the perspective of ego consciousness alone, we are rightly suspicious of the whole idea – we are bound to find it simply unbelievable. Ego knows only too well that, even when it tries its hardest to control situations, it is thwarted. The ability to create our lives does not, cannot, occur at the level of ego control; this creative capacity involves all aspects of the self and the many different modes of human consciousness.

We cannot hope to find the idea of self-generation meaningful unless we begin to explore the operational richness of that consciousness – unless we come to know ourselves more fully. All the time we, in common with the other creatures that share this earth, are each in our own way appropriating to ourselves everything that we need from the environment, from the universe, in order to actualize our own natures. The more comprehensive our consciousness, the more power we have consciously to direct this process.

Thus do we seek those who hold the same beliefs as we do, or open ourselves to those with different beliefs – depending on how we wish to develop ourselves. It is not that people with the same beliefs condition us, nor that people with different beliefs 'take away' our old beliefs and make us accept new ones. It is all a matter of connecting resonances, and particular resonances are either ripe or dormant, depending on what aspect of ourselves we are giving weight at any given moment. Change can never be forced on anyone – as every psychotherapist knows.

It is hard to affirm the notion that we create our own reality in the face of brutal instances of captivity and torture – those most extreme situations of loss of freedom and subjection to external power. It feels extremely distasteful and presumptuous to discuss such appalling tests of our humanness from the safe comfort of sitting at my desk. And so I simply put before you, to ponder for yourself, the fact that people respond very differently to these outrageous and horrifying occurrences. Some do, we know, manage to resist the most devastating and skilled brainwashing techniques that the inventive human mind can devise. It is awe-inspiring. It is a mystery. It unequivocally shows forth the self as more than just ego. Such people must call on a very profound level within themselves: the level of the deepest intention of spirit?

Just because it is, indeed, awesome to claim this level in ourselves, as a species we find it easier and 'more natural' to project our self-causing efficacy on to the world outside us. We thus secure the belief, and the experience, of 'being caused' instead, and can settle for the illusory safety of non-responsibility which this notion allows. We fight for 'cause' to belong 'out there' as ardently as Hitler fought to place on to the Jews those parts of his nature that he had rejected. He highlights, in a particularly challenging and sobering manner, the great thrust of projection in which we are all involved at this stage of our evolution.

If there is a part of ourselves that we do not want to accept, then we place it elsewhere – we project it outwards on to the world and other people. Energy has to go somewhere, and our feelings are energies, as also are our thoughts. When we disown a thought or feeling, for instance anger, we experience that anger as residing in another rather than ourselves. We can then no longer handle and deal with it.

We have literally lost our grasp on reality. Obviously the other person cannot handle it either; it isn't theirs. Confusion sets in when they are treated as if the anger were theirs. By this time a similar emotion may well be stimulated in them, and the stupefying complexity of the exchange escalates still further.

Distortion after distortion results from this disowning process. Increasingly tangled interactions and miscommunications arise when we disown a far larger aspect of self: our instinctual self, our whole emotional and physical self, our feminine or our masculine self, or that most fundamental organizing principle of our humanity – our power to determine ourselves. And then, when large groups of us do this together, doctrines and dogmas and ideologies evolve and, eventually, concretize into institutions to delineate our confusion and protect us from what flows from the cultural imbalances brought about by these splits in our psyche. All this arises from our habit of projection and our refusal to stay in contact with our own feelings and wishes – our reluctance to be at the centre of our own activities.

No wonder the mass collective projection of our intrinsic power to cause ourselves, rendering the power of self-generation an external phenomenon, has left us deeply confused about the very nature of our species. We have turned ourselves inside out. This core projection, or projection of our core activity, has dictated the structure of our thinking. It is not surprising that it eventually became overtly intellectualized into powerful theories of external causation. It is fundamental to all other projections. It upholds the very process of projection itself.

The consolidation of all our projections is captured by the notion of Fate. If we remain limited to ego consciousness and a linear view of reality, then we shall remain victims on all levels of our being except, perhaps, the most trivial. In the age-old opposition between Fate and free will, Fate will come out the victor. But with a more extended consciousness of self, the opposition falls away. There is no conflict between mature responsibility and destiny; freedom and fate are reconciled.

Destiny is but the projection on to the external world of our own deepest intention, and it unfolds as such as the seed of individuation unfolds. The more we obey our essence, the more gracefully and creatively we 'fit' and actively contribute to the movements of the universe around us. And we come to have an ever-more profound sense that what is 'right' for us has a rightness for all those with whom we interact. Although much disturbance or misfit of the various 'wants' of our egos may occur on the surface level, ultimately, whenever we are true to ourselves, we find that other people are offered some opportunity or release on the deeper level of *their* being. In the subtler domain of our existence our choices are complementary. In other words, that to which we each are called to give our obedience has found a joint resonance.

The more comprehensive our consciousness, the more we can view fate as the unfolding of an inner phenomenon, and the less we come up against it as a hard, relentless force out there in the world. The troublesome concepts of premonition and predestination can lie at peace with that of choice: they can be understood as the viewing of one of the many strands in our life from a trans-temporal perspective (through the activity of our Eastern aspect of consciousness). The more we know of ourselves, the less we experience having to contend with our fate; we can recognize and take responsibility for what we are creating. We come to experience our destiny as indeed ours – our unique path – arising from within, from our deepest being. And in obeying it so we fulfil ourselves.

How, Then, Can Life Be So Unfair?

As events directly present themselves, 'life' is often 'not fair'. How do we square this with personal responsibility? The point is that life responds to the whole person, not just to the level of rational consciousness; the level of good and bad behaviour. And so 'good guys' seem to have bad luck, and 'baddies' get away with it. Many events do, indeed, seem to occur in an arbitrary fashion, and on the level on which they occur, taking responsibility for them would be ridiculous. In such cases, the explicit realm in which we usually search for causes and reasons seems completely barren soil for even the most inventive of moral theorists. Things just don't seem to tie up. There is no justice in this world. Are there not times when people really do seem to have no power or say over their lives? And without choice, how can they

Chapter Ten: Freedom and Destiny

be responsible? On this level it is best not to see life as fair, nor expect it to be.

We have to go deeper and discover the organizing beliefs of that person. Many will be 'programmes' of tangled outdated thoughts and unfinished feelings. Others will be of a more profound nature; the deeper intentionality of the incarnated being. Together they fashion the responses and reactions, the decisions and actions that make up our interpersonal relationships, drawing specific responses, reactions, decisions and actions in others – as well as a vast array of other kinds of events.

To take an example. A really generous, talented, hard-working and 'worthy' man has a life punctuated by unexpected trials and difficulties. His qualities set him towards success, and he overcomes ordinary obstacles without much trouble. But his deeper need is for struggle. His response to difficulties in early life had been to engage with them as a challenge – this had eased the pain and given meaning to negative experiences, and so 'paid off', but then became a set model of how things *had* to be, if he was to feel 'all right'.

Given this need, the relative ease with which he attains success is somehow disturbing. He is only really 'at home' if he has to contend with something that seems to be too much for him. To be really tested, he requires to be taken by surprise and thrown off balance – devastated – as only then can he meet his deeper need and fulfil his intention to triumph in the most adverse of circumstances. And so this configuration in his psyche resonates with some unknown belief in someone else's psyche (for example – that only through disruption is one really alive), and a 'hard time' is created. It seems to come from nowhere – to miraculously appear on the scene unbidden. There is no obvious link on the manifest level, and he is thought to be very unlucky.

Alternatively, this man will take a holiday in a place where an earthquake occurs, while some heroin pusher will be relaxing in the sun at a safe distance from the area of destruction and upheaval. No one would say it was the good man's fault. How could he have anything to do with such events? Incredibly bad luck. A crazy universe. But it could be that his psyche, at an extremely subtle level, had tuned in with the subtle level of disturbance in the earth, and that he was thus attracted to choose to go and visit that area. Often our choice seems quite arbitrary to us, or some surface connection looks like the only reason for our decision, when in fact the power behind the choice is our deeper need, belief or intention.

In this case, the earthquake could provide exactly the kind of struggle the man was needing at that point in his development. It could awaken him, revitalize him. Or what if he tragically lost his wife in the disaster? Perhaps, unknown to his ego consciousness, he was ready for the most testing challenge imaginable for his particular personality – he was ready at that time to work with issues of dependency. And his wife, for her part, was living out her subtlest level of all. Who are we to judge?

We can only see the relative surface of both the psyches of others and the material universe. We usually have limited and fairly crude data at our disposal, unless we access subtler layers through intuition and extension of consciousness. Certainly, we can learn to use and develop these attributes to inform us of our own deep inner connectedness to our outer reality. The whole orbit of the self is ultimately available to each of us.

Although it may seem utterly unfair or absurd that a certain person be subjected to a particular event, their response to it can be such an important expression of who they are that it further develops their special qualities, and confirms their approach to life. Or we may detect a general coincidence of inner attitude and outer events; a person's overall life situation can be one of success, whatever the outcome of a particular event. Someone deeply willing to succeed will always pick up again after a failure of any kind, try out a new approach, or switch directions if one avenue is blocked. Such a person is seen to be ever resourceful; in charge of the basic quality of her life, even though she can be frustrated by certain unexpected and apparently 'unfitting' events.

Even when we take responsibility for our lives, at times we are bound to have the experience of things 'happening to us'. Just because we are not a victim of life, it doesn't mean that we are in charge of the external world – of all outside circumstances. We don't control the whole vast context of our being – we are of it, in it, and have to express ourselves through and in and beyond it. Pressures from

Chapter Ten: Freedom and Destiny

without can be 'too much' and destroy our plans and divert our actions. We are but one subject in, and therefore in a sense subject to, the interplay of collective energies which may suddenly alter direction, or polarize in such a way that our context lurches – and we with it. By definition our context extends beyond us, and this larger field of our being may throw up undesirable and unchosen features for us. Ego choice may be shattered.

None of these considerations makes us a mere victim of circumstances. It is only the ego, with its focus on temporal sequence and overt appearances, that demands that we either fulfil our decisions *in this mode* or else we are proved helpless. We may be 'casualties' of a certain context and not succeed in materializing our conscious intentions, but nothing (except ourselves) can stop us from being true to who we really are, nor prevent us from playing our unique part within that context – nothing has the power to wipe out our contribution to collective consciousness. It is just that we cannot fix or control exactly how this contribution may manifest. That does not make us a victim, or mean that fate rules over freedom in human affairs.

The activity of risk-taking demonstrates in a useful manner the relationship between deeply personal choice and our interdependence within a wider context. It seems that it is essential to our nature as human beings to take risks – at least some of the time. Is it not part of the very movement of life in its evolutionary mode? Now we *choose* to take a particular risk – without the act of choice, an action cannot be defined as taking a risk. But equally fundamental to this phenomenon of risk-taking is the fact that we cannot control its outcome – we cannot know what the consequences of our action will be. Indeed, we choose to take the act in the full knowledge of its unknown outcome.

If our risk-taking 'fails' (i.e. does not go the way we had hoped), then we are not therein victims of the external world. The choice lay in taking the risk itself – not in its outcome. And the choice expresses our self-being. Its importance for us lies in our being able to take that particular risk at a given time in a specific situation; the preparedness to act on unsafe ground and stretch out towards the new; the willingness to let go into the unknown. Such activity is the antithesis of victimhood.

If we feel cheated by the outcome, then we were deluding ourselves in our risk-taking – we were really involved in an attempt to control the unknown. Many a risk may appear to flounder, or not pay off in an obvious way for the individual that undertook the risk; but as a creative act, it is likely to play a part not only in the unfolding development of that person but also in the collective development of the human psyche.

We evolve new forms through witnessing the mistakes of our fellows as well as our own. We learn through putting forward hypotheses into the world of our shared experience and receiving the world's feedback. If we *receive* that feedback, then we are not a victim of it. We have fulfilled our purpose of learning something more of how to live in the world as the unique being that we are. Our great misunderstanding is to consider that we are a victim of that which we cannot control, and to limit ourselves to our ego perspective of success or failure measured in terms of immediate, explicit results.

The Greater Clarity Afforded by a Multi-dimensional Model of the Self

In the light of connection theory (which rests on a multi-dimensional concept of the self, the structure of consciousness and the nature of reality), it is perfectly feasible, as well as richly meaningful, to posit that we are each responsible for how we live our lives and that we carry our destiny within us.

Meanwhile, however, during this transition stage in our evolutionary development we hold ourselves in confusion. And we imagine that complex models of our nature – all that 'multi-dimensional stuff' – only accentuate this confusion. We hate being confused; it frightens us. It also undermines the hubris of our species. After all, if our rational consciousness makes us the crown of all creation, how can it lead us to muddle and ignorance? To fight confusion and uncertainty, we become readily defensive of the particular level which we have singled out as relevant at any given moment. We can feel so much more sure on a linear mono-dimensional path. We can then be 'right'. What is more, we can be 'in the right', which gives us an illusory security as long as we hold on to it. It also means, of course, that we can be 'wrong', but at least we know where we are. Our habit of taking up simplistic positions dictates the nature of our interactions, from the purely intimate and personal to those on political and international levels.

It is impossible to have rewarding or even workable relationships unless we do admit to our multi-layered nature. The fact is that we can love and enjoy someone on one level while on another we can hate that person because, for example, we perceive them as more powerful than we are. Many men feel this about 'Woman' and therefore hate them while also adoring them, or deeply need them while regarding them as burdensome. Both levels have their truth; one does not negate the other. But if we insist on a mono-level reality, then we either have to repress the hate (which, of course, does not relieve us of its presence; it leaks out in indirect and destructive ways and we end up more confused than ever); or we take on board the hate at the expense of our loving feelings, casting doubt on them and distrusting ourselves.

We are not only impoverished by linear models of the psyche, therefore; we are thrown into tortuous complexity and have no means of extricating ourselves from the muddle. Simple models do not simplify the psyche; they complicate its expression. A flexible clarity is only born out of an appreciation of our actual nature.

We cannot be true to ourselves, then, unless we accept the multi-layered operations of our psyche. Here is another example. We can feel outrage at someone's behaviour on one level and yet understand it on another. An oversimplified view of the psyche traps us in *either* the outrage (usually righteous and unbending in quality in order to fend off the denied levels which appear to oppose it), *or* the understanding – which locks us 'in our head' and very likely leaves us with a headache, then falling prey to odd bouts of irritation and a strange need to criticize, making it increasingly difficult to understand *ourselves*.

Once we admit to the true complexity of our nature, everything becomes clearer, and 'cleaner'. We can acknowledge our ability to use our rationality and draw on our compassion, and then suspend those levels of our being while we allow our outrage to flow. Having done so, we shall not only be energized but free to pick up the rational level again, without having to keep 'obstructive' material at bay. We shall also be relaxed enough to sink into that place deep within ourselves from whence true compassion unfolds. After 'being' our outrage, we can then come to rest in our understanding of the other. But so often we flee to the safety of our understanding in order to escape our outrage, and call it 'being grown up'.

The dynamics of our social and political activities become ever-more obscured and remote, the more we insist that we are operating solely on sound, rational principles. If we acknowledge only one level of consciousness, believing that we are being logical just because we veto those other levels that interrupt our line of argument or action – levels that cannot help but interweave with the perspective we have selected – then we remove ourselves from reality. We thus become less in charge of events, rather than remaining 'on top of them' as we fondly imagine we are doing. So when we engage in advanced agriculture or industrial development, pursuing rational short-term economic gains while losing touch with the life in all things, we ultimately impoverish the earth and alter the climate.

Modern civilization, in attempting to tame the intricately balanced and benign environment out of which we emerged, is busy turning the planet into a potentially life-threatening, chaotic, hostile human habitat. We become utterly illogical if we stick purely to the logic of one domain of our being. We become utterly stupid if we insist on following only our intellect. (Intelligence is born of our conscious appreciation of the interplay of our multi-dimensional nature.) As long as ego rules the psyche and we pour our energy into one mode of being, we create enormous complexity on that one level. We then become ever-more bemused as our modern solutions, aided by brilliant technology, fail to deliver the well-being for which we long.

Our fearful lack of recognition of the nature of our multi-layered psyche operating within a multi-layered reality has led us into futile oppositions, polarizations and contradictions, rather than creative paradoxes that reveal the relationship between the levels and the marvels of their interaction. Once good and evil are separated, we are lost. *A false simplicity generates irrelevant and dangerous complexity, whereas the graceful intricacy of the interplay of many complementary dimensions creates a living, ever-moving order.*

As already mentioned in Chapter 7, paradox is the language of wisdom – the language of the soul in its communication of its nature. All great teachers of both the East and the West use it. Christ's very life itself was a paradox. Paradoxes call forth another level of consciousness, and a more comprehensive and trans-verbal context of meaning. As they rely on the appreciation of both the distinction and the connection of the different levels of our being (for without that recognition, we are into contradiction and incoherence), they draw us into a realization of the nature of reality itself. What could be more practical? Illumination of the way we actually operate occurs through apprehension of paradoxical meaning. We human beings can never be reduced to mono-level meanings, and any attempt to explain ourselves by using mono-level modes (such as materialism) is doomed to distort our nature.

The Nature of Self-generation

In a society dominated by the victim/persecutor dynamic, which itself rests on a linear mono-level view of reality, we are bound to divide people up into controllers and the controlled. None are free, although the controllers may have some illusion of freedom. No one is being responsible, although the controllers may appear to be taking responsibility for their actions. (In fact they are driven by fear and the need for power and are compelled to control – they are addicted to it.) Neither knows the peace of obedience to self, the at-one-ness of accepting self and trusting intuition; of going with the Tao. Pushing the world around, or being pushed around, denies our inner transformative energy of Fire. We are trying to achieve change by manipulating externals and everything stays essentially the same, bound by the interweaving of false impotence and false omnipotence. Transformation can only occur at a subtler level of reality.

Because we know little of our true power of self-generation and are more familiar with the dynamic of impotence and control, we assume that it entails causing others to do the things that we want them to do. As I said earlier, however, the process of creating our own reality does not rest on 'making' other people do things. How could it? Those other people are also creating their experience. To take an extremely challenging example. If I need to test myself with a tragedy of the magnitude of my daughter's death, then it does not mean that I caused her death, or even that I chose her death. This level of connection has little to do with the ego consciousness of the North.

Furthermore, I may not even choose my own cancer. By the time my body is riddled with malignant cells I have moved beyond a situation which is amenable to the conscious activity of choosing. I do not, therefore, choose cancer in the same way that I choose a house. I shall by then have so successfully embodied old choices, which themselves were limited by my frozen responses, that unless I open to the very depths of myself in the West and contact the energy emanating from the source of all being, I cannot heal myself or be healed by others. It is a cruel misunderstanding of levels to talk of such things in terms of simple choice, although highly individual connections will have taken place to allow the cancer to emerge.

I equally violate the complexities of human connection and interaction if, just because I acknowledge that I am not a mere victim of my daughter's death, I then assume that I have somehow caused it. Connection theory frees us from the guilt-inducing, blame-provoking causal model. Seen in the light of connection theory, her death indicates that some deep need of mine, at an extremely subtle level of my being, resonated with a need of her's at the most subtle and profound level of her being. That would be the level of the connection around this issue; the ego is not activated to deliberate and come to a decision. I 'cause' who I am through the connections I make – through the connections I attract and repel and pass by. And so does she. The universe is one great self-happening. And so is each one of us; we are source points of life energy. We connect with, move with, make patterns with other source points – other infinite points of 'God' expressed in matter. These may be people, animals, plants, stones; all life is of God if God is All-That-Is. All is spirit at its subtlest level. All is one.

The scientific medical description of the cause of my daughter's hypothetical death would be genetic weaknesses, or the virus that caused it. The sociological description may include environmental influences that made her vulnerable to disease or affected the

Chapter Ten: Freedom and Destiny

standard of nursing. The psychological description may include her lack of will to fight for her life because she had always been indulged by her mother – or because she had been abandoned by her mother at an early age when her mother went back to work. All these would be looked on as the cause of her death.

The idea that she drew her death to herself for some profound reason of her own seems shocking, and could be seen as a way of evading responsibility by those around her. Once again, the different *levels* of responsibility are being collapsed into one another. A careless or over-harassed nurse certainly needs to be aware of her participation in the unfolding event, and it would be to her advantage to trace further connections with other similar events in her life, or familiar patterns of feeling, and from such connections subtler ones could emerge into consciousness. All participants in an episode do well to explore their particular connections with it from as many different aspects as possible. And so, as mother, if I wish not just to be a victim of circumstances, I need to discover how I actively connect with my daughter's death and what specific learning it offers me. None of which cancels out intense grief and shock and loss. We are not exempt from any human feeling just because we are choosing and responsible beings. In fact, we make ourselves available to feel all emotions fully. What we are no longer vulnerable to is the terror of annihilation, or ontological despair.

There is a great taboo about the idea of consenting to our own death. Death is meant to befall us – the one absolutely certain thing which we cannot help. That is perhaps why, in infant defiance, we ward it off so vigorously. Suicide is the special name used to mark off chosen death and separate it from respectably unwelcome and unchosen deaths. And then we declare even those committing suicide as victims of an unsound mind, or impossible conditions, or some harsh cultural perversion. We have an aversion against the very idea of participating in our dying and our time of death.

All the causes that we list for the diverse happenings in our lives give us a sense of 'knowing' the world, a world which we, at the same time, experience as cruel and arbitrary. We delude ourselves that what we name, we understand, or at least partly understand. We feel that we are more in control of things if we are able to label them.

And so we extend our ingenuity to name causes, especially in the face of fear and the unpredictable. However, those events which we mark as 'causes' are merely elements in the self-generation process. They are the material that the entity, the agent, appropriates to create her or his intention, just as a plant appropriates to itself what it needs from the soil, water, air and sun. These 'causes' are merely evidence of some of the connections that the entity attracts and forges on all levels of its being, from the subtlest to the most explicit.

Given that it is so difficult to free ourselves from causal thinking, I believe it is worth stating yet again that we do not, as the agents and generators of our own lives, cause others to be the way they are in the service of this creation of our reality. As self-generating beings themselves, they are co-operators with us in our creative endeavour (or they are colluders with us in our avoidance or self-sabotage). Self-generation is something very different from manipulation. It is those who feel impotent who manipulate and attract collusion; who harness their creativity to try and find ways and means of having power over others; who seek to control the world in order to compensate for that power to be themselves which they have given away and placed erroneously on to others.

Self-generation has nothing to do with controlling others at the manifest level; it has to do with connecting with others at the level of possibility, that fluid level of living energy at a point prior to the actual manifestation of an event. It is just because of the oppressive connotations of impotence, blame and control around the word 'cause' that I prefer to use the term 'self-generation' when describing our process of being in the world. It has a more creative ring. And we are essentially creators of our lives, of ourselves, and co-creators of a shared reality.

If we insist on holding to a mono-level causal approach when looking at the dynamics within a relationship, designating cause (and thus guilt and responsibility) either to one person or to the other, then we are bound to validate the victim position and, in so doing, reinforce the belief in a general lack of choice and responsibility. We cannot help but negate both participants in the interaction. Even in particular episodes where one party is obviously active while the other is passive, or there is an imbalance of power between them, it is still unwise to define the interaction in terms of one person *causing* the behaviour of the other, because we then not only affirm the 'reality' of victimhood but designate the less active person as a non-self.

On the other hand, reversing the emphasis and loading the receiver of physical assault with the causal efficacy of the action not only strains credulity, but then simply classifies the *attacker* as a victim – a victim of his victim's unseen powers. However, if we say they both equally caused the action, then we render the meaning of cause vacuous because the notion of cause rests on an inequality of power – an inequality of agency. A new concept with which to organize our understanding is obviously called for.

The act of intuitively recognizing the various levels of our particular connections with other people and external events not only releases us from the impossible dilemmas that abound if we apportion blame, but also offers us the opportunity of self-healing rather than the limitation of merely resorting to punishment. Only if we see and experience our interactions and relationships 'in the round', as it were, in their completeness, are we in a position to come into our own wholeness. Even if the filled-out self that we then experience contains some shocking elements, we are far freer than when locked in denial. Once integrated and at one with ourselves, our energy is released, it can move, and change then becomes possible; transformation can take place. When we refuse to acknowledge our highly individual and specific network of connections with other people and events, we leave ourselves diminished, not more intact.

However, given that the atmosphere in which we live as social beings is permeated by the fear of blame and guilt and the assumption that someone must be to blame, we easily slip into a judgemental mode. Recognizing connections then becomes a process of confession, an invitation to be blamed, or an inner witch-hunt for the culprit. If insight is reduced to 'finding fault', then we are hardly likely to open up to our own awareness, let alone to feedback from others. Why should we render ourselves a target for conviction? Keen awareness flourishes only in a climate of acceptance and compassion. If we regard *any* connection, *any* feeling, *any* attitude that we may discover (however forbidden in the eyes of society) as simply part of the process of rounding out our awareness so that we can come into our fullness, then we can let ourselves see and feel and know. But equally, we can only let go of judgementalism through a similar acceptance, and by acknowledging and experiencing our continual making of judgements. We then find that a particular judgement either dissolves (because with our awareness and acceptance its energy clears out of our system, allowing us to move beyond it), or that we can, having given it recognition and clarification, consciously suspend it. Only by not judging our judgements can we have some say in handling them or transcending them. And the more we let go of our habit of making judgements, and allow unimpeded awareness of the complexity and specific quality of our participation in life, the more directly we contact our energy, experience our richness and know ourselves as part of the operations of the universe itself.

An Example of the Transformation of a Frozen Response

Our movement into adulthood, difficult enough for the human species at this stage of our development, is hardly aided by the fact that the area of study labelled 'psychology' is still struggling to extend beyond its reductionist base, and that psychoanalysis and much of psychotherapeutic theory and practice attributes *fundamental* status to the wounds of childhood. We are offered a linear road forward which has most of its signposts pointing backwards.

Given this compelling emphasis on wounding parents and the inevitably damaged infant, together with a general reluctance to note and experience the self-evident fact of our resourcefulness and resilience, it seems that the most responsible approach is to note when our repetitive patterns erupt into the present so that we can gradually uncover at least some of the most crucial of the frozen responses of our early days. In this way, we can come to experience real choice in significant areas of our lives, and enjoy the satisfaction of conscious creation, in spite of the fears and traumas of our youth.

I wish to emphasize, however, that it is not so much our wounds that we need to re-experience as *our initial modes of handling them* – our own unique style of dealing with the natural pains and vicissitudes of life. Past hurts can heal, but only if we stop sustaining them by our fixed reactions to them. We have to know and accept the particular method of defence evolved by the child in each of us, and sometimes in specific and immediate detail, in order to leave victimhood behind.

I should like to share an example of a frozen response, first exposing the way in which it can interrupt and obstruct the full functioning of choice, and then tracing the process of its release. A friend of mine (whom I shall call David), after some years of therapy, was still thwarted by acute anxiety in any situation of assessment – in any test or examination – even though he was talented and, on the conscious level, reasonably confident. And then he decided to use just such an occasion as an opportunity to explore what lay beneath his anxiety, to try and discover what generated this unfitting reaction; a reaction tailored to fit another set of circumstances in the distant past.

From very early in life, he grew to believe that his mother wanted him to be different from the way he was: she liked strong, macho males, and approved of his 'tough' elder brother. As an adult he came to realize that he had always swung from desperately trying to please her and gain her approval to withdrawing into himself. He had set up a split between what he called his 'true self' (which he could only be if he was on his own or did the things he imagined she didn't like), and the self that he felt she demanded him to be. He couldn't be both true to himself and appreciated. Over time it came to the point that whenever he pleased someone, he feared that he was 'a phoney'; he had the sneaking feeling that he was being unreal. This dilemma was accentuated if he gained approval from authority figures – he could never fully receive or be nourished by their love or praise, and would become strangely anxious if he was favoured in any way. He thus developed tactics for diverting such approval.

Again and again he would seek new challenges, only to bump up against what his psyche perceived were the demands of his mother ('men must be successful...'), whereupon he'd find a way back to the safety of failure and the moral satisfaction of being his 'true self once more. At the same time, however, he also plunged into the desolation of feeling abandoned and rejected. His life script evolved into, 'To be true to myself, I have to be not wanted, lonely and unsatisfied'. But of course this position was, in fact, a betrayal of his real self, and so he sensed that something was deeply wrong. Either way, then, he betrayed himself – caught in a contradiction that readily generated anxiety and paralysis.

David came to see why examination situations were a hotline to his old dilemma; he was not true to himself if he engineered failure (because he wanted, for his own sake, to pass the exam), and yet the old frozen response was still lodged in his psyche and held by his body, generating an updated version of, 'She'll approve of me if I succeed, and therefore I won't be my true self if I do'. The 'double bind' he had created set off a chain of responses at the hormonal level and rendered him helpless – choiceless. Once he was in this anxiety state, he genuinely felt that he was without choice. And so, as an interim measure, he 'reframed' the situation in such a way as to by-pass the notion of success or failure altogether. He told himself that *whatever* happened – whether the examiners passed or failed him, were pleased with him or disappointed in him – he would learn something of crucial importance about himself from undergoing the examination. This released him from the inevitable experience of self-betrayal. His anxiety level was lowered, and he passed the exam.

On the surface, it was impossible to see why David made things so difficult for himself. He was an extremely attractive and gifted person. Only as he gradually extended the range of his consciousness, and experienced and understood the nature of the dilemma that he had set up for himself, could he freely choose to be successful in life in his own way. He came to see that elements of what his mother wanted of him were exactly what he also wanted for himself, and he could be true to himself even if his actions did 'please' her too. She had been dead many years, but lived on for him in the repetitive dynamic of his frozen response to her. What had held his false 'choice' so firmly in place was the fact that whenever he retreated into what he called his 'true self', he had also felt abandoned and rejected. Because this was such an old and familiar feeling, he was convinced that it was a place of truth; it was more real to him than anything else.

Over time, David learnt not to give the weight of reality to his repetitive feelings of abandonment and not to associate truth with familiarity. He thus assimilated more and more deeply the fact that his 'true self' did not rest on what his mother wanted or did not want of him – or what any other significant figure wanted or did not want. No agonizing decision between impossible alternatives was necessary. There was no need to resist anyone. All that time, he had only been resisting the mother within himself.

The Physical Experience of Releasing a Frozen Response

We experience the conscious meeting with one of our underlying modes of response physically; we feel touched on that organismic, preverbal level from which it originally sprang. It is on this level, also, that we can let it go. If we give due attention to our inner process, then we will experience a deep and subtle easing right through our body. A release occurs on the tissue level which is almost imperceptible but very profound. We are likely to sigh out gently and find that our body tingles and streams with energy – again, almost below the threshold of sensation. It is not a loud, cathartic realization. Simple wonder and recognition: 'Yes, yes, that is it....'. Wonder and simplicity combined. Silence, as a new rhythm of breathing takes over. It is a meeting with ourselves at the original point of responsibility. From this meeting we can reclaim our true responsiveness: we unite with that initial response which later became fixated into a position of reaction; and as we unite with it, so we integrate and become whole at a profound and primal level. This integration allows our energy to flow and clear and move in more appropriate ways in future. A full and aware acceptance of self is the most potent tool of change.

As long as we are caught in debilitating responses from the past, we cannot effectively live out our adult responsibility or fully enjoy our ability to act. But if we connect with that point where we took up a set position, and include the old formative decision in our awareness, then we can reclaim our responsive nature and become capable of making fresh choices in the present. Troublesome primal responses cannot be defeated or overcome; but they can be discovered, respectfully uncovered and recognized. Recognized with compassion for the infant self, or child, that responded so, and froze so.

Recognized with the calm which comes from really knowing; from knowing our reality, and resting in our reality. The security of truth. 'This is my life position, fashioned by me and given energy by me, expressing my dilemma and my fear.' Freedom from blame. The sureness of ownership. We have a sense of fitting together, of fittingness, of re-membering ourselves. The old frozen position softens as we contemplate it. Gradually we find that it has lost its compelling power, its relentless attraction, its inevitability. Our whole being feels lighter and, indeed, is enlightened. We find ourselves saying, 'I don't need to go on doing this. I don't have to do it any more.' The most blessed of conversations. It is, quite suddenly, no big deal. We release ourselves from repeating that old response and, in so doing, come into the fullness of our conscious ability to choose.

Accepting the Damaged Self

It is not the wounds of the past that damage us so much as our taking up set positions against them. It is not the deeds of our parents that harm us so much as our perpetuation of the hurt we once experienced. The act of our parent occurs as a passing temporal episode – our reaction, guarded by hidden remembrance, is out of time, and stretches its influence over countless moments.

No parent can punish us as thoroughly as we do ourselves. We torture ourselves by keeping alive our parents' mistakes and inadequacies, continually updating the most agonizing encounters from childhood. Our self-cruelty is immense, both crude and subtle in expression, and inexhaustible. In this way the sins of the parents are indeed visited on the children – invited to remain eternally with us. We find it astonishingly difficult to let them, and therefore ourselves, off the hook. We are relentless in our pursuit of lost causes, of what can never be. We refuse to rejoice in the fact that what once hurt so dreadfully, or raised such terror in us, is now no longer occurring; we give more weight to the fact that it *did* happen.

If we dealt with physical wounds in this way, would we not be incredulous at our own obvious folly? Yet we use enormous energy to preserve the pain of the past, and systematically refuse to allow the powerful process of healing to take its course. Again and again, I have witnessed people being so absorbed with what they didn't have as a child that they miss what is readily available to them in the present: they mourn their past deprivation even when in a situation of plenty.

Chapter Ten: Freedom and Destiny

Of course, it can never serve us to pretend that the past wasn't painful or frightening, desolate or frustrating; to insist that it was 'fine'. As I discussed earlier, denial of our true feelings, of our reality, only distorts and wastes our energy. But the value of actively re-experiencing such episodes lies not only in affording ourselves the opportunity for such feelings to flow and clear, but also because we can at the same time learn of our particular inventive response to these old hurts, and know precisely *how* we keep recycling what we most objected to when a child. It serves us best to re-connect with our own activity: we can never be in charge of our lives if the accent of our attention is always focused on the energy of the 'other' – on what they did to us.

The subtle processes of transformation or healing – involving as they do the letting go of old formations within the psyche, old formative energies – require far more of us than the employment of our ego, or our will. Certainly, if we rely only on ego consciousness, then we are likely merely to take up a new counter choice *on top of* the old position, perhaps even hiding it more craftily if our deeper intention is to remain defended. We may give the old fixed position a fresh burst of secret affirmation by this counter choice – yet another way of covering itself and preserving its influence. Our many-layered psyche is incredibly complex in its operations. We are still orientated around the old position if we are busy refuting it. Only acceptance brings change.

Will and choice are not synonymous; we use our will in the service of choice, to fulfil and implement our choice. If we merely *will* new behaviour while holding to old beliefs and emotional positions, we shall find ways of subverting that behaviour. And if this does not occur, then we may do well to consider whether it really is new behaviour – perhaps it is simply appearing in a new guise. So much surface change can, at first, look very impressive. We can say with conviction, 'I would never have done or said that before'. And it is true. Our primal response has found a different means of expression. We are enormously inventive. It often takes decades to clear a key fixation or old choice of its power to influence us. We come to a point when we can expand no further from its base, and that is our opportunity for transformation, for healing, although more often experienced as an unwelcome crisis. (It is worth noting that in Chinese, the word 'crisis' is the same as the word for opportunity.)

Meanwhile, these apparent changes are still valuable. They give immediate relief and solve certain relatively superficial, but nevertheless urgent, problems. Perhaps they are even necessary staging posts – the ego feels more secure if it can mark development in some way. Such changes also take us finally towards discovery of the original position which supplies their countering energy. For although at first they might deceive us, and we perhaps imagine that they are proof of the death or demise of our troublesome neurotic stance, in the end we are disappointed, as we hit some breed of the old familiar sabotage tactics at a more profound level, and know that we haven't really freed ourselves, or changed in the way that we had hoped.

There may come a time when the only means of opening up the undermining frozen response is to acknowledge that we do not wish to change after all. However much we think that we want to change on a rational level, and desperately desire and need to do so, the balance of our energy is obviously with non-change. In order to be at one with ourselves in that given moment, we must consciously connect with our powerful underlying determination to remain the same (usually in the hope that the world around us will move and 'bring' the change to us). We want change without ourselves changing.

Once we accept our reality, whatever it might be, and connect with our ruling energy at that moment, we in fact cannot help but change. That is the great paradox of human development. Trying to change, we remain fixed, because our energy is split and thus held and ineffective. No real movement can take place if we are at war with ourselves – albeit in a good and just cause. But once we accept our reality, even if it be the very refusal to change, then we integrate our energy and the life in us, being dynamic in nature, moves us on. We are changed. The process of change is freed.

With acceptance of our true state, we become fully present, and aware, with nothing more to lose, nothing to resist. We are then available not just for mere surface change and immediate relief of some kind (involving only a rejuggling of old patterns and a minimal sense of loss), but for true transformation. This is the place of creative despair. We are available for the dismantling of our original position, which we have finally laid bare. This is the place of humility, of nakedness. From here we can, indeed, start afresh, for we are at one with ourselves; we have dared to acknowledge the seed of our dysfunctioning. With complete self-acceptance, our energy gently disengages from this distorting 'seed' so that it loses its formative power. We no longer attempt to flower in the same old self-defeating ways. Having extended our consciousness to our beginnings, to the ground of our choice, we are ready to come into our true adulthood. We can become actively choosing beings.

Our fixated responses must thus be accepted, not refused; appreciated, not berated. They can never be conquered. If we try to defeat them, they will only hide more skilfully. We must enter into their energy – not set ourselves against them; only then can they loosen and begin to move. The old formation undoes itself, un-forms, only in a climate of full acceptance and a situation of non-resistance; and we are then freed to respond and shape our lives differently from that moment onwards. Having seen how we have created our reality up to this point, we know from direct experience that we can continue to create it – but now with fresh responses, and conscious choices based on these more fitting responses. We are open to making different kinds of choices which draw on a variety of ever-changing responses. This realization fills us with a subtle sense of exhilaration. If the experience does not contain this quality of subtle vitality and immediacy (which indicates the level at which the original response was made), then in all probability we have not quite got there.

We have to face the fact that some patterns are extremely tenacious – bonded, perhaps, by a complex combination of frozen responses which are reinforced over many years of systematic provocation and reaction. It could be that such patterns are unlikely ever to unfreeze and dissolve but, rather, form a scar that must be acknowledged, and respected as such. Each time this damaged spot is touched, we will experience being 'in its power' as vividly as ever; but we can at least learn not to exacerbate the old wound, not to deal roughly or carelessly with it so as to set it gushing forth with renewed energy. The scar lives on in us, a witness to the past and playing but a part in the shaping of our life – as a tree is shaped by a series of severe winters or dry summers; but the growing tip of our being, like the shoot and leaves and buds of the tree, is as new and flexible as ever.

We can learn how to stay with the growing tip of the self. And the more we expand and enter into other areas of our being, claiming our 'roundness' as an individual and opening to the rich spectrum of possible ways to be, the less dominant is the scar. It becomes scarcely noteworthy, and it no longer commands our present. We become ever less attracted to our wounds, less bound up with them, the more we fill out our experience and appreciate other aspects of ourselves. Old reactions may always be triggered by certain situations, but once we are aware of our damaged areas and are familiar with their ways, once we respect our specific vulnerabilities and do not condemn ourselves for feeling and acting in 'the same old way' when these sensitive areas are touched, then we learn how to process or step aside from the old material and move on to other things. We no longer get stuck in our stuckness.

It is important to note that it is not only lack of awareness or denial, but also condemnation, that ensures a continuing emphasis and, thus, a further fixation on those very fixations that we cannot dissolve. Blaming can never free us. If we can say with lightness, humour and compassion, 'Here I go again' ... 'This old thing back again!...', then the dynamic in question will have short-lived influence and will fail to divert the general thrust of life towards fulfilment. It is at first disconcerting that each time a scar of the psyche is touched, or bumped, it can yield the familiar pain, or fear, or compulsive behaviour *at the same level of intensity*. However, once the scar is 'placed' and contained within the ever-growing context afforded by an increased experience of our potentialities as an individual, this old reaction, as intense as it may be, soon sweeps through us and is gone.

Once we know our neurotic areas and sense when we are 'in them' – recognize as soon as we are operating neurotically – then we can live as a healthily neurotic being. We learn how to skirt around the 'swamps' of our nature; and if we do inadvertently step into them, at such times we know that we do well to refrain from making important decisions, or performing certain actions. There comes a point when the less attention we give to our neuroses, the better; we can then keep our energy for the more open and free aspects of our psyche – the 'mountains' and vast 'planes', intimate 'valleys' and interesting 'caverns'. Such choices are the antithesis of denial, for they rest on deep acceptance and familiarity with our own unique modes of response and our own entrapping fixations. We don't have to be clear of our neurotic habits before we can describe or experience ourselves as a responsible human being – we simply have to be aware enough not to let our neurotic patterns call the tune and dominate our lives.

The most common 'scarring' seems to centre around the notion of abandonment. As long as we as a species are *totally* dependent during our early days of infanthood (not only biologically but psychically dependent, as discussed earlier), we are all too likely to feel abandoned. No mother or father can be 'there' just for us. A sense of being abandoned is one of the most primary of all frozen responses to life, one of the most frequent of fixated emotional states to which we return time and again. This position is intimately interwoven with our deep resistance to taking responsibility for ourselves later in life. If we keep alive the experience of being abandoned, of being left helpless and alone, then we carry an in-built justification for all those other versions of victimhood in which we so readily and 'naturally' engage as we go through life. How can an abandoned infant ever be expected to become a fully functioning, responsible human being? We believe that we are owed something. We must have our due from our parents, and the world, before we can grow up.

Surely, however, those of us who are now alive (which includes all those reading this book) were obviously *not* abandoned. We were given enough care to survive. The rest is up to us. No one else *can* do it for us. As alive human beings, were we not carried by life's natural unfolding into countless opportunities for self-being? The experience of abandonment rests on the deeply entrenched and mistaken idea that we have to be 'attached' to someone to be safe, that we *ought* to be attached. This is one of the fundamental beliefs that needs to be cleared from our bodies and minds, or at least not given weight and substance, so that we can truly develop psychologically, and leave the womb behind. If we refuse to forfeit our demands on mother or father – which so often continue unabated long after we are children – we will cheat ourselves of the experience of our true place of being at the living source of our own reality. We will cheat ourselves of adulthood.

Chapter Eleven
Towards Full Adulthood

I want to draw a distinction between the freedom of responsibility and the 'freedom' of irresponsibility.

The freedom of responsibility is the freedom we take, we make, for ourselves by knowing that we are the source of our own reality. We therefore do not let externals determine us, however profoundly we interact with others and draw on the world around us. Put in other terms, we no longer have an 'authority problem'. We stand in our own authority, speak with our own authentic voice. We are free in that we do not mind about our reputation or our image. While accepting others as mirrors and valuing their feedback, we do not let the fear that we may be judged as rash, selfish, inconsistent or foolish influence our decisions and actions. We do not limit ourselves by identifying with any stance or institution, sect or nation, social role or past state. We draw on the wisdom of different or ancient cultures, and are enriched by the talents of other people. In touch with our needs, we easily offer and receive support and help from others when appropriate. Not burdened by competition or the making of comparisons, we seek to discover and express our own contribution to the world, however ordinary or extraordinary that may be. We give ourselves the freedom to follow our 'inner voice' and allow our own particular, and often unexpected, unfolding of being.

As our consciousness extends and more of our self comes into view, as new energies and different qualities become available, so, too, our contact with the world around us clears and deepens. Whenever we experience our inner reality directly, we find that we also experience our outer reality more directly. They increasingly become one experience. At moments of clarity, the division between internal and external is perceived as illusory, although the facility to distinguish between the two in an appropriate way remains. (Contemplative and mystical approaches to human experience deliberately set out to invoke and develop such immediate unitary apprehension.)

We take up our freedom through being at one with self (which entails differentiating the various levels and modes of expression through which self manifests); and if we are at one with self, we cannot help but be at one with the larger reality within which we have our being. In our essence, we fit the universe: both unfold in one movement. This fittingness, this lack of constraint and obstruction of our deepest intentionality, gives us the living experience of freedom. We do not *feel* restricted by the world – we feel met by it; nourished by it, challenged by it, shaped and extended by it. Freedom is the experience of at-one-ment with All-That-Is.

The 'freedom' of irresponsibility is born of the blissful sensation of letting go into fusion, which in turn allows us the 'innocence' afforded by introjection and projection. It is the ecstatic descent into the illusion of oneness *at the ego level* – which in reality is simply a confusion of boundaries. In the midst of the turmoil and conflict of competing realities – a condition which cannot help but arise in societies whose members are dominated by ego consciousness – we feel that we must 'have' a special friend, mate, partner, object, security blanket, teddy, to support our position and confirm our reality. (And while we are in this situation, thank god for teddies!) Later, we can turn around and use this special co-dependent fellow ego as an ever-available and handy peg on which to hang all blame, thus' freeing' us from the burden of blaming ourselves.

It is important to make a distinction between the experience of oneness and that of fusion. The experience of oneness with all things could not be further from that familiar desire to be the same as another – or to reside within the orbit of another particular person. Being at one with *any* other manifestation of the ONE is a very different state of consciousness from fusion with another one being. The former is an actualizing activity which calls on the full self; the latter is the concern of the trapped infant in us.

Fusion is sought by the disconnected, ego-dominated self wishing to escape its belief in isolation. For all those short-lived dips into bliss, a need for fusion expresses fear, emptiness, longing and dependency. On the other hand, being at one with another arises from the knowledge that separation is an illusion and draws on the aspect of consciousness that experiences connection: it expresses love, fulfilment, peace and freedom. Being in oneness is the resonating movement of spirit, whereas fusion is the preoccupation of a psyche that has forgotten its original source of being and remembers only the biological pre-definition of the womb. The more we experience at-one-ment with all things, the less we feel the compensatory tug towards fusion with one special other. Oneness is inclusive and fusion is exclusive. Our development as individuals, and as a species, depends on not confusing the two.

Meanwhile, as we tentatively oscillate on the brink of the next stage of evolution, it is hardly surprising that we are tempted to flee from the mode of separation that ego has brought to our attention. It is natural to seek out a state of fusion – to join the collective dive back to the womb in search for a lost continuity. But ego consciousness, designed to serve our need for differentiation (which is where its true power lies), can never fuse with another ego without also bringing up fears of oblivion; hence the close association between death and sex. This very fear then exacerbates a renewed drive to regress; an even greater urge to seek the old safe place of fusion in the womb.

A self-destructive reflexive loop occurs whenever we treat our ego as our whole self. Preoccupation with fusion is a retrograde step: it attempts to turn back the arrow of time. Our apprehension of unity is appropriately experienced by other aspects of consciousness, not our ego consciousness. Both the deep consciousness of our Western Adult Spirit self and the all-inclusive consciousness of our Eastern Child Spirit self tune in to other entities at the subtle level of shared being. It is not a matter of attempting to fuse what has necessarily been given distinction. Individuation requires that we hold awareness of both our given connectedness to all things and our differentiation within all things – hence our multi-dimensional consciousness.

Given that so many of us are still centred in ego, however – terrified by that very state of separation to which, as egos, we are bound to attribute false ontological status – we claim the freedom of irresponsibility and abandon ourselves to attachment. (Of course we need, instead, to abandon our attachment – but that is a lot to expect of a self that is largely constricted to ego consciousness.) The attachment, although entered into in order to supply permanent security and 'fix' everything, is ever vulnerable because egos believe deeply in separation – hence their absorption with attachment. Once again we can witness the blind, ego-referring loop in operation.

Thus it is that we are frequently driven to repeat the sexual act in a false flight into union even while filled with hatred and resentment. 'I must have you.' Abandoning ourselves for brief spells in this way gives us a regressed and infantile *sensation of freedom*. When an opportunity for achieving intense fusion seems on the cards, we allow ourselves anything and take stock of nothing; we risk all. We throw restraint to the winds. Such bravado is admired and envied by all other fellow 'infants', and condemned by the 'parent' in us. The 'freedom' of irresponsibility springs from our terror of, and a desire to fill, the empty vacuum which is left by our flight from taking responsibility and claiming our full selves. The hunger to 'have another' or, if that is too frightening, to go for the bottle, or a 'fix' to fill the void and gain a fleeting release into carelessness, is as powerful as is the legitimate biological hunger that the infant has for the breast.

Having equated the hunger of the fragmented ego for attachment with our original biological need for nourishment, as a species we have tended to hold our energy at this point. We continue, generation after generation, to live out our fixation on the 'psychic breast'. We believe that our necessary psychic nourishment – our self-esteem – must be imbibed from outside of us, from a specially selected 'other' who will make *us* special. We hold to the idea that we must drink in energy and meaning from this 'other', fill ourselves with her (or his) urgent need for us. And so we occupy ourselves in obsessive searching, or hopeless longing, for such an other with whom to fall in love: a fall into intense and socially approved regression. We take delight in their elevated and elated view of us; drink in the tempting fantasy image of ourselves which they offer us (arising out of *their* desire for such an image).

We get intoxicated with the hope that we are, indeed, this figment of our lover's imagination, while all the time it is merely a construction fired by the unlived aspects of themselves. And in our longing for a fixed state of attachment, we promise love for ever more.

It has *got* to last, though we fear and sense that it can't and won't. This is the currency of abandonment to attachment; and when we empty the bank – when the energy of being in love suddenly goes bankrupt and the cold light of reality creeps in – we simply open another account elsewhere. We fall in love all over again with a new fellow image-maker. This choice (compulsion) is counted our highest and most daring freedom, although many soon settle for the safer freedom to choose and consume material 'goods' instead. Both are compensations for true freedom and true fulfilment.

Being in love is an exchange, not of selves (that is impossible) but of fantasies of self. 'If you think that I am the most wonderful person in the whole world, then I'll think that you are.' Absorbed in this exchange of self-image, locked together in our specialness, we feel set apart from and different from everyone else in the world. For a time, no one else matters. Fusion equals isolationism. This particular kind of enclosed and exclusive passion gives us permission to do 'anything', to go 'mad', to lose ourselves in another. We suspend our habitual constraints and inhibitions, and imagine that we have found our freedom. Because all the rest of the world is placed outside of this magic circle of infantile absorption, we don't mind what other people think – not even our parents or our own children. We delude ourselves that we are self-determined at last. Isn't it true that we don't care about anyone else's opinion? And even their feelings don't seem so important any more. We are no longer trapped by our old concerns. We've 'made it'. We're free – except that we *have* to be with the loved one.

Of course, beneath this 'love' lies fury – not only the impotent fury of dependence but also the fury that arises out of the omnipotent belief that we should 'have it all our own way'. At this stage of our development, our sexuality is streaked with a resentment that we should have to consider the other at all in the midst of our abandoned, passionate love-making. Of course we are equally anxious to accommodate the other's fancies because we must please them and 'keep' them and impress them, but we resent that they don't just 'know' and fit our needs exactly. Isn't that what being good lovers is all about? We can see how this position has a shadow likeness with that sense of 'fitting' the universe which we experience when we take up the freedom of responsibility.

We lurch between a state of complete self-absorption and demand for our needs to be met whatever they may be (persecutor/sadist), and the opposite pole of service and self-subjugation (victim/masochist). At this stage of evolution, it seems that our sexuality stems fundamentally from our infant selves; we engage in physically adult genital sex expressed via the infant psyche. It is fired by the dynamic of separation and fusion within a framework of perceived inequality, and this combination can easily give rise to the experience of devouring and being devoured. Courtship is all too often based on power games; the perpetual dance of the disclaiming and reclaiming of power in relation to another. Only the crown of the 'in love' experience gives us a brief respite – a truce of equality in mutual absorption, but destined to revert to the power struggle that underpins it.

All the time we sincerely believe that we are following the life force, our libido, as we fall backwards into regression and clutch at our once-blissful state of physical fusion. Daunted by the prospect of the freedom of responsibility, we prefer to seek freedom, for which we inevitably long, by means of abandonment to infantile irresponsibility – ending up enslaved. The two opposite freedoms (and if they are opposite, then one must be a non-freedom) do indeed share many resonances with each other. Unable to bear a stage of difficult transition which has no reference points, we slip backwards in order to pick up resonances from our past, rather than venture into new territory to discover fulfilment and true freedom.

Yet at the same time, in our half-evolved and incomplete state, our hearts know something of mutuality and respect for self and other – of that nourishing, joyful, expansive exchange of energy between two selves in intimate acknowledgment, honesty, compassion and delight – just as we also intuit something of our true freedom and glimpse our power of self-generation. How hard it is at this transitional stage of development to combine the needs and knowing of our hearts with the thrust of our still-infant sexuality. Our more mature needs urge for expression alongside the voracious infant desire to be filled by another. We can never reach satisfaction or fulfilment if we settle for remaining an infant, and yet this obvious truth is cloaked by our mistaken belief that we are, psycho-sexually, adults. Are we not only too ready to accuse the 'other' of being the childish one? In so doing, we seal our own infant state.

Of course, in daring to 'go with' a deep passion for another, there could well be an overlapping of both 'freedoms'. We could indeed be giving ourselves the opportunity of discovering and expressing ourselves more fully at the same time as being drawn into fusion and obsession. With awareness and discernment, it is possible to work through the regressed aspect of the process and move beyond it. We can learn to let go of the obsessional element in a relationship and come to honour our own boundaries in a new way, recovering a sense of self even while experiencing the pull towards fusion. It is not an easy road and never automatic, because, along with the stretching and the challenge, old material is not only called up, but is given an added charge of energy. All aspects of self are required – our Southern, Northern, Western and Eastern modes of consciousness – to steer us through the compelling pitfalls until we gain a resilient sense of choice. Thus we can grow in our ability to be active in our own self-fulfilment, which will of course include open exchanges with our loved one.

The 'in love' experience can also be an important catalyst; it can bring us to life. A powerful opening of the psyche takes place, affording access to a stream of energy strong enough to help us move beyond a present 'safe' arrangement. Is not this the 'biological' reason for falling in love? A special energy is required if we are to be lifted out of our intense absorption in the dynamics with mother and father and siblings in 'the nest' – an energy which holds a greater and more immediate attracting force. And just such energy is provided by the 'in love' condition.

For this reason it is enormously important, as an adolescent and young adult, to fall in love. This is a time of extravagant discovery – we need to 'go over the top' and break, and lose, and find, and form boundaries. But it has its proper place in our lives. We move from those sweet, intensely serious childhood 'crushes' that interweave with summers that seem to go on for ever and which lighten our school years, until suddenly we are hit by the impact of full sexually charged romantic passion for another. And we think, 'Ah, it has happened to me too – now I know', as the blood rushes through our

Chapter Eleven: Towards Full Adulthood

whole being. Of course, as the psyche is unconcerned with chronological age, adolescence can occur at any age. But this captivating liberation loses its natural developing force if it becomes an addiction. If endlessly sought, it is no longer a soaring flight from the nest: adulthood remains an elusive state, receding ever-further from the lover's grasp.

Herein resides a paradox: 'falling in love' goes straight to the centre of our defence system, touching the point around which our sexual energy originally fixated; and therefore while acting as a life-giving explosion of energy that releases us from the confines of our external material home, taking us beyond its bounds, at the same time it drags us right back to the core of our inner psychological home. It can be an example of creative regression; an opportunity to pick up on our original passion for mother or father. The organizing matrix of our sexuality, our erotic blueprint, is revealed – its specific quality and nature... – if we care to see it. Thus, we gain the possibility not only of repeating, but also of releasing ourselves from set modes of expressing our sexuality. We can come to let go of that which we can now experience from another perspective, with the greater security of having achieved at least some of the practical aspects of adulthood.

Any fixation precludes satisfaction because to be fully alive, we need to allow change, and most of our present sexuality is based on fixations of one kind or another. Don't we talk of 'our type' and aim always to re-create, again and again, what once 'turned us on'? Much of our sexual energy becomes switched to our heads – it spends itself in clamouring and insistent fantasies, and has little to do with the person breathing and moving in and around us. No nourishment is then possible. Or we may seek specialness by dissociating ourselves from physical connection and turning to the 'intellectual breast'. We thus demand, with a similar fervour, to be 'understood' by a significant other. We crave their understanding, and feel abandoned and isolated if we do not receive it. How common and how emotionally charged is the indignant cry that we have been misunderstood. Of course we can also alternate between these hungers, as well as combining the two.

Nothing renders us more lonely than misdirected sexuality. In the end, we find that it feeds, not our sense of specialness, but our self-hate. Only as a unique being – in the company of others and in communion with others – experiencing life in an unfolding and ever-flexible immediacy, do we *live* our natural specialness. Only then are we released from the pain-filled demand to be 'made special' by the obsessive attention of another. The specialness for which we so yearn, and compulsively seek, is intrinsic; a given.

The freedom of responsibility entails freedom from dependence, attachment, and thus from the experience of abandonment. It is the freedom to be who we are through the conscious acceptance of who we are; daring to be true to ourselves, unhampered by the unnecessary constraints of others' attitudes as well as our own outdated defensive positions. Once we take on our freedom to be a unique self, knowing that as such we also serve the Whole and are upheld by the Whole, then we can love another rather than attach ourselves to them. We can enjoy and appreciate others, rather than hunger after them and attempt to possess them. Human sexuality will then be a mode of individual expression in relationship with another – an I/Thou experience – rather than misused as an escape from full self-hood and a transient means of gaining approval, pseudo-power and comfort (which can eventually lead to the appalling quagmire of abuse and protection of others). Only by moving on into becoming a fully individuated being, not by losing ourselves in another or using another, can we experience true fulfilment.

The Tide of Life

While aspects of us wish to commit ourselves to follow the direction of life forwards, simultaneously we give way to the strong backwash of that immense tide of energy needed to carry our human species into the next stage of our development. It seems easier to go with this backwash and to let ourselves be pulled, against life's main flow, towards the infant freedom of irresponsibility, than it is to allow the forward movement into completely unknown territory. It seems more desirable to return to the familiar than to risk the radical newness that unfolds, once we take up the freedom of full responsibility. We dare not go through the 'no-man's land' of unknown psychic experience which inevitably lies before us as soon as we let go of our infant sexuality and our power games – that stubbornly idealized drive towards fusion which also brings rejection and warfare in its wake.

We mistake the letting go as an expression of cynicism – the embittered consolation of those who have denied their sexuality, or have never dared to 'fall in love' and experience its blissful agonies. We are reluctant to enter the disconcerting period of transition that is bound to follow the relinquishing of our old preoccupations, and which somehow we must find a way of living through. (Many women wish they could die during the transition stage of labour, but luckily are carried by their biology which, during birth, seems at the peak of its power.)

Perhaps any transition reminds us of that original transition at incarnation – that hiatus in being, that point of suspension when, for an instant, we were neither substance nor non-substance. And because we are so familiar with the state of stuckness (which is the very nub of all neurosis), do we fear that we shall get stuck at this point of suspension? The ego cannot know that the creative void is the womb of new being – that once it is entered, the actualization of potential is assured. The ego has no meta-view that can span across both being and non-being, and perceives any gap in knowing as the 'black hole' of its darkest nightmare. Transition is thus anathema to ego consciousness. It is the all-inclusive, trans-temporal consciousness of our Eastern self that bridges the gaps; that knows beyond the nothingness, knows the integration of being and non-being, and envisions the simultaneous expression of the whole.

Thus, we ego-dominated, linear-orientated beings are wary of this time of transition, fearful of trusting and going with the tide of life. We abhor the imagined nothingness of waiting, as we go through the actual processes of change, before we find new points of reference and a new means of expression. It seems too much to expect of human beings that we should wait until we discover how to be equal beings: touching. meeting, being present and open to one another, but not fusing or devouring or controlling – on either the personal or the political level. We are used to searching for immediate satisfaction of our ego energy and seeking instant release for our sexual energy. (Is not that one of the main freedoms of irresponsibility?) Why should we wait?

As the freedom of irresponsibility shares undertones with the mature freedom of full responsibility, we go for that echo – even when we learn that it is hollow. For the no-man's land ahead is silent and void of familiar resonances – utterly new and unknown. We balk at the silence. We regress backwards, going with the backwash rather than holding firm on the empty clear-washed sand, biding our time, trusting, until we move forward with the tide of life into that fuller consciousness of our multi-layered self which alone can bring us into freedom.

At this stage of evolution – this transition stage – we are not yet fully evolved, and yet we are evolved enough to know that we are not fully evolved. Witnessing this state is so costly, brings us so close to madness, that we prize illusion and diversion. We sense dimly our fulfilment as free beings, glimpse it – and yet do not feel ready to actualize it. Or rather, we cannot hope to actualize it unless we let go of all echos and allow old reference points to dissolve. But we are so terrified of the unknown that we do almost anything to avoid it. Is it because it reminds us of that great and inevitable Unknown that lies before us at death? To the ego, which always identifies with the known, death speaks of oblivion. (Also, as the delineator of boundaries, ego naturally abhors that which is beyond boundaries.) Therefore ego-dominated beings must always connect death, and the unknown, with nothingness. No wonder we feel the pull of the old known fusion of the womb. It has the power of a magnet drawing us ever backwards to the familiar.

So we dress up this regressive urge in the guise of love (for a person, nation, sect or group), and we value 'being in love' more highly than any other state. Our music, art, drama, literature, religions – all pour out the message of dependent love from morning til night, either in crude and brash form or on levels of beauteous subtlety. The words of our pop songs, that are the back drop of so many peoples' lives, all shout at us of neediness and possession: 'Love only me for ever' is the continual refrain. They lure us with false expectations, and invite us to remain ever 'young'. They attempt to immortalize infanthood. Such visions of intermingling, such stories of entanglement, divert our energy, and protect us from insight; from the shocking clarity of a deeper awareness that cannot help but also take us into the dreaded unknown. Coiled blindly in the orbit of another (or the cohesive passion of national pride), we cannot see either them or ourselves. We seek the false freedom of illusion (even though it soon becomes a prison and a trap), rather than let go and step forwards into empty silence, waiting in openness until we discover the new freedom of creativity and self-expression.

The attraction of the freedom of irresponsibility is so compelling just because it touches off the same harmonics as the fully resonating state of true human freedom. We genuinely experience being called backwards to our beginnings. It feels so much more natural to slip back into the known, to pick up the old buzz that we get from attachment and the intensity of neurotic involvement. It feels so much easier to be drawn back with the retreating waves into the ocean of original bliss, rather than thrust forward further up the shore where no woman or man ever trod before; and where we fear we could be left stranded and alone. The human species is being urged into new consciousness, creativity and freedom and that, by definition, *must* feel too much for us if we are also endeavouring to remain the same as we always have been. It has come to a point in our story when life demands expansion of consciousness or extinction.

We can trace the same regression on the political front – the same aversion to transition, the same lurch backwards to old 'solutions'. Did not the loosening of old repressive structures in Eastern Europe immediately evoke a preoccupation with fusion along old nationalist lines, with the concomitant resurgence and validation of racism? (racism being a good barometer of national regression). Freedom is being identified with the maintenance of national groupings and free-market economies. We refuse the new. Release from the clear familiar enmities of the 'Cold War', although opening up a possible way forward, sent us scuttling pell-mell backwards into the least original of all methods of gaining what we want – war.

In the Gulf, the crude clash of male egos – of siblings fighting for control of access to the rich black 'milk' from the breast of mother earth – was dressed to look like global co-operation; for we know perfectly well that such must be the way forward. Cheating ourselves in this manner, our actions are all too likely to give birth to a mere re-arrangement of enmities. Rather than daring to let go of our infant obsession with power and possessions, rather than falteringly trying out something new which we cannot be sure will work and may leave us feeling inept, we revert to tried old methods; it feels 'safer'. And so the sibling which lost the battle took revenge on Mother, as he had threatened to do, resorting yet again to an act of violation born of impotent infant rage. He struck at the breast he so desired and the oil wells blazed. Better no-one have that which we cannot have ourselves. The more we attempt to avoid what we assume is the chaos of the unknown, the more we hold fast to the obsolete, the more surely we shall bring on ourselves the very chaos we so fear. We cannot control life. If we are not prepared to risk uncertainty then we can never gain maturity or enjoy the full benefits of adulthood.

Just as we as individuals slip back into our old neurotic patterns when we reach that precarious threshold which marks the possibility of the new, so too on a collective level, we seem to have taken a great collective lurch backwards. It is clear that ego consciousness alone is not enough. Indeed, have we ever before had such comprehensive and detailed information at our disposal? On the psychological level, we have more 'facts' to aid us than ever before, but they avail us nothing if they cannot be placed within a more integrated consciousness. If we continue to resist the tide of life and flinch from experiencing the yet-to-be-known, our species may never reach its adult state; and we may not manifest the fulfilment for which we were born. However, given our stupendous inheritance expressed through all living form, I find it hard to believe that we could finally ignore the creative vitality of this heritage and turn our back on our completion.

So perhaps one of the most important questions to put to ourselves at this point is whether we truly do wish to be rigid – which we are forced to be if we hold on to old positions – when we are so capable of expanding. We don't have to find the answer to life; we simply have to dare to go *with* life. All we have to do is to see our present preoccupations as unfitting – to see attachment, dependence and blame as illusory pursuits. Once we know them as illusions, it is easier to forgo our general commitment to holding things as they are, and the way is opened up for further development. The humility of clear sight is what is required. It is the *seeing* that is the first crucial step – allowing the light of the next stage in the dialectic of human truth to shine on this stage, which is then, in that instant, made redundant. If we can only let ourselves know our dearest beliefs as illusions, then fixed frameworks can begin to dismantle themselves. We must simply recognize them as illusion, or as spent 'truth', and let our frame of reference shift.

It is not a matter of fighting or solving or grappling with illusion – such a relationship only entangles us more subtly in its energy. It does not help to denigrate our out-dated treasured beliefs in yet a further act of blame; old illusions, once known to be illusions, can become a fresh vehicle in the unfurling experience of truth. Is it not the knowledge that our present attitudes are illusion that opens up the possibility for new perceptions of a more relevant truth? And this more fitting and potent truth must then be embraced as a provisional truth. It cannot be held too lightly if it is to work its power: it must excite us, but it must also be seen in the context of life itself which is ever changing. Only when *held* as truth, against the insight of its illusory nature, does illusion work the evil of non-truth. It is when a new unfolding ordering of reality is refused consciousness, so as to maintain the false status of the old reality, that the illusions which once we cherished and lent our belief become the enemy of life.

The dialectic of life calls for the ceaseless transformation of past 'truth' into illusion so that we can move on into a more evolved truth. As a species we are ready, and urgently required by life, to move from false 'freedom' – that encircling trap of infant irresponsibility – into the freedom of full selfhood. The urgency is expressed by the state of our planet; or as some would see it, the responses of Gaia. The whole person is needed by all creation, for only if we are whole ourselves shall we see the planet as a whole.

The Importance of a Non-linear Approach to Change

We have for long enough mistaken control for power, and loss of control for loss of freedom. Of course, keeping things under control could not be further from the true experience of freedom. Fear of loss of control, any hint of diminishment of false power or threat to that elusive freedom we never achieve, play an enormous role in our resistance to change. Change is interpreted as loss in nearly every sense; a loss of being 'on top of things', a loss of what has gone before, of what we had or have. A sequential time-set encourages this experience. In fact, the exact reverse is true. Change cannot help but *add* to our experience of life: it furthers opportunities of self-and-world discovery. Nothing is lost, once we let go of our sequential mode of viewing our lives. All is increase, once we stop measuring the riches of the psyche in terms suited only to the workings of the material dimension (and a crude one at that), and hold consciousness as the great gift of being.

It is salutary to note that our fear of change is actually creating a precipitous rate of change in our physical environment – the very level we have chosen as providing the base of our security. Likewise, clinging to what we already have is likely to bring a catastrophic collapse of the present economic system (however ardently we try and lend it our confidence). Such a collapse would demand a sudden and violent adaptation at a material level – the very level which 'takes time' to evolve. We create whatever most engages our energy – in this case, the thing we most fear. Human beings are not just trivially greedy or too 'soft' to give up a bit of pleasure. Deeply intuiting that we are not yet fulfilling our destiny as powerful and free beings, we are all the more frightened of losing our illusory power – the power of control – which requires the arena of the already known. And so we tend to resist rather than celebrate change, and the psyche struggles to remain a closed system within an intrinsically expanding universe.

One of the great assets of the Native American model of the self is that it offers each individual a fresh *non-linear* approach to change; to the inner change that is our only starting point. Given our deep resistance to change while so patently requiring new ways of being, such an approach could ease us out of our present predicament. Change need no longer be seen in terms of negating the past or berating what is, but rather as the clearing and melting away of the barriers which hide the unclaimed aspects of ourselves so that more and more of the whole 'sphere of the self' is illuminated. Change then becomes a phenomenon that allows us to move more freely within the possibilities of all that we are, and have been, and could be. It need not be understood in terms of *discarding*, but in terms of *expanding* and extending.

Nothing is lost – the ego's great fear – in this view of change. It does not demand that we be something else or something other. We may, if we claim more of ourselves, choose not to keep repeating old tried ways, but these are still part of who we now are. We may discontinue our habit of operating only from certain parts of ourselves while denying others, but these aspects remain available to us; they are not wiped out just because they receive less attention. Nothing is lost and nothing is fixed. It is only limitation and denial that we leave behind, while we ever increase our range of experience and action.

From our Eastern self, aided by our trans-temporal consciousness, we can see that we are everything that we are – it is an 'all-at-once' vision. Thus, when we change, we merely move through our 'isness', illuminating different aspects of our being. We know change as a varying emphasis of what is, which itself is limitless because we partake of the infinite. Our 'isness' therefore includes the utterly new. The rational mind of the North then arranges our discoveries – our uncoverings – into historical sequences and developmental stages, and this procedure has its place. But if it is given the stamp of ultimate reality, then rather than making ego feel at home, it can instead evoke intense fear of loss every time we are challenged or required to move further along this linear path – as indeed must occur, because life is not static. And so we hold against the movement of life and, puzzled by our resistance, we may even consolidate our stuckness by berating ourselves for not changing!

Perhaps, therefore, it would be more productive to think in terms of *claiming* ourselves rather than changing ourselves; we need to conceive of change as an openness and readiness to see and live more of ourselves, rather than as an endeavour to alter what already is. Put in the language of the Medicine Wheel, we would do well to see change from our Eastern perspective rather than from our Northern one. We have reached the limits of ego understanding – rationality, on its own, can take us no further. A linear conception of development will always cheat us of the ever-available experience of fulfilment which a non-linear perspective affords. A sense of completeness need not forever be postponed. We can participate in this state at any time – a state of lacking nothing – utterly satisfying and filled with joy, but never fixed or finished. We have always 'arrived' if we live our full self in the present.

But while we are still operating with such a focus on ego, and so often enclosed within it, transformation (moving across the inner barriers of the psyche), while being essential, will also still be *experienced* as change in the old linear historical sense, and thus associated with loss and so feared. Ego is by its very nature a closed system, and as such is unsuited to be the leader of human consciousness. It is hardly surprising that ego has an aversion to change when change is seen only as moving 'ahead' and losing what it already has, and with an aversion to change it will have a preference for getting stuck. And so, perhaps, in order to bypass automatic resistance, it would be better to pose our questions and challenges differently. Rather than ask whether we are prepared to change or stay stuck (which hardly invites honesty and catches us in a 'double bind'), we could ask ourselves whether we wish to stay empty and frightened or become full; whether we wish to be blanked out or alight; shrunk into a confined space or free to move and explore.

The Part Ego Plays in Our Fulfilment

Simply to heap blame on the ego for our misconceptions is not only pointless but ill-conceived. For too long the ego has been used as a scapegoat – especially by those involved in spirituality. It seems that we either let our egos dominate us or try and get rid of them; both activities equally violate our psyches and sabotage our ability to live well on earth. It is the ego, with its power to give distinction within the continuum of life, that contributed to the phenomenon of personal responsibility; and the ability to delineate boundaries and distinguish differences is as necessary to the act of taking responsibility for ourselves as is the apprehension of our essential interconnectedness. Ego plays a crucial part in the process of choice and decision-making. It is only when the ego is erroneously isolated from the rest of the self, and we attempt to function thus, that it then leads us into irresponsibility. If we dare to move into our fullness instead of trying to regain a lost past state, then the ego shall come into its own and we will be able to enjoy the challenge afforded by conscious distinction within the whole: individuation. We shall come to appreciate the true value and essential nature of the ego's contribution to our maturity as individuals.

However, although ego plays a part in the process of individuation, it does not itself provide our uniqueness nor our essence. In fact, an ego-dominated person, far from expressing individuality, copies others and takes on roles. But a supported ego, integrated within a larger concept and deeper experience of self, is free to drop its entwining concern with separation and fusion, and concentrate on its proper function of delineating boundaries on the appropriate level. With conscious recognition of our distinction as an embodied singularity, willing to avail ourselves of the many different layers of human consciousness, we know the source of self as spirit. True individuals, undivided in themselves, cannot be divided from the universe. And knowing this we are deeply safe. What need then to fuse and lose our precious boundaries, blur our distinction, when we can directly experience a far more profound oneness?

A Brief Recap of Our Present Predicament

Meanwhile, we cannot experience our oneness with the universe if we continue to see the self as a separate unit that must attach itself to another unit, if all our energy revolves around just one specific bit of the universe, as if 'she' or 'he' (perhaps translated later into nation, party, sect or 'cause') were the only source of life and well-being. If this remains the emotional matrix of most adults, let alone infants, then our creative libido will be left swirling endlessly around variations on this theme.

It is both a terrifying state of affairs and a fragmenting one, dividing us both from our source and from the rest of our environment, to be fully preoccupied with attachment to one being. We cannot be the individual that we are. Such a dependency situation also, all too frequently, traps us into the unfortunate choice of dubbing ourselves 'bad' when the relationship proves unsatisfactory in any way – as it is bound to do. The only alternative is to declare the treasured 'other' bad, and that is too appalling to contemplate if she or he is the centre of our life. Better to be 'bad' ourselves. However ardent our blaming of the one to whom we would be attached, it usually covers a deep, hidden or secret self-hate. How, as a hated self, can we hope to reach fulfilment?

Yet all the time, we could be supported by any number of different expressions of the field of life energy into which we are born; any number of individual human beings, as well as the rich sustenance afforded by nature, music, play – the list is endless. The extraordinary vitality of life both within us and all around us, *if we do but connect with it*, is far more reliable than any parent could hope to be. It alone is always 'there', unfailingly present, available in the way that we wish mother would be. Whenever we open our awareness to its movements, we no longer feel isolated. But the energy of attachment is so absorbing that we are blind to the opportunities life offers, and we obstinately try and hold on to our selected 'love object'. It is hardly surprising, therefore, that we are fundamentally insecure and prone to neurotic adaptation. The fragmentation from the rest of the world brought about by our attachment obsession evokes terror that needs continually to be kept at bay. We contract our bodies in order to create the necessary tension to block the terror and, in so doing, become physically as well as mentally rigid, and fixate our energy around the notion of abandonment.

It is ourselves we have abandoned in that primal veiling of the knowledge of our whole nature. With that forgetting of our spirit we abandon ourselves, also, to a world bereft of spirit, because spirit is one. Once we know ourselves as multi-dimensional beings, then we not only know that we cannot help but exist in some mode or other, and that all does not rest on our bio-survival alone, but also we actually experience our connectedness to all things, and so can allow mother (or any 'other') to fall into her rightful place in the unfolding of our lives.

Spirit-in-matter

However, at this transition period of evolution, when we do not retrieve a full experience of spirit immediately and start life strongly focused on our biological nature, we are going to have to come to terms with existence in the realm of matter. It is essential, therefore, that we change our attitude towards matter itself. For some people, this transformation may be most vitally understood in terms of engagement with the archetypal energy of the Goddess. To know the Goddess is to know spirit-in-matter. And once we know matter as inspirited, we can begin to resonate with the spirit in our biological nature.

But for centuries matter, 'materia', has carried connotations of corruption and inferiority. Its only access to purification has been its depowering delegation to inert meaninglessness: only as the subject of physics is matter cleansed – cleansed at the price of being declared dead. If we are indeed biologically orientated at the moment of incarnation, then we put ourselves in an almost impossible situation if we see body, in itself, as bad. And what is more, we put ourselves in this unacceptable position at the very time when our physical growth is at its most urgent and vital; when the consequences of fixating energy are most dire. We fix our defensive personality in our body structure.

The true fall from grace is brought about not by coming *into* bio-life, but by interrupting the flow of bio-life; that flow of life which brings security, and lets us know that all is well in the physical mode of being. Indeed, our libido, so often associated with bringing about the Fall, could help transform our sense of fallen-ness. As infants we could begin to sense again our cosmic connections as we experience our 'cosmic' sexuality – that exquisite sensation of life's flow which is common to us all. In other words, we rest in the arms of the Goddess. Thus, when we are born, we could trust life and breath fully, for we would know of the divinity harboured in all things. Fear of death would gently ease from our system. Complete dependence on our particular mother, with her own fears and needs, would diminish. The libidinous circuit is perhaps an expression of cosmic love offered by life to see us through those times of inevitable separation from mother, for it gives us a profound sense of inner well-being. Indeed, the infant is sexually potent in a very special way.

If the taking on of fleshly form is welcomed, then the one-way valve, the shutter, the period of forgetfulness, can be more easily refined to its rightful function. Evolution can take its course. And so the new stage of evolution depends as much on love of matter as on love of spirit. It is not matter that blocks the dawning awareness of our wholeness, but our reluctance to embrace matter. It is essential that we flow gladly, not sadly, into matter, and experience the living ocean rather than the vale of tears. Here lies our redemption, rather than in striving for release from that which we have never fully entered, and never fully known. Is this what is meant by the resurrection of the Body?

If we continue to give matter negative power (which has been going on for centuries, and is now done quite unconsciously), then we will be locked in matter, and made its prisoner, instead of flowing through matter and shaping matter as it, too, shapes us. We shall be in wrong relationship from our very first contact with it – at that crucial moment, poised to take on human-beingness, when our bio-focus is most urgent. We cannot effectively honour one mode of being at the expense of the other because human beings span both. And if we try to separate matter and spirit, then we are torn on the cross of both dimensions. We need to see matter as the expression of spirit in space and time and form. In other words, we need to recognize, re-cognize, re-know, the archetypal energy of the Goddess: spirit-in-matter.

Only with this power, this archetypal power, can we unlock the archetypal collusion of Infant and Mother which has dominated our history. This is the level at which it has to be. Filled with the power of the Goddess – which means entering into a living knowledge of spirit-in-matter – we can release ourselves from dependence and annihilation terror, attachment and a sense of abandonment. We can free ourselves from blaming and blame. By experiencing the Goddess within all things we gain cosmic security, a natural security, which enables us to let go of Mother. And so we are free to come of age and enter the new Archetype of Self-generation.

We need to experience entry into matter as a welcome into the Divine, and not as an expulsion from the Divine: a well-coming, and thus a coming into wellness. If we continue to hold a negative view of matter, thus accentuating 'Incarnation Shock', we shall hinder, not help, our rapid remembrance of spirit. We cannot be terrorized into wholeness; we cannot flee into wholeness; we can only claim our wholeness. And we do well to start with matter.

It is possible to rediscover spirit by gently allowing contact with, and thus directly experiencing, the movements of life within our own unique body. Through knowing matter in its fullness – through fully being matter – and through letting ourselves be tended by the deeply pleasurable and satisfying inner movements of our biological being, we know, too, that we are spirit and connected to All-That-Is. Could it be that only when matter really matters, and is given its true value by our species at a collective level, that our knowledge of spirit will be freed from the vale of forgetfulness at an early enough point in our engagement with physical form for the un-neurotic infant to be born? No longer, then, will so much time and energy be dedicated to the 'wounded child' for we will start life free to live it.

So a new consciousness – of matter, of the Goddess, of Infant, of Mother, of Father – is vital to the continuing process of maturation of the human being. From this release into a fuller knowledge and experience of who and what we each are, from our first moments on, adulthood, with its freedom of responsibility, will beckon us, not threaten us. New modes of human relating, with radically different social and political arrangements, will begin to emerge as victimhood ceases to be.

Appendices

Appendix One

The Power of the Child

Jill Hall

Article originally published in Self & Society: An International Journal for Humanistic Psychology, 23 (1), 1995, pp. 34–6

Yes (I wish to say to Alice Miller and others), it is important to pay attention to the experience of the wounded child in each of us, but only as a stage in the process of healing. It is equally important to ensure that attempts to understand human nature are not being made from that same wounded place.

There is an urgent need to expand our framework of thought beyond that of linear causality and develop a new way of viewing who we are and how we relate to the world. If our energy is focussed on how mother and father failed us, we can never grow up, nor can there be a tenable solution to our ills. After all, mother and father also had it 'done wrong' to them, and mass psychotherapy for prospective parents is not only impossible but shows little sign that it would make everything better. Even when we give up our initial demand for perfect parents and talk in more reasonable terms of 'good enough' mothering, we are nonetheless placing all power in our parents' hands. This is serious. As long as we do this – as long as our consciousness is caught in this mode of thinking – we render each and every one of us psychic victims.

I believe that we are misreading the nature of the psyche and, for all our sophistication, we are still approaching it as we would a material object or a mechanical system. The psyche, although interacting with events in time, is itself atemporal and multi-dimensional. We are only dealing with the 'tip of the iceberg' when we trace linear causal chains back to our childhood wounds; such knowledge has value of a limited nature only. It is distorting if such an activity is taken as fundamental.

The more we see ourselves as a mere result of other people's actions and attitudes, the more we generate a culture of blame, shame and guilt. And adulthood will elude us. As I see it, the only way out of our predicament is to reframe our thinking about infant and mother. If we start life with an intense and all-pervading power imbalance, we shall create relationships and societies obsessed with power issues, and the male of the species will be stuck with a profound and primal fear of the feminine. And we shall all be stuck with what flows from this: the fury and confusion, violence and pain.

I have become engaged in the project of empowering the infant, an issue I explore in my book *The Reluctant Adult*. If we acknowledge that we start life as a being of equal status to mother, then a different human story can emerge. Of course this is not possible if we see ourselves only as biological beings: on this level, she does hold the power, and our initial biological dependence gives her an awesome place in our psyche. In order to know ourselves as essentially equal beings, we have to embrace an extended view of self and affirm our atemporal or spiritual nature. I wish to stress that it is not so that we can rise above our biology and earthly condition that we need to know ourselves as spirit, but so that we can release ourselves from our blaming mode of thought. The way is then cleared for the next step in the fulfilment of our biological heritage and our ability to live well on earth.

Once we consider the existence of a spiritual reality, we see that if spirit exists at all, then spirit must exist from the start. When we contemplate the nature of spirit, we apprehend that spirit simply is. It may manifest physically in time, space and process, but it is not subject to these aspects of life. Therefore we do not develop a spirit. It doesn't pop out of a mid-life crisis, though we can, of course, develop our awareness of spirit. Once we really seriously take on this notion, the relationship between mother and infant shifts. We begin to see and treat and experience the infant as a full spiritual being, having mutuality with mother on this level. Both are whole beings. And with such acknowledgement, the primal underpinning of our present power relationships can begin to loosen.

No person is in a better position to influence another person as profoundly as a mother her child. Yet it was as a mother that I experienced just how much less power I had in relation to my children than their own power to be themselves.

However great my influence – and I do not want to dismiss the importance of this influence – it was secondary. Their responses to all my actions and qualities, ideas and beliefs, neuroses and hopes, were uniquely their own. Each drew from the spectrum of what I had to offer – 'good' or 'bad' – to build their own psychological schema and life story in their own, special way. Things that I liked or valued most about myself were not necessarily helpful to them – or were a comfort to one and a stumbling block to the other.

My faults, it appears, were sometimes just what they needed. My children are each a starting point in their own right. It seems quite unfitting to take either blame or credit for them. I do, of course, have responsibilities towards them, but I do not cause and cannot control their personhood or their destinies.

When our thinking opens to the idea that the infant is empowered at this most basic and essential level, we can begin to break the cycle of insecurity, blame and victimhood that rules so many of our interactions – and ease the sense of self-betrayal that feeds self-hate. Freedom from blaming is an even greater gift than freedom from being blamed; it allows us to reclaim our energy and power as our own.

The infant-in-us-all is indeed more powerful than 'mother' or 'other' because an infant experiences itself directly. Its power lies in its immediacy. The infant is raw consciousness free of concepts and words, at the centre of the experienced universe and utterly focussed on its being.

In addition, the infant is someone because an infant is whole spirit, freshly and uniquely embodied. Have you ever experienced the aura of a newborn baby? Our 'isness' shines before we take our first suck of mother's milk. Our particular way of being has an immediate and profound impact on others from our first moment on. We are all source points of energy.

If we deny this 'source' energy, then we become selfish, not selfless. We become suckers of others' energy, dependent and attached;

self-absorbed in our emptiness and generators of an addictive consumer society. Furthermore, if we continue to experience ourselves as a victim of mother, then it is hardly surprising that we should later retaliate by victimising Mother Earth. A primal state of blaming passivity leads to exploitation and a fanatical desire to control when, with our grown bodies, we eventually stir to action. Unless we grow up psychologically, by claiming our intrinsic and initial wholeness, we shall remain compulsive consumers. We need to stop going back to mother (or, rather, not stop at going back to mother), and re-enter our essential infant power so that we can begin to water the seed of the full adult woman or man in us.

Further Reading

Jill Hall, *The Reluctant Adult,* Prism Press, 1993.
Alice Miller, *The Drama of Being a Child: The Search for the True Self,* Virago, 1995.

Appendix Two
Victims Can't Forgive

Jill Hall

Article originally published in *Self & Society: An International Journal for Humanistic Psychology,* 24 (2), 1996, pp. 13-16

I want to explore the mind-set of the victim position – a framework within which any one of us might operate. This position does have its own logic. However, I believe that this logic to be incompatible with the state of consciousness from which forgiveness flows. Once trapped in the logic of victimhood, forgiveness is edged out of action. I want to make it clear that I am not claiming that everyone who has been on the receiving end of abusive action, whether from another person or persons, an institution or a political system, never forgives; I am only saying that where victims do forgive, I am pretty sure that they have not at the time of the abuse experienced themselves as victims or, at any rate, not primarily as victims. They will have experienced themselves as more than victims, and their abusers as more than their abusive behaviour.

One of the striking features of Nelson Mandela is that he does not have a hint of the victim about him, although for so many years he struggled within the horrific limitations of an appallingly victimizing economic, social and political setup. By any external reckoning, he qualified as a victim; yet he did not, apparently, take up the victim position on the psychological level, but chose instead to embrace a wider and more empowering perspective. Would he have been able to work closely and creatively with his former enemies (a convincing indication of forgiveness having taken place) if he had been feeling their victim?

What is the logic of victimhood? And how is it incompatible

with that state of heart and mind which is a prerequisite for the exchange involved in forgiveness: the experience of openness, wholeness, connectedness and compassion?

A victim implies a persecutor. Not a helpful start. Indeed, once we define someone as our persecutor, not only are we unlikely to forgive them, but we will find the very idea distasteful. We will have narrowed our entire area of awareness, and lost both the experience of our own wholeness and the acknowledgement of the other in their full being. It is a restricted viewpoint. The viewpoint required for forgiveness is expansive and inclusive, to allow for the activity of one whole being recognizing the wholeness (including the abusive behaviour) of the other.

Another aspect of the victim/persecutor perspective is that it is all about apportioning blame – this is what the labelling is for; and blame and forgiveness do not sit together. Forgiveness is not about being kind or 'understanding' to the one whom we believe is to blame, while still holding on to the blaming. Such activity is usually a protection of some kind from the pain of the event, if the persecutor is a loved one, or from the fear of not being loved or wanted. Or it might be a flight from blame, or a denial of blame – very different from moving into a framework where blame is not what it's all about. To enter into forgiveness we need to go beyond the partiality of blame, and embrace the entirety of 'what is'. It is the ultimate in realism. (Again, witness Mandela. He does not deny the wrongdoing he and numerous others suffered, but neither does he give it his prime energy, nor build a world upon it.)

The victim/persecutor perspective is a highly defined and selective viewpoint which fixes people in their 'innocent' or 'bad' place, and blots out all else. It thus divides and separates the two parties as if they were different kinds of people – and the sense of connectedness essential to release forgiveness is diverted. The victim/persecutor approach to life places us in different categories, and tends to keep us there.

Those identifying themselves as victims are not likely to know the persecutor in themselves: the mirrors of learning are not only misted, but are turned around, so that no light can be reflected from them. From such ways of seeing are generated hate, fear, blame and blind pain; not forgiveness. Not 'there, but for the grace of God, go I'; but 'Me' and 'Them' and never the twain shall see one another (or, indeed, their own selves), despite being locked together in the same dynamic.

How can this division nurture compassion? What meaning would forgiving our persecutors hold if we still felt ourselves the victim of their damaging acts? Only by stepping beyond the victim position would it attain meaning. Only by letting go of the restricted views of both victim and persecutor, by entering a state of consciousness that illuminates our essential wholeness and our interconnectedness with all others, can we make compassion both fitting and a reality.

It seems to me that forgiveness is the inevitable result of the experience of oneness, and is inevitably blocked by a perspective that draws from, and maintains, a sense of alienation and separation.

It is so unpleasant and unrewarding to feel a victim. Such feelings couldn't be further from those that accompany a state of forgiveness. Victimhood is the 'hard done by' position, all contraction and diminution – a far cry from the sense of peace, integration, expansiveness and freedom that forgiveness both requires and generates.

What else is implied by the victim position? It is essentially passive. A victim is 'done to', and any sense of agency is dismantled. It is the persecutor who is the dreadful but powerful one. (Indeed it gives power a bad name, which is a great disservice to the human race.) Victimhood creates and confirms a sense of impotence and insecurity, and therefore breeds fear, fury, defensiveness (and thus possible attack), resentment, misery, blame and shame – hardly the climate conducive to forgiveness.

Shame is perhaps our greatest secret enemy, and any mode of thinking that feeds shame is worth challenging. It may seem extraordinary that a victim, who is after all defined as innocent, should feel shame; but the fact is that we, as victims, feel just that – and in no small measure.

If we experience ourselves as powerless, if we feel helpless, if we seem to be only acted upon – if we are victims – then we tend to feel shame. Perhaps it is because we have unwittingly betrayed that fuller self which knows of our intrinsic power to be who we are, even if we have been ill-treated and abused. We sense something is wrong, out of order. So we blame, and then, to our surprise, we feel more shame.

The burden is not lifted. Blame never releases us from shame; they are born from the same source, and both confirm our impotence. Empowerment, responsibility and freedom elude us. Declaring that 'it's not my fault – it's theirs' may afford temporary relief, but the shame and dislike of ourselves persist.

We, as victims, are not known for our self-acceptance, although that is what we long for. Apportioning blame to a transgressor may be a necessary step in the process of healing – for self-blame breeds more shame, and is more constricting than any other form of blame; but we are still stuck in less than who we really are. This is immensely painful. It is like trying to move in a very tight and shrinking shoe; difficult to stand up straight, let alone dance.

The trouble with shame is that it not only paralyses us but is morally counter-productive. It doesn't help us behave better and thus gain in self-esteem. In fact, the more shame we feel, the more we tend to behave in shameful ways. We feel we deserve to be punished, and can feel compelled to bring about our own humiliation. Then we are even more ashamed and think we deserve more punishment. And so we devise, and continue to allow, shaming acts. The victim and persecutor in us have a heyday, and forgiveness doesn't get much of a look-in.

So I believe that it is a matter of some urgency that we let go these modes of defining and identifying ourselves. They keep us from experiencing our wholeness and interconnectedness, which alone can liberate us into forgiveness; forgiveness of self and others and the ways of the world. It is only within that same limited mode of definition that letting go of victimhood is seen to justify the persecutor. The act of transgression is not 'made alright', but is seen in a larger and fuller context which has nothing to do with trading blame. Forgiveness is only appropriate, and only flourishes, when we give our attention to more than the victim or persecutor in us, while not denying either of them.

As you may have noticed, I am reluctant to define the word 'forgive'. I have simply alluded to the conditions out of which forgiveness emerges, and I have not attempted to describe what it is in itself. I hope I have indicated something of its meaning in what I have written; but as with 'love', I believe forgiveness does not lend itself to definition – it is recognized and known when it is touched or received or entered into, and is a grace. And I deliberately use the word 'forgiveness' to include both the forgiver and the forgiven, or to refer to either. This is not a confusion but an attempt to express its essential 'we-ness' or 'us-ness'.

I hope it is clear that I have not been talking about formal acts of forgiveness or apology (although they have their place in social discourse). I am not referring to something bestowed on the malefactor, as a kind of favour or act of generosity. Nor is it a matter of trying to make the wrong-doer 'feel better'. I am writing of something that requires a shift to a more inclusive mode of consciousness (unknown by the victim part of us, which is a fragmented aspect of the self, however charged and prevalent it may be). And when we enter that willingness to see what is, in its entirety, forgiveness naturally comes forth. It flows from an inner state of heart, an integration of being, and an extended awareness. Feeling a victim obstructs access to this ever-living potential in us.

APPENDIX THREE

THE VICTIMHOOD ARCHETYPE:
HEALTH, ILLNESS, COMPLIANCE, CAUSALITY AND HUMAN CONSCIOUSNESS

An interview with Jill Hall

Article originally published in *Self & Society: An International Journal for Humanistic, Existential and Transpersonal Psychology*, 50 (1-2), 2022, pp. 73-86

Note: this interview was hand-written and conducted by post during 2021 – hence, it was written before more recent developments in the unfolding coronavirus story, and so should be read in that light as, to some extent at least, an historical document – albeit an important one. However, the discussion of the dynamics of the pandemic experience is just as valid and compelling today as I write, as it was last year – and especially so, if Covid-19 proves to be just the first episode in a new 'Era of The Pandemic'. [Editor, Richard House]

Richard House [RH]: Jill, your book *The Reluctant Adult* (Hall, 1993) had a profound influence on many people when it came out nearly 30 years ago; and I think the momentous issues about what you call 'the Victimhood Archetype' and the evolution of human consciousness are perhaps even more relevant today in the 'Age of Covid' than they were when you wrote your path-breaking book. Can we begin this interview by you sharing how you see the global response to Covid in terms of the Victimhood Archetype, and all the associated dynamics around it (i.e. the so-called 'Drama Triangle' of Persecutor–Victim–Rescuer, or P–V–R).[1]

I'm also wondering how it was that you came to realise that

'victimhood' is a core dynamic at this juncture in the evolution of consciousness. A definition of the Victimhood Archetype might also be helpful for readers not acquainted with these ideas – though of course I'm aware that definitions can be dangerous things!

Jill Hall [JH]: Yes, our response to Covid is a wonderfully powerful illustration of the Victimhood Archetype, and the device of Lockdown literally breeds it and requires it of us – sprinkled with ever-changing little tit-bits of freedom. Trust of any kind thrown into chaos, as people flee to Persecutor or Rescuer within their confinement, or when let loose for a spell, as if for a treat. An alarming number of youngsters have decided that if this is 'life', they'd rather not be here at all. It is not a farce – it is tragic.

Meanwhile, to put it crudely, our political leaders also flounder and play out Persecutor in the name of Rescuer, fleeing to Victim when the consequences of all this doesn't deliver in the way they hoped for or intended. They rush to 'the science', pick out bits of it and re-arrange 'the facts' which were already frail.

All this can divert many of us from examining ourselves according to our own values. We can so easily slip into our most familiar compulsion – or compulsions – and be diverted from genuine unclouded self-reflection. It is not easy to take responsibility for ourselves in non-reactive ways when we are being subjected to an unprecedented worldwide 'epidemic' of control far more damaging than any virus, and more widespread over the entire world than any war. The most natural aspects of our humanity, from when we first evolved on this planet, have been violated.

When has a warm, comforting hug been vetoed? No access to people we love when they are dying or most in need of us? Or just for the joy or pleasure of it. And the rituals, that are so part of every culture at those moments of prime significance such as births, marriages, funerals. The decisions no longer up to us. Surely a violation of our basic Human Rights, to which 'Western' nations love to lay claim. What an invitation for anyone prone to the lure of Victimhood, when our natural instinctive human responses are crippled, and forbidden, and dubbed irresponsible. It is an insult to our very humanity.

I'm pretty confident in asserting that there has never before in history been such a worldwide fixation on controlling others, and at such a cost to their mental and physical well-being and other health issues and vital concerns. Multiple interference in the name of protection.

Our challenge is how, nevertheless, not to be a victim. No-one can prevent us from thinking for ourselves. We are creative beings, and could devise all sorts of ways to bypass the reactive behaviour of the persecutor in others.

RH: Thank you for articulating my hunches about Victimhood and the current Covid experience so clearly, Jill. This is the first time we've communicated since the beginning of the 'Covid psychodrama' (as I perhaps controversially term it), and it's very affirming that we see things similarly. What you say here is one of the most resounding and authoritative critiques I've seen or heard anywhere, at the time of writing.

I think it's a crucial insight that we can slip into our most familiar compulsions in the face of all this. And of course that will include (and perhaps especially) our leaders and 'scientific experts', and not merely us 'ordinary' citizens! So the need for leaders with a deep and mature self-awareness about all these dynamics becomes all the more essential (assuming they are not using and deploying such understandings for nefarious purposes, that is).

Again, many of our readers won't necessarily be acquainted with the Persecutor–Victim–Rescuer (P–V–R) dynamic/model that's so well known in Humanistic Psychology circles. Could you say something succinct and 'in a nutshell' that summarizes the P–V–R dynamic, and its importance and relevance for understanding human relationships and experience?

I'd really like to get into dialoguing with you about science, medical science, and ill-health and well-being. But first, could you say something about this: 'our challenge is how not to be a victim'. I realise that this is perhaps akin to a Krishnamurti-like 'impossible question'! – but can you share your thoughts on what we need to do, individually and as a species, to transcend Victimhood and step forward into genuine, responsible adulthood (which is of course the core theme of your 1993 book *The Reluctant Adult*).

JH: Well, what a challenge! You ask if I could say something 'succinct' and 'in a nutshell' about the P–V–R dynamic (the Drama Triangle). Yes, it can be immensely dynamic in the sense that we can whip from one 'position' on the triangle to another in a kind of reactive dance in some circumstances, although of course many settle into, or get addicted to, their favourite mode. So identified with rescuer, for example, that they believe or assume that to be a rescuer is their true character, and that it is a commendable way of being and acting in the world. What is wrong with caring and being willing to help those who can't help themselves? Someone entrenched in rescuer can't see it as collusion – indeed, few caught up in the Persecutor–Victim–Rescuer dynamic are drawn to self-reflection.

It is such a relief, such a blessing for all concerned, when we manage to become aware of what we're up to, and get a sense that we could perhaps even choose to step out of our familiar role in the dynamic. The more clearly someone consciously abdicates their position on the Triangle, the more likely that the whole dynamic can be undermined. It is a very transformative step. If we could dare face it and name it as a compulsion, the road to freedom has begun. The dynamic in which we'd been participating loses its grip somewhat – its attraction. The Triangle goes wobbly, losing its set shape, leaving the participants somewhat lost and disconcerted, but also released in some way – even relieved. Compulsions are both limiting and exhausting.

However, it is hard to imagine a person naming him- or herself as a persecutor – not even Hitler! We can simply embrace a position on the Triangle as if it is who we are, without ever naming ourselves as such and using the term. And it is indeed true: neither the role nor the label is who we are. Every human being is a one-off unique being, and we must treat them as such when working together as their therapist. Not that a person established on the top of the Triangle, in the persecutor position, is likely to seek a therapist. But they could possibly, through a conversation with a caring friend, manage to own up to a persecutory action. If that friend can simply listen, appreciating the courage inherent in such a disclosure and the increased intimacy involved in such a sharing, a vital shift could occur. There is always some wounding fuelling all our destructive behaviours. If we can only acknowledge the vulnerability that lies beneath them – a courageous step to take, and then a shift becomes possible.

So, how to release ourselves from our unhelpful compulsion or habit? First, by sensing that there is something repetitive going on – all too familiar – and stepping aside and pondering on things; realising that one is missing out on something. Am I really happy? Fulfilled? I'm feeling lonely yet I'm busy enough. I'm relating to people. It can all feel thoroughly disconcerting.

It is helpful to visualize this 'Trinity of Compulsions' as an equilateral triangle, as follows:

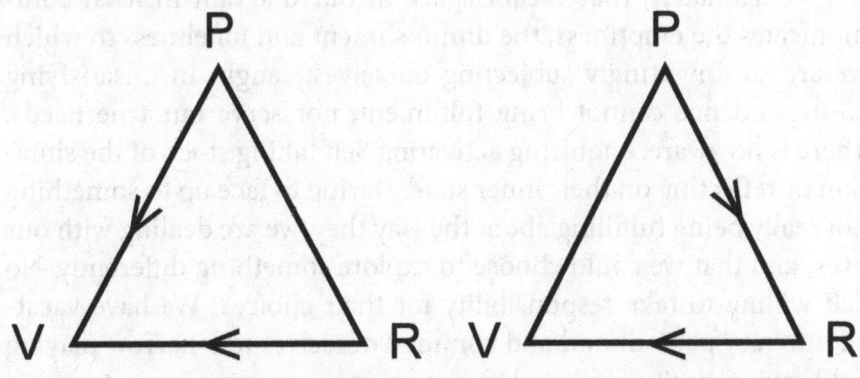

Note: Persecutor domination at the top of each triangle; rescuer fixated on the victim at the bottom of both triangles; victim remains passive, and yet – unless a child – still an unwitting player colluding in the dynamic with the other two.

We can see why the rescuer would want to keep well clear of a persecutor and divert their attention to the 'good role' of helping an unfortunate victim, just waiting to collude with the rescuer with relief.

It's also worth noting that the persecutor remains unchallenged at the pinnacle of the structure, with no arrows going in his or her direction. Thus, it can remain the most inherently lonely and addictive of all the positions on the Drama Triangle. What a paradox; how complex we human beings are! Stuck being a king-pin of the Triangle could be the most isolating of conditions, yet the hardest to let go of.

The inner emptiness of the first two diagrams speaks volumes.

We are by nature immensely complex and amazing beings. What's most striking about the Triangle is that it is empty – vacant. But what about the core self within us? Each one of us is a unique being – even expressed in our finger-prints. The Triangle is empty because the dynamic it is charting is an ego–persona interaction driven by reactive energy, resulting in flitting around like a moth with nothing of true substance to act as a reference point. It is bereft of complexity (as opposed to the complicated wiles of manipulation of the players in the Triangle). It does not invite reflection, but only either flight or fixation – or wobbling between the two.

Fortunately, that vacant space in our diagram in itself communicates the emptiness, the diminishment and loneliness to which we are so unwittingly subjecting ourselves: caught in unsatisfying co-dependence cannot bring fulfilment, nor serve our true needs. There is no aware, enquiring activating Self taking stock of the situation or reflecting on their inner state. Daring to face up to something not really being fulfilling about the way they/we are dealing with our lives, and that we could choose to explore something differently. No Self willing to take responsibility for their choices. We have vacated our very personhood and confined ourselves to a narrow playing field: our capacity for love left unwatered; our most important and vital relationships unable to flourish. Perhaps wilting, or even dying.

If we place this substantial core of our being within the empty space, the triangle of compulsions dissolves, thus:

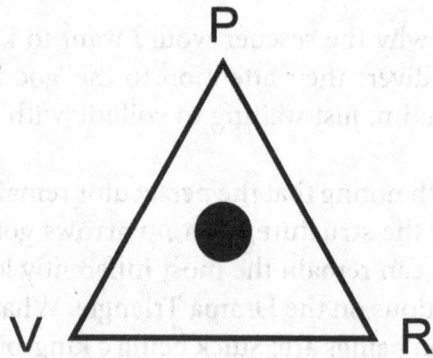

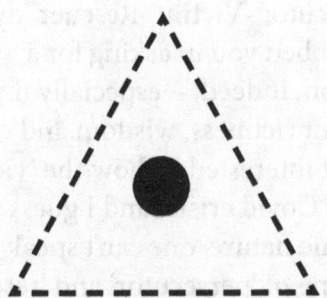

And we are forced to relate in a variety of different ways drawing on who we more truly are – • – a unique human being gifted with an inborn capacity to love. And what's more, so much better equipped to handle the distorting effects of social Lockdowns – and who knows what is yet to come.

However, the most sneaky yet relentless persecutor is the superego. Why would we suppose that our ego, when elevated in status, would possess wisdom of any kind? A very poor advisor. When we flounder somewhat, feeling a bit anxious and unsure – on the brink, perhaps, of attempting to explore something new and a bit risky – we are only too likely to receive a barrage of discouraging and/or distracting 'put-downs'.

Cynicism is another of its ploys. It is an inner voice that can work so stealthily, informed and infected by our earliest woundings and fears – using the tool of shaming, which paralyses action of any kind. We are bound to flounder and feel undermined.

And all this goes on in an isolated inner region of our being. It is such a liberation when we can learn to recognize the input of this adept persecutor, and dismiss it before it gets further into its wily ways. Especially as we are likely to fall prey to it unconsciously, and automatically find ourselves turning it on others – often in our most intimate and important relationships. It's helpful first to notice the 'shoulds' and 'oughts', as they emerge. Not to condemn ourselves, but to release us from the unwelcome repercussions. To free ourselves from being its victim – or identifying with it and patronising others with its diminishing advice.

RH: Thank you so much for such a comprehensive and insightful outline of the Persecutor–Victim–Rescuer dynamic, Jill. I realise what a curve-ball I lobbed you in asking for a 'succinct' description – an impossible question, indeed! – especially if you were to do justice to the model's inherent richness, wisdom and complexity.

I'm particularly interested in how the 'victim' position is playing out in the current Covid crisis (and I guess that precisely because of the system's dynamic nature, one can't speak about the 'victim' position without speaking of 'persecutor' and 'rescuer', too).

As I understand it, a 'victim' pre-supposes a 'persecutor'; so how do you see the various Persecutor–Victim–Rescuer roles playing out in the main actors / protagonists of this unfolding Covid psychodrama? (another simple question for you!). And I'm especially interested in the medical/health system, and its accompanying 'science' and scientific and medical 'experts'. Can you weave into your answer how illness, and fear of illness / death, and orthodox medicine's patriarchal 'war-like' response to the virus, might fit into the P–V–R framework?

JH: What excellent questions – thank you, Richard. As I see it, the whole Persecutor– Victim–Rescuer dynamic is running rampant right now, however unwelcome to many of its players. We are being controlled by those in power in various ways over the entire planet as never before in human history – utterly driven by the obsession with controlling the virus. Possible freedoms stipulated and then suddenly reversed. Domination is seldom so chaotic. A veritable plague of 'dictators', even if some are reluctant and well-meaning in intention. The trouble is that whatever they do, they are thwarted.

The virus will never respond as a victim, and is never stuck waiting to be rescued – it simply morphs into another form. It is a most dynamic invader whose requirement is finding a home in a living entity. Domestic birds and animals are an obvious 'mistake', as then their owners are required to kill them all. However, human beings rally into action to save themselves, and this makes them a much better bet. Hospitals are perfect – fine if people die, but even better if they survive – a home for the virus thus assured.

Perhaps it could then have continued morphing into causing

far less lethal ailments for us human beings, if things had been handled in a more holistic way. Accepting that death is part of life – as essential occurrence – not the worst thing that could befall us and to be deferred at all costs. It is the *quality* of life that matters – its meaningfulness. And especially for the aged, whose options and opportunities might well have shrunk.

What a grandiose idea that we should be able to defeat death. (One of those sneaky intrusions from the superego, taking us off course as usual.) Naturally, we welcome what means of protection and healing are possible, but death as a phenomenon is not some kind of outrage. It is an aspect of life itself; and we'd be in a right old pickle without it. So death is not some kind of persecutor, and we are not victims if we die a natural death (which might well be due to a virus). The carers and healers who offer their services in the hope of relieving suffering are not bound to be compulsive rescuers. People who love us, comfort us, and accompany us during the dying process if they can, aided by carers perhaps, are simply living out their natural human impulses, as they have done throughout the ages. Often a time when differences and past woundings can be shared and forgiven, and in the dying one can slip away peacefully.

As I write I feel a sense of outrage that this profound and natural process has been ruled out of order in the name of 'protecting the aged'. I know my daughter could not bear it if that situation were to be imposed on us.

Yes, I'm also interested in the medical/health system and medical 'experts' and our 'war' on the virus, rather than treating it as a player in Nature that we must respect as such and work with, in as informed a way as possible, as we do with flu and AIDS. Viruses are part of Nature, and we need to learn as much as we can about them in an unhurried and rigorous manner. Our bodies are full of them, and bacteria, and we wouldn't be here, we wouldn't exist, let alone flourish, without them.

And of course we shall get ill at times, and every single one of us will die. What matters is our quality of life as we live our lives in the fullness of the complexity of what it is to be a human being – creative beings, ever evolving and curious beings with a wonderful complexity – and most important of all, an inborn capacity to love.

Nurturing our unique potential, and how we relate to our fellow human beings and the natural world, are far more important than how long we live for. And people have lived enriching lives with all sorts of ailments and disabilities.

These things are not some kind of insult to our humanity – such as unnecessary poverty, or homelessness and Lockdowns, the rules themselves often being an absolute impossibility to live on a practical level anyway. Much easier for the well-housed and wealthy. But it seems that death from 'the virus' is somehow something that shouldn't occur (that arrogant superego slipping in again).

Thus, all this focus on how not to die. We have to put the elderly first at all costs – the ailments of others, who are forming their lives, and are profoundly harmed by interrupting all the natural stages in infant and child development in ways that cannot be remedied, are given scant attention. Their mothers – parents – left without support. The old must come first. And then the hypocrisy of not caring one jot for the quality of life of the old when isolated at home by decree to save them – never mind if their lives are bereft of meaning, and visitors and grandchildren, or terrified of contact because of all the fear being generated about this crafty invader, the virus, hyped up by the approach of our politicians acting as persecutors and rescuers at the same time. We now have a truly crazy-making dynamic!

And even worse in care homes, where rules cannot be surreptitiously circumvented. The outrage of expelling Covid sufferers from hospital straight into care homes, endangering both inmates and care-workers in the initial chaos of 'Twin Dictatorship'. It's interesting what decisions are never put to a vote in Parliament. And noteworthy that we don't get suicide figures reported every day. Quick, efficient methods easy to access online. All therapeutic help offered by city councils shrunk to a bare minimum.

To my mind, no virus could be so harmful or as disruptive to our well-being as the 'solutions' thought up by our highly privileged leaders who claim to be saving us from them. They seem utterly oblivious of the fact that the material conditions necessary for keeping the 'Rules of Protection' simply don't exist for a vast number of our society. They have spent years in power failing to build houses more amenable to being locked down in. And what are called 'state benefits' simply reveal a complete lack of respect for people less fortunate than themselves. The hypocrisy of that hand-clapping for the NHS, and then refusing those exhausted nurses a pay rise, is another sickening example. At least the virus has no prejudices.

Is it perhaps our fear and outrage that the virus is a secret and invisible killer – such a stealthy persecutor, as it seeks to outwit even our brilliant and recently 'knighted' rescuers by whipping across from the other side of the world with this Delta variant, just as our final liberation day is in sight. Trust India – no idea about hygiene and washing their hands etc. But we won't enlarge on that one. Our team of vaccines will soon be topped up to deal with things. We know how to handle things.

RH: Thank you for this resounding response, Jill. I'm reminded of what Laura Dodsworth writes in her book *A State of Fear* – that the government made sure that none of 'the science' that they commandeered was argued against, with all '"wild cards" and dissenters edged out of advisory panels' (p. 256). How different it could all have been if the perspective and insights you're sharing here would have been allowed a voice in the policy-making process!

Would you agree that 'the Covid vaccine' has become the rescuer of us (potential) Covid victims in the Covid psychodrama? And that it is people's assumed and encouraged victimhood in relation to the virus that has been a major aspect of the vaccine being seen and positioned as our salvation? – rescuing us all from death and mortality. I can't help wondering what the overall response to the virus might have looked like if we hadn't taken up a collective victim position in relation to this persecutor! I'd love to hear your views on this. (I even can't help wondering, in passing, whether the high-powered team of behavioural scientists that have been advising government on how to keep us scared and compliant (Dodsworth, 2021) might even have been aware of the P–R–V dynamic and its archetypal power, and deliberately used and exploited it in order to engineer the compliance outcome they required.)

And finally, is there a lesson for humanity here on how we urgently need to move beyond the P-R-V / Victimhood Archetype in relation to our understanding of, and relationship with, well-being, illness and disease? Because it seems to me that the current prevailing 'medical science' approach and worldview are (unconsciously?) steeped in P–R–V metaphysical assumptions about reality. And what might a post-P–R–V medical system look like, I'm wondering? Big questions, I know!...

JH: I appreciated the quotation by Laura Dodsworth, Richard – thank you.

In answer to your first question: behind all the crazy-making obsession with control (however erratically implemented) is this obsession with defeating death, rather than giving value to life. What an utter waste, when we could instead give our focus and attention to how to enhance the quality of life at all levels of society – expand opportunities not only to achieve viable living standards for everyone, but also for exploring our talents and creativity, and all that gives joy and meaning to our lives. A sense of hope and purpose. I believe that fear is a most pernicious, destructive and disrespectful means of control, and one of the greatest of all threats to our well-being. Its dominance is crippling – diminishing. No wonder fears about humanity's extinction and wild conspiracy theories – and even wilder solutions – are proliferating.

Meanwhile, with all this emphasis on Collective Victimhood, it is important that we defy any slippage into victim-like resignation and despair. Resignation is especially dangerous because it is devoid of all energy! Many people have lost the will to venture out of doors at all – Lockdown or no. Their lives have become stale and meaningless. Can't even be bothered to commit suicide. We have been utterly messed around, as if in some horrendous experiment, rather than being encouraged to adapt to the presence of the virus in our lives in sound, respectful and creative ways. Common-sense care for each other by checking ventilation and not getting too close to each other. You can have a good warm hug while looking over someone's shoulder. Ever-morphing viruses simply are a part of Nature, and need to be accepted as such.

Was perhaps the drive and rush to hurry forward 'the science' so as to achieve the invention, trials and production of vaccines by our acclaimed team of 'vaccine researchers' in record-breaking time

– and thus the UK as World Rescuers (even if somewhat stingy about sharing with less well-endowed nations) – an attempt to divert attention from the bumbling lack of attention given by Prime Minister Boris Johnson and his 'advisors' in the early days of the pandemic? No concern to check that all the front-line workers of the soon-to-be-lauded NHS had adequate means of protection. Slip in a quick bit of trade with Turkey who want a load of masks, as Europe is being so tiresome at the moment. What a damn nuisance this all is; let's just carry on and see what happens. Pretty well exactly what Johnson is saying today as we're enticed (as I write) towards Liberation Day on 19 July [2021]. Meanwhile, if People of Colour and Muslims refuse our gallant Vaccine Rescuers, what can you do about such ignorance? We'll keep up our good work, dealing out fresh jabs in the autumn in readiness for the winter onslaught. As you say, Richard, an assumed and encouraged 'Mass Victimhood' in relation to the virus, rather than a focus on those responsible for handling our welfare – our elected government.

It can never suddenly be OK. Positivity can't be turned on like a tap. Seeds of fear have been systematically scattered throughout the entire population, touching the vulnerability that lies in every human being, even if they refuse to recognize it. Serial Lockdowns breed and rely upon fear; what could be more corrosive to our general health and well-being? Breeding distrust in the resilience of life itself and the spirit of hope that sustains us in times of challenge.

To respond to your ponderings about whether the high-powered team of behavioural scientists, whose advice the government has been following, might have known about the P–R–V dynamic and its archetypal power. Highly unlikely – it's not a subject they'd be tempted to explore or research. The P–R–V dynamic is a somewhat automatic and unrecognized phenomenon, especially if we are principally, or most used to, operating from ego. As I've mentioned before in a previous dialogue with you, what dispels the compulsions played out on the Triangle is when we access, or return to, what I call 'Activating Self'. A centring experience – drawing on the energy of our Heart Chakra combined with that of our solar plexus, which empowers the actualization of our gifts in the world.

We have a core, an inner reference point, from which to take responsibility for our choices. If we can bear to embrace our Truer Self, the Triangle dissolves and disintegrates. And thus it is urgent, now as never before, that we claim our more authentic and fuller selves; refuse to be worn down into Victimhood by accessing the richness of who we can become as continually evolving conscious beings – free to explore and discover, if we wish, more of who we are.

Our failures teach us even more, perhaps, than our successes. It is our ego that seeks to dismiss them – sees them as somehow shameful. However, they are intrinsic to the learning process, and inspired by the enlivening spark of curiosity. A baby needs to roll around and explore on the floor, discover how to grasp on to something so as to stand, only to topple around until he or she can walk. Mother and father responding with pleasure and/or comfort, if need be. Experiencing delight in learning is such a vital part of our development.

We are such extraordinary beings, but we pay the price for our complex and rich potential. For we are also wounded beings. Our challenges of such a different order once we, as a species, evolved beyond our tribal heritage, with shared beliefs and common aims grounded in a respectful partnership with the natural world. The development of ego defining us as separate, even though inter-dependent beings, not yet come into play. Ego, however, is far too flimsy a construct to be awarded a position of dominance in our psychological make-up. It is fatal to place our sense of identity in its hands. It lacks substance, and is unduly concerned with our image in the eyes of others.

I believe that the ethos of English Public Schools has wrought great harm in our society. Far from serving the general public, these schools harbour a culture of elitism along with emotional deprivation; arrogance combined with humiliating practices; entitlement, along with a lack of physical and emotional nurturing in their early years. The caned wait apprehensively to become the caners, while all too likely holding inside themselves a terrible shame of unwanted sexual abuse from their teachers. A continual exchange between persecutors and victims, bereft of rescuers. Their parents all the while believing that they had acted in their offsprings' best interest by sending them there; mothers often deprived of fulfilling an inner longing to nurture their children.

What a tragic mess. Their sense of entitlement has, however, enabled them to side-step the detrimental psychological and economic aspects of Lockdown. It has yet to emerge into our collective consciousness just how inhumane the 'solution' of Lockdown has been. It has so reduced our sense of agency: everyone except the privileged minority has been subjected to the likelihood of a de-evolutionary backward state of being, and many well-functioning relationships have been ruined beyond repair.

The natural stages of infant, child and adolescent development have been 'put on pause' by decree – even though it is impossible to put time on pause. Crucial processes thus interrupted, delayed, and all too likely to be radically distorted; so many left confused as to how to handle dealing with the world, the obsession with defeating 'the virus' blocking and diverting awareness of the profound harm and disorientation that the proclaimed 'Rescue Strategy' has had, and will continue to go on having, on millions of our fellow citizens.

My own work as a psychotherapist is increasing, not easing, as is the number of telephone calls late into the night. Much of the damage is irretrievable, however many serial 'jabs' are rolled out.

And yet as always, some people have accessed resources they never knew they possessed, and want to share their new insights and integrate them, and I feel a lift in my heart.

I wake up to the new day. What a rapidly shifting world. Even 'the science' is losing its grip, with various 'experts' doling out conflicting advice. Switching Cabinet roles is also wearing a bit thin. Attempting to keep their nerve as the virulence of the Delta variant outwits the lauded band of rescuers, and turning their attention to the economy instead. Stay upbeat, and talk about business and commercial life expanding once more during the summertime, when we are out of doors and can ease up on wearing masks etc. And we won't worry too much right now about schools and education because it's the holidays soon.

And what about the glory of our footballers? Of course their loyal supporters and fans, with their double-jab status, will be cheering them on on behalf of all of us – shouting and singing and hugging each other in celebration. (Oh dear; damn penalties again….)

Meanwhile, how is it for the unsung? – for the millions of neglected and struggling and deprived members of society, including those who are soon to have even their £20 of Universal Benefit withdrawn that only just enabled them to keep an adequate amount of food on the table, and who were never privileged enough to fulfil the Lockdown rules? No hope or chance to 'get out there' and spend and eat out and play their part in getting the economy going, as if it is our civic duty. Not enough food on their own tables.

RH: Thank you for these searing insights, Jill. I often think that the Victimhood Archetype is surreptitiously embedded into the very language we use in everyday life. I recently came across a book about Covid that I think illustrates this, with its tell-tale title, *Covid-19 – **How It Made Us Feel**: Life in Lockdown during the CoronaVirus Pandemic* (my bold emphasis). I also find myself wondering whether those who experience themselves as victims of Covid and the pandemic are actually those who are constitutionally far more susceptible to falling ill from Covid, than are those who are not consumed by fear and foreboding (notwithstanding the government's determination to scare us 'optimally'... – Dodsworth, 2021). Anyone who has worked closely and deeply with people's well-being and ill-being – as psychotherapists like yourself do all the time – will surely know that illness and disease are infinitely more subtle and complex than materialist medical science can ever comprehend.

And so to several final questions for you! I'm wondering what all that we've touched upon in this conversation might mean for the evolution of human consciousness that you and me have spoken about a lot over the years. You were writing and lecturing about the Victimhood Archetype well over three decades ago, Jill. Do you think that the human species is any closer to being able to evolve beyond the Victimhood Archetype today, compared with when you first started thinking, writing and lecturing on this question all those years ago?

And with specific reference to medicine, health, well-being and dis(-)ease: I wonder whether you have any vision of what a 'post-Victimhood' medical system and truly holistic 'medical science' might begin to look like, in broad (paradigmatic) terms? You say that

'Ego... is far too flimsy a construct to be awarded a position of dominance in our psychological make-up. It is fatal to place our sense of identity in its hands.' Is it perhaps also 'fatal' to have a medical system that is created, and maintained from, the place of ego alone? Or put differently, what might a 'post-ego' Health and Well-being Service (as distinct from a National Disease Service) look like, I'm wondering? – taking account, perhaps, of the traps and machinations of the P–R–V Drama Triangle and its neurotic positions, which can of course manifest institutionally, as well as at an individual level. I know you'll have much of interest to say about these questions! – some simple ones for you, to end with! ;-)

As always, it's an undiluted pleasure to have the opportunity to dialogue with you, Jill, and to co-create an opportunity for you to share your great wisdom and insight. I leave the final words with you.

JH: Thank you for your final question, Richard. You wonder what all we've touched on in this conversation might mean for the evolution of human consciousness, and whether I think the human species is any closer to being able to evolve beyond the Victimhood Archetype today.

Having been subjected to bouts of enforced Victimhood by serial Lockdowns could, I think, possibly catapult a substantial number of people forward on a truly radical path, albeit with many left tragically wounded in a manner never before lived. It isn't easy to take responsibility for ourselves when we are being treated in a fundamentally inhumane way. Whole societies have never before been subjected to such extreme and bizarre and intrusive modes of control. A Pandemic of Victim Creation. Even people who would never have been prone to Victimhood. Reluctant Victims rather than The Reluctant Adult! Any stranger can become viewed as a possible threat.

Perhaps the greatest danger of being manipulated into so many situations that invite Victimhood is resignation – a plight into which all too many may have slipped. Resignation is devoid of any energy whatsoever. The most limiting state of all human beings is when nothing really matters any more. The light of hope is then dimming, flickering, and then turned off.

Depression is really grim, but people really mind if they feel depressed and can seek therapy and/or medication which can make a significant difference. If into resignation, you probably wouldn't bother. Just keep plodding on, regardless. I've heard of so many people who say they no longer listen to the news – they don't want to know. Just a brief summary will do so as to check on the latest 'rules'. And I'm speaking here of fairly privileged members of society, not people who aren't even in a position to be able to follow the rules.

The tragedy is that it is the young, who most urgently require the opportunity to explore their way forward in life, whose path is most seriously blocked and distorted. It is them who most need to be free to make their own mistakes and enter into intimate relationships of their choice, as well as discovering what kind of work could fit their needs and talents.

Furthermore, if you are blocked going forwards in your development, you're likely to slip or sink backwards, and find yourself at the mercy of past woundings that you're not yet ready to process. What must it feel like for them, knowing that they are the least likely to be seriously affected by catching the virus (unless they have some prior condition), or take up hospital beds if they did. It is they who are our future. It is their state of physical and psychological well-being that needs to be our social priority, not delaying the final stretch of life in the old.

It's positively cruel to meet our end in a ventilator. (The son of a friend of mine, who is a doctor, spoke of 'the hell' of being in a ventilator.) It is likely that there will be plenty of life-loving, long-living elderly people, both here and in societies all over the world, who would, as a matter of course, add their experience, wisdom and insight to the mix.

I do believe, with millions of others, that this is indeed a critical point in the evolution of humankind, as more and more of us wake up and learn to honour and care for, and wish to restore, the balance of life on this planet. There is increasing discovery and exploration of Nature's auto-restorative potency at the same time as the most drastically extreme temperatures, gales, fires and floods in more and more parts of the world at this very juncture in time/space, calling and urging us to wake up.

We could be in for another dose of Lockdown this autumn after our short, jab-won burst of freedom; some of the most obedient rushing around like children given a treat. The Delta variant perhaps outwitting our Vaccine Solution, and ordinary old flu activated as usual, especially if the weather begins upping the stakes. Another frozen and enforced P–V–R dynamic, our worn-out NHS over-stretched yet again, and more destructive to our well-being than ever – sick and sick-making in its consequences. Our modes of coping wearing thin.

Fortunately, life itself is dynamic, and at some point – drawing ever closer – we can't help but move on, whatever we get up to, and even if only by default. Life itself can't be put in a deliberately engineered freezer; it can only unfold. That is why eventually, 'All shall be well, and all manner of things shall be well'. There's nothing starry-eyed or ungrounded about Julian of Norwich. It's interesting that she was never persecuted by the Church at the peak of its Persecutory Epidemic and preoccupation with Satan as its chair-leader.

Julian would never be 'locked down'. She chose solitude plus individual contact with people through her window into the world – a literal window on to the street in the heart of Norwich, and she was thus available to those who were drawn to stop and speak to her. And at some point she wrote a book – not in the acceptable Latin, but in English – the language of the people – and she was the first woman to do such a thing. In it she offered her vision of love to the world and God's Hand in All Things through her delight in holding and beholding the wonder of contemplating a little chestnut in the palm of her hand.

Julian never criticized the Church, which had slipped to its lowest depths at that period of its history with its revelling preoccupation with persecutory devices. She had no draw to martyrdom. She experienced suffering, yes, in common with us all, but she carried on living her unique path through those dark times. Her deepest pains arose in her visions of the wounds of Jesus on the Cross – his living out in actual and symbolic terms the five archetypal wounds that we human beings undergo in our journey through life: Abandonment, Rejection, Betrayal, Injustice and Denial – the prices of our multidimensional complexity. It is why, as love is the living source and Spark of Creation, I believe we are already forgiven for all our stumbling mess, but still invited to embrace the journey. Furthermore, this belief nurtures humility and a willingness to learn from our mistakes. It is the truth that sets us free, and love that crowns our life with meaning.

After the shame I felt in being a white citizen of South Africa in the 1930s, I never thought I'd feel a shame in being a British citizen, led by the most arrogant band of wounded egos imaginable. I am struck by the pure ineptitude of ego-led politicians, their policies so bereft of wisdom. But this very pandemic is serving as a world-wide Pan-Revealer of every culture and nation in the world, including our own. Not a Rescuer but a Revealer. And on a world-wide scale – each nation and culture presented with different challenges and hurdles to overcome.

I believe we could take a spurt forward as never before. A strangely cruel wake-up, but also a blessing. A coming together to save the only home we have – this Earth. Pan Co-operation. The nations of the world coming together to work with what we share in common as a species, but aware of certain radical differences so as not to collude with what we discern as unjust without fighting wars about such things. After all, there are shadow sides to every society (I cringe when I think of British arrogance and pride in their erstwhile Empire).

Let us each, and each nation, deal with our own wounded histories. We all have plenty to get on with – in ourselves as individuals and as diverse societies and cultures and nations. Just as we are all suffering from this epidemic of control, we will all benefit from choosing to co-operate and go beyond blaming, while not colluding with that with which we strongly disagree.

So yes, I do believe, along with countless others, that this is a critical point in the evolution of humankind, as more and more of us also face the reality of climate change, and wish to support every means to restore balance of all living creatures and plants and lifeforms on this wonderful planet. Many have been stirred and disturbed and awakened by our bold young activists such as Greta Thunberg, daring to speak up before the Swedish Parliament and inspiring school children to follow her. And the vision, courage and commitment, and imagination and daring of another order of those involved in Extinction Rebellion.

We have so needed to be jolted awake, and I am convinced it's not too late. What amazing people they are. We human beings can be enormously creative and determined, once we combine all our varied gifts and talents. And for the first time in history, drawing on Global Co-operation. No place for Victimhood or being caught in, and reduced to, the P–V–R Drama Triangle, that takes us nowhere.

I have perhaps not given sufficient attention to the extremity of the Lockdown conditions imposed on all places of worship – and just when people's need for that aspect of their being would likely have been most urgent. Doors ordered to be kept locked and bolted except for the briefest of windows, not even to enable people to sit in silence way apart from each other in the beauty and peace of the many ancient buildings in this country. And never allowed to sing until the Sunday after Liberation Day on 21 July (2021) – and then only with masks on.

Zoom is no substitute in matters spiritual, which is all about a state of full presence; being with others in a shared recognition and sense of Mystery that is beyond words, while still, being human, needing to use words. And singing lifts their resonance and takes us beyond those words, as also occurs with chanting together, which is so central to many faiths. And just when solace in loss of loved ones was so profound for so many people. All through the thousands of centuries human beings have been on earth, they have sung and chanted together. They sang when they gathered food and worked on the land, made their pots and tools and weapons, and wove their cloth. Even slaves in the cotton fields of America were allowed to sing – free to express the anguish in their hearts and the hope in their souls. Humankind has sung while they worked, or celebrated, or worshipped, or buried their dead together, from their earliest days on this Earth – this life-giving planet. Until Lockdowns. A deprivation of the very thing that would have sustained and nourished people in a way that completely transcended the P–V–R construction.

So to bring this interchange between us to a close, Richard. This is a time in our world history like none other. Humanity is confronted with two strands of threat to their existence at the same time, and at a global level: climate change and the pandemic. And they are both progressing rapidly, denial requiring somewhat deranged use of our gift of imagination or the folly of avoidance. Once fear takes over, we can so easily lose ourselves, along with all spark of hope.

The fact that those in powerful positions of political leadership have been pushed and stimulated into facing the plight of this planet, and are meeting together from all over the world in full realization that it is essential to co-operate together to begin dealing with it, at least sparks hope in me – and no doubt in many others – that we human beings will now give priority to maintaining a home for us and our descendents not only to survive, but to thrive and flourish. We have the intelligence and creativity, imagination and resourcefulness to fulfil this task if we really take it on board and, at long last, we have dared to face it.

What a paradox that it was the operation of President Trump's bloated ego, spewing out any handy lie as required which happened to include climate-change denial, that became so gross that he lost the election to Biden, who has embraced the reality of climate change and taken action to consult with China, which had already done so and was getting on with creating solutions. Their political system is ideally suited to actualizing them. (Can it be 'The flutter of the butterfly's wings' within the potency of our Collective Unconscious?)

So I believe that we are not just poised, but are geared to create a better world. It has become a necessity. However, it can only be transformed into actuality if we are to tolerate radically diverse cultural norms and socio-political arrangements – and we human beings have not to date shown much propensity to do so. It will, no doubt, be an exacting and bumpy ride, and it will need the co-operation of all nations who have the vote. That means it is up to us to play our part. We will each have the responsibility to keep our eye on the bigger picture.

There's not much opportunity for P–V–R compulsions within the emerging new paradigm of co-operation. Could we even end up with transformation? Reality is dynamic, and thus so are we.... As the pandemic has served to subject so many other cultures over the world to Lockdowns, who knows what transformative effects will emerge that will differ from ours, and will possibly serve to enlighten us all?

You wonder in your final question if it is perhaps fatal to have a medical system that is created and maintained from a place of ego alone. Yes, to be sure. But the troubling thing is that our NHS was not conceived and brought into being from a place of ego – it was socialist in conception and realization, and greatly appreciated both here and beyond these shores; so much so that it's stealthy and gradual degeneration took time to reveal itself. Deals with the private sector, among other things. And now it seems that it is only because nurses and doctors are going beyond ego right now, as many always have done, that the NHS is functioning at all.

You then ask what I think a post-ego 'Health and Well-being Service' would look like. The very title offers the answer in itself. I imagine it would be holistic in its ethos and functioning – offering alternative medicines such as homeopathy and plant-based substances, and modes of healing such as shiatsu, reflexology and biodynamic massage. And of course, plain, straightforward compassion and kindness, as so many of our current staff manage to do even now, in these most stressed and over-stretched of circumstances. And the science would be sound, offering the best hypotheses available at the time. The chaplin or chaplins (both genders, if possible) would ideally need to be sensitive to the particularity of the person and their state of being, and offer only that which they could receive – inviting them to unburden themselves of anything undealt with or disturbing to their peace of mind, especially if they are on the point of death.

And so to close with some final thoughts with regard to your first question about whether I think that the human species is any closer to being able to evolve beyond the Victimhood Archetype today, compared to when I first started exploring it some decades ago. Yes. Paradoxically, the very imposition of the unprecedented means of control to which we have been subjected since March 2020 is likely to stimulate a longing to be free to make our own choices. This could give rise to a more keen sense that it could also mean we'd be more responsible for the outcome of those choices. This in turn would involve more self-reflection, and a realization that we can participate in creating our reality, thus experiencing a greater sense of fulfilment. It would also transform the quality of our relationships. Blaming others would become redundant, a passing slip when stressed or frustrated. Our most intimate relationships would be greatly enriched, and the love in us freed to flower.

Note

1 Throughout the interview, lower-case letters will be used to denote the terms 'persecutor', 'victim' and 'rescuer', even though capitals are used in relation to the Drama Triangle of Persecutor–Victim–Rescuer (P–V–R), which is a key theme of the interview. This follows the publishing convention that capital letters should only be used when absolutely necessary. However, when the terms 'persecutor', 'victim' and 'rescuer' are used, they do refer to dynamic positions in the Drama Triangle.

References

Dodsworth, L. (2021). *A State of Fear: How the UK Government Weaponised Fear during the Covid-19 Pandemic*. London: Pinter & Martin.

Hall, J. (1993). *The Reluctant Adult: The Problem of Choice*. Bridport, Dorset: Prism Press.

Usher, L. & others (2021). *Covid-19 – How It Made Us Feel: Life in Lockdown during the CoronaVirus Pandemic*. Lusher Living.

Richard House edited for many years the Humanistic Psychology journal *Self & Society* and its online sister magazine.

About the Author

Jill Hall was born in Cape Town in the 1930's into an environment of extreme inequality and oppression, which remained unrecognised by all those around her. It was a relief to move to London in her late teens to train as an actress at the Royal Central School of Speech and Drama. In her thirties she married and became the mother of two daughters. Attracted to the world of self-development in the early days of the Growth Movement, she decided to become a psychotherapist, later to become a tutor at the Institute of Biodynamic Psychology in London.

Following the death of her husband in 1993, Jill continued her work as an holistic therapist, while at the same time attending Residential Science and Mystic Conferences. She will never forget the evening when the scientist Glen Schaffer shared with the audience the realisation that spirit was prior to matter.

She currently lives and works in Norwich.

INDEX

A

Abandonment: Wound of, 202, 265, 284
abuse: *see* child abuse, incest, rape, sexual abuse
acceptance: bringing change, 261; climate of full, 263
actualization: experience of, 171; of self in the East, 171–5
Adam and Eve, 47
Adult Spirit (Shield), 132, 150
Adult Substance man and woman, 136
'Adult Substance Shield', 128
adulthood: fear of, 48; towards full, 266–87; true, 16, 136
AIDS, 220
Air – element of the North, 128
alignment: coming into, 170
All-inclusive Consciousness, 158
alternative medicines, 321
American Indian peoples, 23, 115–43 *passim*, 280; Great-Great-Great-Grandmother space, 143; and the Human Realm, 159; model of the self, 114
anger, 86
animals: as receivers of energy, 129
annihilation terror, 88, 187, 253; physical dependence and, 82–3; *see also* fear
Answer to Job (The) (Jung), 36
anxiety, 162, 220; state of, 160; *see also* fear

Archetype of Self-generation: *see* self-generation
archetypes, 92; Christ, 55, 56; defined, 104; Infant, 40; Mother, 40; *see also* Self-generation, Archetype of; Victim(hood) Archetype
art: greatest, 85
assumptions: making of, 21, 22
attachment, 268–9; confused with survival, 43; and detachment, 100; energy of, 284; fixed state of, 269–70; obsession, 284; old buzz from, 277; as our preoccupation, 42; seeking, 30
aura of a new-born, 292
Autumn as season of the North, 131
awareness: of spirit, 50; prolonged eclipse of, 81–2; *see also* core-awareness, meta-awareness

B

baby: isness of a, 70
'bad breast' (Klein), 35
Bear as animal in the West, 133–4
beating up on ourselves, 179
becoming whole, 100–2
behaviourism: theories of, 171–2
being: accessing other levels of, 228–34; and doing, 27; *see also* being in the now, being in the right, 'Beingness'
being in the now, 18
being in the right, 235–6
'Beingness', 142

Bettelheim, Bruno, 225
Big Bang (the), 62; *see also* first second of existence
bio-life: interrupting the flow of, 285
Biodynamic Psychology, 23
biological vulnerability, 74
birth, 43
black as colour of the West, 134
'black' peoples, 134
blame, 15–16; acceptance of, 47; apportioning, 295; beyond, 16, 17; causal ontology and need to, 27–34; culture of, 291; flight from, 57; freedom from, 292; freedom from in South, 127; regression, and licence to, 45–7; taking, 211–13; vs responsibility, 46; *see also* blaming, self-blame
blaming, 34, 264; addiction to, 18; freedom from, 70; syndrome, 23, 27; *see also* blame
body, 107–9; continuum with spirit, 108; perfectly designed, 137; resurrection of the, 286; spirit and, 76; in the West, 132–3; *see also* mind/body split
Bohm, David, 143, 173
'bounded singularity', 71; seeing ourselves as, 62
Bowlby, John, 23
Boyesen, Gerda, 23, 35
brain function: and consciousness, 65
breast: primal need for, 37; *see also* 'bad breast'
Buddhism, 52; 'No Mind', 142
Buffalo – animal of the North, 130
buffalo: horns of the, 130–1, 136, 146, 149–50
'building block' model, 94

C

cancer: and choice, 252
capitalism, 218–19; and ego domination, 218, 219; *see also* capitalist ideological framework
capitalist ideological framework, 35–6; *see also* capitalism
care homes, 308
causal ontology: and need to blame, 27–34; *see also* linear causal models
causal thinking, 18; biologists on, 29; dangerous, 30; going beyond, 24; isolating a definite cause, 31; and the subject/object split, 32–4 *passim*; *see also* cause and effect, linear causal models
cause and effect: external cause, 25; notion of, 23, 254–5; *see also* causal thinking, effect
ceremony, 116
change: acceptance bringing, 261; being essential, 113; fear of, 49; non-linear approach to, 279–82; openness to, 113; radical, 223–6; resistance to, 48–51, 280; as threat to the system, 110–14; trying to, 262; *see also* transformation
child: power of the, 290–3; *see also* infancy, infant; other 'child' entries
child abuse: impossible to write about, 204
child energy, 122, 123: intrinsic, 44
Child Spirit (Shield), 138, 139, 150, 159, 175; our origins in, 176
Child Substance Shield, 122, 126
child within: *see* inner child
choice, 33, 102, 113, 172; cancer and, 252; choosing process, 144, 146; complexity of, 17; confusing control with, 151; different levels in, 153–4; fixed, 162; identified

with ego, 172; multi-dimensional model of, 155; North as place of, 164–8; as part of our nature, 184; and rape, 192–200; resistance to choosing, 157; source of, in the East, 156–60; will and, 261
Christ, 207, 251; archetypal figure of, 55, 56; *see also* Jesus
circle(s): sacred, 115; of the self, 115–43; circular system, 147; *see also* Circle of Reaction
Circle of Reaction: 180–1; distinguished from the Wheel of Responsibility, 187–90
Clarity as enemy of the North, 129
climate change, 318, 320; *see also* ecological crises
Cold War, 277
collective psyche: Victim Archetype and the, 37–41
Collective Unconscious, 66
communism, 218–19
community: being in, 231
comparisons: redundancy of, 236–9
competition: redundancy of, 236–9
completion: participation in our own, 85–6
concentration-camp experience, 225
conception: bio-focus at, 76–7; moment of, 79–80
condemnation: energy of total, 203; self-, 204
confusion, 248
connection theory/theories, 66, 172, 248, 252
consciousness: and brain function, 65; from conception onwards, 64, 66; different aspects of, 65; as gift of being, 280; infant, 63–6; refusal of, in the West, 184–5; *see also* All-inclusive Consciousness, Cosmic Consciousness in the East, ego consciousness, pure consciousness, trans-temporal consciousness
consumerism, 78; addictive, 102, 292; insecurity and, 217–22
contemplative life, 267; Western, 96
control, 76, 315; and the concept of cause, 33; confusing choice with, 151; desire to, 293; enemy of obedience, 188; global epidemic of, 300–1, 318; loss of, 279; mounting need to, 83; without responsibility, 145; *see also* controlling others
controlling others, 151–3
co-operation: emerging paradigm of, 320
core-awareness, 232
Cosmic Consciousness in the East, 138–9
Cosmic Law in the East, 139
cot deaths, 75
courage, 228
courtship, 271
Covid (crisis): generation of fear in, 308, 310, 311; global epidemic of control, 300–1, 318; medicine's response to, 306; vaccine, 309; and the Victimhood Archetype, 299, 306; 'war' on the virus, 307; *see also* hand-clapping for the NHS, Lockdown(s), viruses
creating our reality/lives, 151–3, 241–4; ego consciousness and, 200
creativity: divine, 85; *see also* regression (creative)
'crisis': in Chinese, 262
crystal as mineral of the West, 135

D

damaged self: *see* self (accepting the damaged)

Dark Mirrors: domination of the, 188
Darwin, Charles, 81
Davies, Paul, 61, 66
death, 64, 65, 253; acceptance of, 100; cot-, 75; defeating, 307; ego and, 276; fear of, 136-7; freedom from fear of, 82; instinct, 84; obsessive avoidance of, 77-9, 310; and the psyche, 74, 75; and sex, 268; surrendering to, 74, 78; terror at start of life, 81; *see also* dying, near-death experiences
decision-making: in the North, 161, 164-8
defence: devising modes of, 216; special styles of, 51; *see also* defended personality, defensiveness
defended personality, 285; prevalence of, 83-4
defensiveness, 30
defiance: path to self-definition, 207
dependence(y), 24; biological, 70-1; complete, on mother, 215; and domination, 76; fundamental place in psyche, 127; fury of, 270; and independence, 93; myth of total, 71-2; physical, and annihilation terror, 82-3; *see also* interdependence
depression, 316
desire to be rescued, 227
destiny: defined, 243; freedom and, 241-65
destructiveness, 107; *see also* weapons of destruction
detachment: and attachment, 100
determinism, 144-6; opposition with free will, 115, 146-8; the rational mind and, 165; theories of, 171-2
Dharma wheel, 52
distinction: confused with separation, 28, 71

divisiveness, 24; creating, 130
Dodsworth, Laura, 309, 310, 314
dogmas, 130
domination: dependency and, 76
'double bind', 112, 258
Drama Triangle: *see* persecutor/victim/rescuer Drama Triangle
dualism, 117; entrenched thought, 109; and the Victim Archetype, 102-5
dying: participating in our, 253; *see also* death

E

Eagle as animal of the East, 140
East: Cosmic Consciousness in the, 138-9; Cosmic Law in the, 139; direction of the, 138-42; Eagle as animal of the, 140; ego consciousness in the, 138-9; escapism in the, 188; fanciful dictator of the, 186-7; Fire as element of the, 138; freedom to actualize self in the, 171-5; the Human Realm in the, 140; Illumination in the, 138; information in the, 138; Love of Power in the, 140; Pride in the, 140, 186; source of choice, 156-60; Summer as season of the, 139; superego and the, 139; Timelessness in the, 138; /West axis of the self, 231; Yellow as colour of the, 138
Eastern Europe, 277
Eastern monotheism, 99
Eastern mystical traditions, 95
ecological crises, 145; *see also* climate change, Extinction Rebellion
economic collapse: catastrophic, 280
effect: viewing ourselves as an, 34
ego (the), 24-6 *passim*, 77, 100, 104,

199, 247, 275, 305, 312; antics of the, 101; -based concept of self, 92-8; as closed system, 282; cradled in the West, 99; death as oblivion to the, 276; delineating boundaries, 282; denial of the, 96-7; development of the, 56, 57; dictatorship of the, 94; discarding the, 96; domination, 24, 97; domination, and capitalism, 218, 219; -imperialism, 101; integration of, 25, 73, 74, 77, 81-2; -led politicians, 318; limits of understanding, 281; in the North, 131; over-reach of the, 101; role in fulfilment, 282-3; and separation, 268; weak, 96; in the West, 133; *see also* ego consciousness

ego consciousness, 92, 141, 241, 261, 268, 278; in the East, 138-9; in the North, 130, 131; over-weighting of, 218; slipping into, 170; in social context, 165; transition anathema to, 275; *see also* ego

Einstein, Albert, 24, 189

either/or logic, 26

emotional cycles: uncompleted, 43-5 *passim*

emotional regulation: use/misuse of, 86-8

empowering: of the infant, 291, 292; ourselves, 222; *see also* self-empowerment

emptiness: fleeing from, 229

energy: child, 122; in continual movement, 121

English Public Schools: ethos of, 312-13; sense of entitlement, 313

entities: defined as separate, 149-51 *passim*

environment: human impact of, 63

evolution: next stage of, 40, 51; of a self-conscious universe, 85

evolutionary transition: state of, 76

experience: different levels of, 27

Extinction Rebellion, 318-19

F

failure of mother, 34-7

Fall (The), 48, 52, 285; powerful myth of, 53

fanciful dictator of the East, 186-7

Fate: notion of, 243; vs free will, 243

father (the), 35

fear of death: as enemy of the West, 136

fear(s); of adulthood, 48; of being our self, 178; of change, 49; as enemy in the South, 124; of growing up, 48-51; and international relationships, 30; as means of control, 310; from mothering, 86; and old programmes, 44; and powerlessness, 210; psychological, 75; trapping other feelings, 124-5; *see also* anxiety, fear of death

feelings, 86, 168; as enemies, 83-4; guilt and, 87; making judgements about, 87; need to flow, 45

Fire: as element of the East, 138; elemental energy of, 172

first second of existence, 61; *see also* Big Bang

fixation, 76, 129; on the 'psychic breast', 268; state of, 197

fixed positions in the North, 182-4

fixed thought: as great danger, 129

foregiveness: beyond definition, 298; victimhood and, 294-8 *passim*

Forster, E.M., 100

four directions (the): and aspects of the psyche, 118-20; balancing the powers of, 121; confusing the, 132, 160; the East, 138-42; the North, 128-32 the South, 122-7; the West, 132-7

four elements, 122; water, 122; *see also* fire
fragmentation: state of, 92–3
free child, 123
free will, 33; challenge of, 144; contradictions of, 172; Fate vs. 243; necessary conditions of, 52; opposition with determinism, 115, 146–8; paradox as elucidating, 148–9
freedom: birthright of creative, 208; to create, 173; and destiny, 241–65; escapism as enemy of, 188; of full selfhood, 278; infantile sensation of, 268; of irresponsibility, 267, 274, 276, 277; living experience of, 267; psychic protectionism, as death of, 208; responsibility and, 16, 266, 274; *see also* freedom from blame
freedom from blame, 292; in the South, 127
frozen responses: releasing a, 259–60; of the South, 181–2
Freud, Sigmund, 23, 24, 36, 84; on energy in the psyche, 91; equals isolationism, 270; as patriarchal thinker, 24; *see also* Id, Oedipus Complex, superego
fusion, 133; experience of oneness, 267; idealized drive towards, 275; in love with, 216; prolonged, 42; pull towards, 272; as retrograde step, 268; safety of, 50
Future in the North, 128

G

Gaia, 278
Garden of Eden, 125
'Geist' (the German word), 60
Gnostic Gospel of Thomas, 47
God, 69–70; externalized, 99; meta-explanatory, 52; objectified, 98; relationship with concept of self, 98–100
Goddess (the), 70; archetypal energy of, 285, 286
good-enough mothering, 290
Great-Great-Great-Grandmother space, 143
greed: politics of, 238
Grof, Stanislav, 23
grooming, 201–2
grounding of the mind, 130
growing up: fear of, 48–51
guilt, 46, 84, 204; of the abdicated self, 191; equated with responsibility, 152; and feelings, 87; loaded on to mother, 34; mistaken claims of, 235; -pact, 235; in social context, 203–4
guilty mother, 16, 34
gurus, 99

H

Hall, Jill: beginnings of, 66–8; interview with, 299–323; jealousy, 173
hand-clapping for the NHS: hypocrisy of, 308
hate, 249; of self, 184
Hatfield, Sue, 15–17
healing, 119; *see also* Healing Wheel of Life, self-healing
Healing Wheel of Life, 127
health: obsession with, 220
Health and Well-being Service, 321
health-and-safety culture, 19
Heart Chakra, 311
Hegel, 60
helpless self, 20
helplessness, 20, 21
hierarchical models of the self, 109–10
'higher' and 'lower': terms, 110
Higher Self, 84
Hitler, Adolf, 216, 230, 242:

nationalism of, 210; as victim, 200; war against, 158
Holocaust, the, 157; and impotence/omnipotence, 157–8
House, Richard: foreword, 12–14; interview with Jill Hall, 299–323
hubris, 130
human nature, 41
Humanistic Psychology, 37
humanity: abdication of our, 158

I

'I': self-aware, 58–9; flow and force of the, 125
I/Thou experience, 274
Id, 84
Illumination in the East, 138
illusion: beliefs in, 278; false freedom of, 277
imagination: energized human, 174
impotence: of the all-powerful mother, 68–9; belief in, 221; fury of dependence, 270; power games and, 226–8; and protectionism, 207–9
impotent/omnipotent dynamic, 24; the Holocaust and, 157–8; and the victim, 145
incarnation: intention at, 156–60; passage of, 80; primal repression at, 88; '-shock', 73–6, 286
incest, 184
individuation, 56, 81, 268, 283; circle as symbol of, 115; in the East, 171
infancy: psychology in, 23–41; state of development, 25; see also infant
infant: as all immediacy, 70; consciousness, 63–6; determination to remain an, 54; innate power of the, 64; -mother collusion, 207–9, 286; as raw consciousness, 292; reclaiming the power of the, 60–72; as spiritually 'mature', 62, 291; see also infancy, wounded child
Infinite (the): Beingness, 105; context for self, 59
'infinite regress' problem, 34
information: fields of (Bohm), 173; massive amounts of, 221
initial responses: claiming our, 69–71
inner child: regression and the, 43–5
inner/outer distinction, 28; American Indian view, 116–17
insecurity: chronic, 93; and consumerism, 217–22; seed of our, 207; socio-political arrangements and, 218
integration, 103, 104; integrated self, 237; personal, 238
intellectual knowing, 79–80
intention at incarnation, 156–60
interconnectedness, 18, 25
interdependence: conscious, 93
international relationships: conflict, 210; permeated with fear, 30
Intuition in the West, 134, 135, 169; see also knowing (intuitive)
irresponsibility: freedom of, 267–9 *passim*, 274, 276, 277; infant, 278
isness, 61, 281; of a baby, 70, 292; timeless, 94
isolation, 24

J

jealousy, 173
Jesus, 47; wounds of, 317; see also Christ
Johnson, Boris, 311
joy: spirit bringing, 224
Julian of Norwich, 317
Jung, Carl, 36, 66, 115

K

Klein, Melanie, 23, 35
knowing: intuitive, 225; Right and Left brain, 130–2 *passim*; *see also* not knowing
koans, 149
Krishnamurti, J., 129

L

Laing, R.D., 23, 112
language: and concept of self, 25–7; secondary system of, 27; serving the Victim Archetype, 26
left-brain activity, 131; *see also* Right and Left brain knowing
libidinous well-being, 89, 285; *see also* sexuality
life: being unfair, 244–8; creating our own, 241–4; direction of, 79–80; as essentially flawed, 52, 53; going with, 278; original spark of, 62; tide of, 274–9; *see also* bio-life
linear causal models: expanding beyond, 290; letting go of, 146, 147, 172
linear logic, 26; *see also* linear mode of thought
linear mode of thought, 149; *see also* linear logic
litigation: fear of, 19
Lockdown(s), 300, 305, 308, 311, 313, 317; as enforced Victimhood, 315; of places of worship, 319
love, 70, 215; being/falling in, 270, 272, 273, 276; inborn capacity to, 307; Julian of Norwich's vision of, 317; and meaning, 318; *see also* hate, romantic love

M

Magical Law in the West, 135
Mandela, Nelson, 294, 295
martyrs, 235
Mary (mother of Jesus): qualities of, 207
Maslow, Abraham, 37
maternal deprivation, 36; *see also* mother(s)
materialism, 60; and victimhood, 39
matter: existence in the realm of, 285; as expression of spirit, 286; knowing it in its fullness, 287; love of, 285–6; probing of, 29; reluctance to embrace, 286; spirit prior to, 213; *see also* spirit-in-matter
meaning: hierarchical structure of, 91–2; self-concept and, 91–114
meaningfulness: joy of, 157
'medical science' worldview, 310
medical system: NHS, 321; post-Victimhood, 314–15
Medicine Wheel, 115, 154, 281; and the four directions, 118–20
meditative life, 95–6
memory: organistic, 66
meta-awareness, 232
Miller, Alice, 290; and the hurt child, 35
Mind: grounding of the, 130; in the North, 128; Universal, 142
mind/body split, 54; *see also* dualism
Mineral Realm in the West, 132
mirror(s): dark and the light, 120–1; *see also* Dark Mirrors
money: placing security in, 219
monotheism, 52; personalized Eastern, 99
mother(s): complete dependence on, 215; focus shift to self, 55–9; guilt loaded on to, 34; impotence of the all-powerful, 68–9; inevitable failure of, 32–4; –infant collusion with, 207–9, 212–13, 286; letting go of, 286; needs of, 36; onus always on, 35; rejection

of, 207; unique journey of, 215–16; as whole beings, 208; *see also* guilty mother, maternal deprivation, mother-blame, mothering, primary maternal preoccupation
mother-blame, 15, 37
Mother Earth: victimizing, 293
mothering: good-enough, 290
Mouse as animal of the South, 125
multi-dimensional beings, 147, 148; model of the self, 248–51
mystery, 29
mystical traditions: Eastern, 95

N

naming a human, 58
national 'security', 107
Natural Law in the South, 124–6 *passim*
Nature: self-regulatory genius of, 220, 316
near-death experiences, 64–5
Neo-Freudian age, 23, 34
neurosis, 30, 84, 88–9; as commitment to the outdated, 183; intensity of, 277; 'natural', 216; as the norm, 23
neurotic personality, 83; healthily, 264
'No Mind', 142
non-choice: experience of, 17, 154; and rape, 192–200
non-conscious mind, 68–9
non-linearity, 26
non-resistance, 263
North: Autumn as season of the, 131; being stuck in the, 135; Buffalo as animal of the, 130; Clarity as enemy of the, 129; decision-making in the, 161; direction of the, 128–32; element of Air, 128; the future in the, 128; Mind in the, 128; place of choice and decision-making, 164–8; re-enacting old fixed positions in the, 182–4; social law in the, 128; vagueness of thought in the, 129; White as colour of the, 131; wind in the, 128, 129; wisdom in the, 129
not knowing, 129; *see also* unknown

O

'obedience': control as enemy of, 188; unfortunate connotations of, 169–71; vs victimhood, 170
obedience to voice within: in the West, 168–71
objective knowledge, 28–9
Oedipus Complex, 30
omnipotence: *see* impotent/omnipotent dynamic
open systems, 58

P

pandemic experience: dynamics of the, 299; *see also* Lockdown(s), viruses
paradox: and elucidating free will, 148–9; embracing, 144; of human development, 262; as language of wisdom, 251; Russell's unsolvable, 148
passive resignation in the West, 184–5
past: addressing our, 160; clearing our, 136; coming to terms with our, 123
patriarchy, 110; Freud and, 24
patterns: repetitive, 161
peace: the experience of, 50
perfect society: demand for a, 222–3
persecutor, 295, 302, 303; super-ego as most relentless, 305; *see also* persecutor/victim/rescuer dynamic, victim/persecutor/

rescuer dynamic
persecutor/victim/rescuer (PVR) Drama Triangle, 299, 301, 310, 311, 322
physicality: human, 132
physics, 29: defeating the laws of, 108; modern, 28; of Newton, 24; *see also* Bohm, David; Davies, Paul; quantum mechanics
Piaget, Jean, 23
plants: as givers of energy, 123
political activity: healthy, 214
political realm: ego-led politicians, 318; power struggles in, 238; stepping outside of, 230
power, 24; and ability to trust, 206; of the child, 290–3; claiming out true, 230; dynamics of, 206–40; illusory, 227; of the infant, 60–72; love of, in the East, 140; without intelligence, 206; mistaking control for, 279; -over, 206; over ourselves, 229; and politics, 238; transferring to individuals, 226; *see also* power games, powerlessness
power games: depowering the, 228–34; of the impotent, 226–8
powerlessness: and violence, 209–11
present predicament, 283–4
Present in the West, 134–5
Pride: in the East, 140; enemy of the East, 186
primal self-betrayal, 215–17
primary maternal preoccupation (Winnicott), 36
projection(s), 242–3; : re-owning, 150
psyche: atemporal, 290; divided against itself, 51, 84; ego-dominated, 97; energy within the, 91; as essentially creative, 30; the four directions and the, 118–20; multi-dimensional, 290; Newtons of the, 189; power and complexity of the, 148; sequential model of, 213; split-, 100–2; *see also* collective psyche
psychic brain surgery, 234
psychic protectionism: as death of freedom, 208
psychoanalysis, 256
psychological theory: premises of, 19
psychology, 29, 256; biodynamic, 23; Humanistic, 37; in infancy, 23–41; prior to sociology/politics, 213–15
psychotherapy, 39
PTSD, 202
Public Schools: *see* English Public Schools
pure consciousness: at core of self, 142–3

Q

quantum mechanics, 33
quantum physics, 173; experiments in, 174

R

racism: and national regression, 277
radical change, 223–6, 233–4; *see also* change
rape, 190–200; case study, 192–200; in general, 190–2
rational linguistic model, 25–6
rational mind: misuse of the, 130; and theories of determinism, 165
rational thought, 27: linear nature, of, 26
reaction, 179: Circle of, 180–1; the grip of, 178
receptive mind, 130–1
red as colour of the South, 126
reductionism, 27
regression: and the child within,

43–5; conscious and unconscious, 43–4; creative, 272; the great, 42–59; and licence to blame, 45–7; powerful pull to, 56; racism and national, 277
reincarnation: belief in, 99
relating: fixed modes of, 50
relationship: obsessional element in, 272
religions, 48, 52, 99, 101; see also Buddhism, Christ
religious wars, 78
repression: primal, at incarnation, 88; releasing template of, 88–9
Rescuer(s), 48, 183–4, 234–5, 302, 303; see also desire to be rescued, persecutor/victim/rescuer dynamic, victim/persecutor/rescuer dynamic
resignation, 315: danger of, 310; passive, in the West, 184–5
resilience: intrinsic, 35
resistance, 40; to change, 48–51, 280; to choosing, 157; to psychological growth, 49; see also non-resistance
responsibility: control without, 145; equated with guilt, 152; extent of our, 144–75 passim; and freedom, 16, 266, 274; learning to be responsible, 204; taking, 211–13; vs blame, 46; 'Wheel of', 154–5; see also self-responsibility
responsive self: in the South, 160–4
resurrection of the Body, 286
revolution: true, 230
Right and Left brain knowing, 130–2 passim
rigidity, 129; dogmas, 130
risk-taking, 247–8
ritual, 116
Rogers, Carl, 37
Romanian revolution, 221–2
romantic love, 84; yearning for, 42

Russell, Bertrand, 148

S

St Paul, 78
Sampson, Edward E., 37
science, 29, 146; faith in, 220; limits of, 58; see also scientism
scientism, 28, 29; see also science
security: grasping at physical, 219; money and, 219
self (the), 27, 33, 73; accepting the damaged, 260–5; Activating, 311; Adult Spirit, 168; American Indian peoples' model of, 115–43 passim; as an axion, 59; Child Substance, 160; the circle of, 115–43; compassion for, 199–200; concept of, 103; from conception, 163; dangers of hierarchical models of, 109–10; discovering our Einstein-, 189; divide between other and, 28; ego-based concept of, 92–8, 199; extended view of the, 291; the fallen, 47–8; flight from, 191; focus shift from mother to, 55–9; fresh understanding of, 223; -hate, 184, 216, 274; helpless, 20; Higher, 84; Infinite as context for, 59; integrated, 237; and language, 25–7; the mature, 119–20; mature spirit-, 168; multi-dimensional model of, 248–51; non-linear nature of, 94, 115; pure consciousness in core of, 142–3; relationship with concept of God, 98–100; responsive, in the South, 160–4; as source of energy, 163; split into bits, 103; victim-, 159; West/East axis of the, 231; see also other 'self-' entries
self-acceptance: only safe path, 200
self-aware 'I', 58–9

self-betrayal: primal, 215–17
self-blame, 46
self-concept: based on spirit, 105–7; and meaning, 91–114; victim, 98
self-condemnation, 204
self-empowerment, 239–40; *see also* empowering ourselves
self-generating systems, 29, 34, 69; *see also* self-generation
self-generation, 153–4, 251–6; Archetype of, 104, 208, 213, 223, 286; idea of, 241; *see also* self-generating systems
self-hate, 184, 216, 274
self-healing: rare, 45
self-responsibility, 56
self reflection: the 'shields' of, 116–18
senses: splitting our five, 221
separation: confused with distinction, 28, 71; ego and, 268; preoccupation with, 81; *see also* entities
set conceptual frameworks, 130
sexual abuse, 201–2; *see also* incest, rape
sexual energy: split off from spirit, 88; *see also* sexual expression, sexuality
sexual expression: as flight into union, 268; and the West, 133
sexuality, 270–1; based on fixations, 273; 'cosmic', 285; death and, 268; grace of our initial, 89; misdirected, 273–4; repressed, 89; *see also* sexual energy, sexual expression, libidinous well-being
Shadow: dealing with our, 120
shame: greatest secret enemy, 296–7; tool for shaming, 305
sharing: promoting safety, 219
shield: Adult Spirit, 132; Adult Substance, 128; Child Substance, 122, 126; as a mirror, 117, as our teacher, 117; *see also* 'shields' of

self reflection
'shields' of self reflection, 116–18
Shohet, Robin, 18–19
shutter mechanism, 81–2, 285; and life direction, 79–80
sickness: tendency towards, 220
'sieve of fear', 124
singing, 319
Skinner, B.F., 172
Snake as animal of the South, 125
social law in the North, 128, 165
socio-political arrangements, 287: insecurity undepinning, 218
Sound of One Hand Clapping, 149
source(s): back to the, 73–90; fascination with, 61
South: direction of the, 122–7; fear as enemy in the, 124; frozen responses of the, 181–2; Mouse as animal of the, 125; Natural Law in the, 124–6 *passim*; Power of the, 126; red as colour of the, 126; responsive self in the, 160–4; Snake as animal of the, 125; Spring as season of the, 126; Trust in the, 123
spirit, 141; acknowledging, 86–9; apprehension of, 56, 57; awareness of, 50; and body, 76; bringing joy, 224; experience of, 88; forgetfulness of, 176; matter as expression of, 286; prior to matter, 213; recognition of, 60–3; rightful place of, 18; self-concept based on, 105–7; simply *is*, 60, 291; *see also* spirit-in-matter, spiritual essence
spirit-in-matter, 284–7; *see also* spirit
spiritual essence: recognising our, 106;
split psyche, 100–2
Spring as season of the South, 126
Stalin, Joseph, 142, 227–8, 230

State of Fear, A (Dodsworth), 309, 310
staying the same: determination to, 262
subject/object divide, 28
subjectivity: 'black hole' of, 29
suicide, 253
Sullivan, Harry Stack, 37, 91–2
Summer as season of the East, 139
superego, 84; arrogant, 307, 308; and the East, 139, as most relentless persecutor, 305
survival: confused with attachment, 43
synchronicity, 168

T

'tabula rasa' concept, 64
Tao, 251: universal living principle of, 100
television: programming by, 221
Thanatos, 84
Thunberg, Greta, 318
time: curved, 80
Timelessness in the East, 138
transformation, 251: of a frozen response, 256–9; possibility of, 85–6; resistance to, 40; subtle process, of, 261; true, 224; *see also* change
trans-temporal consciousness, 172, 281
'Trinity of Compulsions', 303
Trump, President, 320
Trust: power and ability to, 206; in the South, 123
truth: more evolved, 278; provisional, 278; setting us free, 318

U

uncertainty: risk of, 278
unconscious mind: power of, 24; see also Freud, Sigmund; psychoanalysis

Universal Mind, 142
unknown: terror of the, 276; *see also* not knowing

V

vaccine: *see* Covid (vaccine)
vagueness of thought in the North, 129
ventilators, 316
Verny, Dr Thomas, 66
Victim(hood) Archetype, 17, 18, 25, 27, 37, 71, 72, 299–323 *passim*; and the collective psyche, 37–41; conceptual backdrop to, 64; and dualism, 102–5; evolving beyond the, 314; language serving the, 26, 314; organizing energy of the, 103; release from the, 101; *see also* victimhood, victims
victimhood: being born info, 103; Collective, 310; denying the reality of, 228; energy of, 16, 17; logic of, 294–5; in a materialist framework, 39; vs obedience, 170; *see also* persecutor/victim/rescuer dynamic, victim/persecutor/rescuer dynamic, Victim(hood) Archetype, victim(s), Wheel of Victimhood
victim/persecutor/rescuer (VPR) dynamic, 103, 189, 226; *see also* persecutor/victim/rescuer dynamic, victimhood, victim(s)
victim(s): calling forth persecutors, 72; can't forgive, 294–8; experiencing ourselves as, 225; pull to be, 104; self-concept, 98; victim self, 159; *see also* persecutor/victim/rescuer dynamic victim/persecutor/rescuer dynamic, victimhood
violence: powerlessness and, 209–11
viruses: Mass Victimhood in

relation to, 311; as part of Nature, 307
vision quest, 117
visualizations: active, 166
vulnerability: biological, 74

W

warrior: the term, 120
water (element), 122; qualities of water, 123; in rituals, 123; in the South, 161
weapons of destruction, 219
West: bear as animal in the, 133–4; black as colour of the, 134; the body in the, 132–3; control in the, 188; crystal as mineral of the, 135; direction of the, 132–7; /East axis of the self, 231; fear of death as enemy of the, 136–7; Intuition in the, 134, 135, 169; Magical Law in the, 135; obedience to the voice within, 168–71, 188; passive resignation in the, 184–5; the Present in the, 134–5; refusal of consciousness in the, 184–5; sexual expression and the, 133; subtle holding of the, 170; Winter as season in the, 134
Western contemplative life, 96; see also meditative life
'Wheel of Responsibility', 154–5, 161; completing the, 174–5; dark mirrors of the, 187–90
Wheel of Victimhood, 176–205
White as colour of the North, 131
wholeness: claiming our, 286; memory of our, 77; state of, 89–90; see also becoming whole
will: and choice, 261
wind: quality, in the North, 128, 129
Winnicott, Donald, 23, 36
Winter as season of the West, 134
wisdom: innate animal, 129; in the North, 129; paradox as language of, 251
womb: only safe place, 42
wounded child, 18, 23, 24, 54, 176–80, 187, 256; the experience of the, 27; and guilty mother, 16; recognizing the wounds, 178

Y

Yellow as colour of the East, 138
'You make me feel...', 26, 314

Index compiled by Richard House